HILDEBRAND

HILDEBRAND

A LIFE OF GREGORY VII

BY

A. J. MACDONALD

RPC RICHWOOD PUBLISHING CO.
MERRICK, NEW YORK

58202

Published by Richwood Publishing Company
Merrick, New York

Reprinted: 1976
Printed in the U.S.A.

Reprinted from the original edition in the
University of Illinois Library.

Library of Congress Cataloging in Publication Data

MacDonald, Allan John MacDonald, 1887-
    Hildebrand: a life of Gregory VII.

    Reprint of the 1932 ed. published by Methuen, London,
in series: Great medieval churchmen.
    Includes index.
    1. Gregorius VII, Saint, Pope, 1015 (ca.)-1085.
2. Popes--Biography. I. Title. II. Series: Great
medieval churchmen.
BX1187.M25 1977 262'.13'0924 [B] 76-30354
ISBN 0-915172-26-7

GENERAL PREFACE

THE aim of the series as a whole is to produce a number of studies of various leading medieval Churchmen, more particularly of those who have not yet received their rightful meed of appreciation. These studies will attempt to view their subjects, not in isolation, but as contributing to the Church's life and thought at some particular epoch.

The responsibility of the general editor has been confined to the choice of subjects and authors : in his own volume each of the latter has been allowed full liberty both of judgement and method.

L. E. B.

AUTHOR'S PREFACE

HILDEBRANDINE studies in England were instituted twenty years ago in Cambridge by the work of Professor Whitney and Mr. Z. N. Brooke. Yet much misunderstanding of the dispute between Gregory VII and Henry IV remains, and still more of the influence of the pre-Gregorian reform movement upon that Pontiff's life and work. Gregory was rather a manipulator of the ideas of others than a creator of new policies—a statement which by no means detracts from the importance of his work. From his era dates the practical foundation of the medieval papal system.

Gregory's life was not a drama in three acts, although there was much that was dramatic in his dispute with Henry IV, and the chronological method has therefore been followed in order to secure a proper perspective for the more important events. In the intervals between the critical periods in his relations with Henry, constant supervision of affairs in other lands was being maintained, and Gregory's despatches to almost every country in Europe illustrate the development and application of his ideas to Germany. Thus it is misleading to group together at the end of the story of the German drama an account of his relations with Sicily, Spain, France, England, Hungary and other kingdoms. The thunder of anathema was being hurled against Philip of France, before it rolled forth against Henry IV.

The chronology followed is mainly that of Meyer von Knonau. For the convenience of the general reader the edition of Gregory's letters quoted in the footnotes is that of Jaffé, *Bibliotheca Rerum Germanicarum II. Monumenta Gregoriana*, but careful students will also use the edition of Caspar in *Monumenta Germaniae Historica*,

vii

Epistolae Selectae II. Fasc. I–II. (1920–1923). This, however, in contrast with Jaffé's edition, does not contain the letters gathered from sources outside the *Register*.

The estimate of Gregory VII offered in my *Lanfranc* and *Berengar* will prove that his career in this book was not approached with any pre-conceived bias against him, and, if a different view of his policy has now been presented, it has been the result of a new and intensive study, especially of his letters. With the exception of Mr. Brooke's chapter in the *Cambridge Medieval History* (*Vol. V.*), Henry IV has hardly received satisfactory treatment from English historians, and, if the present work goes even farther in the direction of vindicating that monarch in his relations with Gregory, it is offered with the conviction that it has not gone too far. It necessarily follows that Gregory does not come well out of the controversy, but it is time that the work of German scholars, who for the last two generations have been adjusting the conclusions of their countrymen drawn in the last century, should be better known by the general reader here. No safer advocate for Henry can be found than the letters of Gregory himself.

From undergraduate days onwards I have owed much to the two Cambridge scholars whose names have been already mentioned, and, although they may not agree with some of the conclusions now put forth, they first introduced me to these studies, and have always offered the greatest encouragement to my work since then.

My friend, the Rev. J. H. McCubbin, Vicar of Kellington, formerly Senior Classical Scholar of Trinity College, Cambridge, has read through the book in proof, and has checked my rendering of Gregory's letters.

I also wish to acknowledge the courtesy of Dr. Binns, the Editor of this series, and Messrs. Methuen & Co., who readily agreed to my request for a fuller treatment of the subject than was originally arranged.

A. J. M.

CONTENTS

HILDEBRAND

CHAPTER ONE

INTRODUCTION

WHAT was it all about—this assembling of
councils and synods—this deposing of Kings
and Popes—this hurling of anathemas and
excommunications—' False monk, come down, come
down ! '—' Let no man serve him as King ! '—this
designation of Gregory as devil, Anti-Christ, lover of
women—this slandering of Henry as adulterer, murderer
or worse—this calling-up of Norman troops from the
South—this movement of Teutonic armies from the
North—this German encirclement of Rome and Norman
storming of the City—this acrid polemic on either side
—Crassus and Wenric and Benzo against Bernard and
Gebhard and Manegold—a hundred and thirty-six
pamphleteers or more ? What was it all about ? In
order to find the beginning of an answer we must go
back five centuries.

The most portentous day in the history of Italy and
of Europe was the day when the kingdom of Theodoric
practically came to an end when the Ostrogoth died in 526.
The influx of Goth and Vandal and Teuton across the
Elbe and the Rhine and the Danube, breaking up, in
their onset, the frontier of the old Roman Empire,
brought with it the downfall of the imperial organization of Europe, and indicated incontestably that its
political future would be conditioned by the principle
and institution of nationality. Rome had successfully

imperialized the Gaul and the Greek, the African and the Asiatic, but when she failed to embrace the northern races within her system, nationalism was the only alternative for the new organization of Europe. Indeed, the true correlative of race is nationalism, not imperialism, and every empire which has sought to merge peoples of foreign blood with its own has sooner or later broken up into the nations which have emerged from its constituent races. The principle of nationalism springing from race is so strong that it always acts as a solvent of imperialism, and recent developments in Ireland and India are only the modern manifestation of an ancient political experience.

Yet the imperial idea is not easily obliterated; it readily seizes upon any opportunity provided by a weak interlude in the development of the rival system of nationality to reassert its sway, and sometimes a reactionary process has been essential to meet current political and social needs, no matter how disastrously the interlude operated for the future and final development of European conditions. Thus the fall of the first Italian monarchy, when Theodoric died, necessitated the development of the temporal power of the Papacy, based upon the inheritance of the old imperial idea—a development which has hindered Italian unity from the days of the Lombards to Frederick II and down to Mussolini.

Nor was the disintegrating influence, initiated by the rise of the temporal papal power, confined to Italy. Germany became involved in papal politics, with results as disastrous to German as to Italian unity. It was bad enough that the revival of the Roman Empire in the person of the German monarch was a mere figment in medieval Europe, entailing all the waste of energy and deflection of motive which the pursuit of a figment always incurs; worse still were the results for Germany of that infatuation with a glittering bauble—the imperial crown—which led the German kings from the Ottos to the Hohenstaufen, across the Alps, luring them away from the home problem, from the repression of feudal anarchy, the taming of German magnates, the conversion of oligarchic self-interest into administrative service on behalf of a united Germany. If England and France, and later Spain, attained national unity long before the German monarchy had defeated the centrifugal forces of the oligarchic principle, that was largely because the monarchy in these lands was not enticed away from the home problem by the figment of ancient imperialism.

The claim to imperial honour set up by the Saxon and the Hohenstaufen was bound to lead to a dispute with the Papacy, not only because the Papacy constituted a rival claimant to the exercise of the imperial principle—thus setting up a dichotomy which made impossible a successful revival of the Roman Empire—but because, in order to make sure of the imperial diadem, it was necessary for the German monarchs always to have some one favourable to German interests in the papal chair. German interests did not usually coincide with papal interests, still less with Italian interests, and the flame of conflict began to smoke when Charles the Great was crowned at Rome on Christmas Day in the year 800. Indeed Europe was waiting for new ideas. The old imperial concept could only hope to succeed when a man with a dominant personality like Charles or Henry III assumed the purple, and then only if the Popes were ready to abandon imperial precedence to the Emperor—a concession which the ablest of the Popes from Gregory VII onwards failed to make.

But if the political development of Europe demanded loyal service to the principle of nationality operating around its chief executive function, the kingship, that was not the only requirement of medieval society. Politicians have always proved singularly incapable of dealing with moral and social problems, and these problems were never more acute than in the early Middle

Ages. The life of the tiller of the soil was almost as insecure as that of a soldier on campaign. Not only was he the victim of devastating invasion conducted by warring kings ; he was at the mercy of every feudal magnate who chose to raid his neighbour, or fill his own barns at the expense of the labouring serfs on his own property. Moreover, morality which had possessed considerable stability, even in the trans-Alpine provinces, under the old Roman regime, had been broken up by the incursions of the Gothic and Teutonic armies. The dissolution of moral sanctions and prohibitions had even spread to the ecclesiastical hierarchy. From bishop to parochial minister, from abbot to monk, from dean to cathedral doorkeeper, the life of the clergy was corrupt. The corruption reached the Papacy, and in the first half both of the tenth and of the eleventh centuries scandal wore the papal tiara. If life for the ordinary man was to become again secure, and if morality was to be re-established, not only must the Papacy be reformed, but an opportunity had to be created for it to supervise the reformation in the dioceses of the Western Church. The conversion of the new races had been inspired and supervised by the Papacy, but no S. Paul had arisen to breathe into the infant churches of the West the spirit of independent growth, once the missionary stage was over. This was indeed largely due to the obliteration of the *Pax Romana*, to the warring as well as the wandering of the nations, to the struggle of race and kingship towards self-expression and the definition of geographical boundaries, and above all to the planting of proprietary churches in all countries occupied by the German stock. But it was also due to the failure of the Papacy to develop, through the episcopate, a strong and healthy provincial church life, a failure which enabled the landlords, as Stutz has shown,[1] to set up and maintain for centuries the institution and theory of the proprietary church.

[1] *Die Eigenkirche* (1895).

Even at Rome by the time of Hincmar of Reims, in
the ninth century, the proprietary church had appeared.
Not Cæsaro-papalism, but ancient Germanic ecclesiastical
theory, lay behind the claim of the Emperor to intervene
in German church life. Thus, if a spiritual, in contrast
with a temporal, empire lay open to the Bishops of
Rome, it was conditioned by the results of their initial
failure during the period of evangelization, and its
development was tracked from the beginning by un-
solved problems. Indeed, but for these early failures
the ecclesiastical domination of Europe by the Papacy
would never have been necessary; for the unit of
Christian organization is the local ecclesia, at its greatest
extent the diocese, with no more than a moral supervision by the Metropolitan bishop. But having left the
diocese and provincial episcopal system unequipped for
their work, the Papacy was bound to intervene, yet
at the cost of bringing a worn-out imperial principle
into conflict with a developing national instinct in the
provincial churches. So the loftiest motive of the
medieval Papacy was doomed to failure, largely by local
conditions which it had helped to create. The only
solution lay in the slow growth of provincial church life
towards independence; that development required the
work of centuries, and, as the event showed, could only
be accomplished by the aid of revolution.

The failure of the medieval Papacy was due to its
blindness to conditions and tendencies. The real possibilities and opportunities for spiritual hegemony are
revealed, on a smaller field, in Sir Samuel Dill's brilliant
sketch of the influence of S. Martin and of his tradition
in Meroving Gaul.[1] The Frankish kings ruled, but
there was no interference with ecclesiastical organization.
This inter-relation of church and state was inherited by
the Carolings. The sword saved the Papacy from the
Lombards, yet there was no voluntary turning from

[1] *Roman Society in Gaul in the Merovingian Age* (1926).

Byzantine rule, because Hadrian I did not approve of the anti-iconoclastic policy of the Isaurian house [1]—indeed Charles the Great was an iconoclast. The church was protected by the secular authority, and, after the coronation of Charles, by imperial sanction. But was not this the original state of the relationship under Constantine ? Was there, at the beginning, or for many centuries, a Holy Empire representing a concordat between Pope and Emperor for the government of Europe ? The theories of pamphleteers seldom enter practical politics whether civil or ecclesiastical, and the only concordats known to history in the relation of church and state were concerned with points of detail, where administrative practice was on the side of the secular authority, and principle—usually strained and short-sighted—was on that of the church. By precedent Henry IV was justified in challenging the papal theory of Gregory VII.

The temptation, sometimes justifiable, to exercise power was continually present to the Papacy. In the era of Gregory the Great the administration of Italy and the supervision of the West by the Roman Pontiff, alone upheld the security of society. But Gregory the Great was an administrator trained in the older secular imperial methods, and his ecclesiastical policy had much of the spirit and attitude of S. Martin ; and, even if in his successors the deference of the Papacy to civil authority was only skin-deep, that deference was shown, and without it the Papacy could not have survived. In truth, from the hands of an able and conscientious King or Emperor the Papacy received back far more than it ever conferred, even though long periods sometimes intervened before the return was made. Henry III repaid the debt of Charles the Great to the Papacy and discharged more than his predecessor had received.

At the time when our story begins, dynastic move-

[1] *Cf.* E. J. Martin *A History of the Iconoclastic Controversy* (1930) p. 224.

ments towards nationality were in operation all over Europe. The Capetian and Angevine in France, the Norman in England, the Saxon and Swabian in Germany were all struggling towards dynastic expression. In Italy Godfrey of Lorraine sought to erect the dukedom of Boniface of Tuscany into an Italian kingship ; while the Normans, Guiscard and Richard, were quartering the body of the south Lombard inheritance, in the effort to form a south Italian kingdom. Whenever a strong ruler seized the mantle of kingship, he was able to impose his will, and the success of William in England, Philip I in France, and Guiscard in South Italy, indicated the true line of political development.

In the first decades of the twelfth century nationality was fostered by the disputes of the commanders on the plains before Acre and Edessa. The crusading knights were no longer mere feudal magnates, but the aspirants to a new vocal French, German and English nationhood. The Latin kingdoms of the East assisted in the development of the idea of national monarchy in the West, except in Germany. Here the rivalry of Saxon and Swabian, Bavarian and Bohemian, a feudal medley, confused by racial instincts in the case of the Saxons and Czechs of Bohemia, proved too strong for the policy of Henry IV and Henry V, but the failure of the Salian emperors to weld Germany into a compact monarchy was due largely to the legacy of the imperial crown, which deflected their attention and that of their successors towards disastrous campaigns in Italy.

The eleventh century was an era of great personalities in church and state. No such galaxy of distinguished rulers and administrators, soldiers and writers had occurred for five hundred years. To find its parallel a return must be made to the era of Justinian and Theodoric, Belisarius and Narses, Gregory the Great, Papinian and Ulpian. In the eighth century two stars of the first magnitude appeared in Charles the Great and John

2

Scotus Erigena.　But with the eleventh century came
Cnut and Godwin and Harold, the Normans William
and Guiscard, the Angevine Geoffrey Martel, Leo IX,
Gregory VII and Urban II, Henry III and Godfrey of
Bouillon, Lanfranc and Berengar, Damiani and Humbert,
Anno II of Köln and Adalbert of Bremen, and among
women, Matilda of Tuscany ; and the greatest of these
was not Hildebrand.

CHAPTER TWO

YOUTH (1025–1048)

THEY said his father was a carpenter, whose shop was in the village of Rovaca in Tuscany, and that as a boy Hildebrand played with the shavings beneath the bench, and although unlettered, formed them into a curious prognostication of the future. But this was only to establish a comparison with the carpenter's shop at Nazareth, and to weave, in view of his single-minded vision and tragic end, a parallel with Him who also scorned the kings of the earth and died for His message. So we discard the tale about the carpenter coming to Rome from Tuscany with a small bright boy, who attracted the attention of a priest by his unusual intelligence, and was hailed as a future Pope of Rome. Hildebrand's father was a Roman citizen named Bonizo, who may have lived in Tuscany, but became the husband of a woman related by marriage to the banker family of Benedict the Christian. His mother's name was Bertha and she lived very near the Church of S. Mary in Portico.[1] Perhaps the child was born at Rovaca near Soana about the year 1025,[2] but they brought him back to Rome as soon as Bertha had recovered. What a Rome it was ! There were married clergy and free-living clergy, dignitaries who had bought their honours and a Pope who was both married and a simonist. The great palaces of old Rome were

---

[1] P. Fedele *Archivio della Reale Società Romana di Storia Patria* XXVII. (1904) pp. 399 ff. followed with some reserve by R. Lane Poole *Proceedings of the Brit. Acad.* VIII. (1917) p. 25.
[2] *Cf.* Martens *Gregor VII* (1894) I. 10.

occupied by the captains and cadets of the noble Roman and Tusculan houses, who turned them into fortresses, manned by armed retainers, from which they sallied forth to make war upon each other, to plunder rich pilgrims to Rome, and to make and un-make Popes. But with it all were two significant facts—the child Hildebrand was being educated under the ægis of the Lateran, and Benedict the Christian, the founder of the great banking family of the Pierleone, was getting richer.

From infancy Hildebrand was educated at Rome, nourished ' with piety beneath the wings of the prince of the apostles, cherished in the bosom of his clemency '.[1] So he himself referred to his earliest years, which could only have been spent at the monastery of S. Mary on the Aventine, where the Cluniac rule was partly in force, and where his maternal uncle, Peter, was abbot. It was unlikely that any other school would be selected by Bertha for her boy, and, as she was a lady of substance in Rome, no doubt the choice lay with her rather than with his father. Peter was still abbot in 1044 when he subscribed the acts of a Roman synod ; and he signed another document, near the signature of Bertha, who is described as *ancilla dei*.[2] But long before that time Hildebrand had been removed from S. Mary's, and when adolescence was over, continued his education at the Lateran Palace, where his associates included Alberic and Cencius, cadets of substantial Roman families.[3] In later days Cencius became Prefect, or Police Commissioner of the city, and Alberic became a Senator, an honorary official possessing a kind of aldermanic rank. So the Lateran Palace, like the abbeys and cathedrals of the time, rendered good public service by the training of young men for civilian as well as ecclesiastical careers. These early associations with the church left an indelible impression on some of the boys, even though they

---

[1] *Reg.* I. 39 ; *cf.* III. 10a, VII. 23. [2] Fedele p. 408 n. 1.
[3] *Reg.* III. 21.

adopted civil careers. Cencius was so devoted to religious exercises in later life that he neglected the duties of his office, and more than one unruly scene in Rome resulted from his dreamy lackadaisical habits. From time to time Hildebrand's family visited Venice. The beauty of the lagoons, the wonder of the ancient church at Murano, the glory of San Marco, and the freedom-loving people attracted his attention and remained a happy memory to the end of life. 'From boyhood I have loved your town and the freedom of its people.'[1]

During this early period Hildebrand was not trained for monkhood. He received instruction in the grammar, rhetoric and logic of the *Trivium*, subjects studied by a well-educated youth in that period, the curriculum on the classical side of a public school to this day. Unless he was already destined for Holy Orders he did not yet pass on to the *Quadrivium*,[2] in which arithmetic and geometry, astronomy and music were chiefly studied for ecclesiastical purposes. The boy's thoughts were wandering outside the walls of the Lateran. The exciting secular and ecclesiastical life of Rome called to his ardent imagination, and the marching and counter-marching, the sieges and war-cries appealed to the military instinct in his own young mind.[3] Yet his soul was unconsciously absorbing the elements of what became later the passion of his life. The glamour of the papal institution slowly cast its spell upon him. It fell upon an impressionable subject. The military instinct seeks out institutions rather than persons as the materials for its thought, hence the conservatism and traditionalism as well as the ceremonialism of soldiers. Certainly not on the papal throne of that era, nor for three decades to come, was there a personality who could

[1] *Reg.* II. 39.
[2] For training in the schools *cf.* my *Lanfranc* (1926) pp. 27 ff. and *Berengar* (1930) pp. 9 ff.
[3] *Cf.* Wido (*Libelli de Lite* I. 554).

win the eager homage of a growing youth. Neither
John XIX nor the infamous Benedict IX could inspire
contemporaries with respect for the Papacy. But from
early years the young Hildebrand was attracted by
tradition and the old customs of the past. As he grew
older, he was often not satisfied with a decision, or a
line of policy, unless he had first consulted the records
of the past, or had referred to those who could make
the search. Precedent was his precept. How like the
military mind! Yet how misleading, for only those
precedents were noticed which supported inclination
and gave wings to aspiration—precedents giving substance to papal authority, culled from collections of
canons and writings of the late Fathers, especially from
Gregory the Great, without any attempt to sweep the
wide European field of vision, past and present, in order
to ascertain the relationship of other centres of authority
to the Roman Pontiff. Yet Conrad the Salian was on
the German throne, and Conrad came to Italy and Rome
during these years, and dealt with Popes as he dealt
with German magnates. Did the young Hildebrand
never ask himself the question why this Emperor was
able to be so effective in action, and what were the
sources of *his* authority? If he had done so, no one
in Rome would have given a satisfactory, still less a true
answer, for the nobles and citizens of Rome hated the
German monarch with all the pride which Romans had
shown towards Teutons from the days of Marius onwards. The influence of the Roman noblesse and
populace upon the contest between Pope and Emperor
was well sketched by Gregorovius, and, if he frequently
wrote bad history of persons and affairs outside Rome,
his work on the city itself deserves wider notice than
it receives to-day.

When quite a small boy Hildebrand may have seen
Odilo, the Abbot of Cluny, who was in Rome not later
than 1032, and he perhaps renewed the acquaintance

when Odilo returned to the City at the end of his life in 1046. At this latter period Hildebrand may have come in contact with Laurence, the Archbishop of Amalfi, who was banished from his see, and sojourned at S. Mary on the Aventine.[1] From them he would learn details of the reformed Benedictine rule, but, if Hildebrand had any inclination towards the monastic life, it was counteracted for the time being by the influence of John Gratian, Archpriest of S. John at the Latin Gate, who may have been one of his masters in the Lateran School. A fast friendship was formed between the two, which ended only with the death of John in Germany.

John Gratian was the son of Benedict the Christian, a converted Jew; John's brother Leo married a sister of Bertha, Hildebrand's mother, and became the father of Peter Leoni, Hildebrand's cousin.[2] Gratian was thus Hildebrand's uncle by marriage, and this relationship no doubt partly accounted for the close friendship between them. Benedict the Christian was a banker who died before 1051, and John Gratian his son had access to some of his father's wealth, and spent a large sum in order to secure a reform of the Papacy. Between 1012 and 1032 the papal chair was occupied by Benedict VIII and John XIX, two brothers of the Count of Tusculum, who for several years wrested the domination of the City from the rival house of the Crescentii. Benedict VIII had already been a Cardinal, and his rule was not inefficient. John XIX was a layman, who had been Senator of Rome. During his pontificate the influence of the Papacy steadily decreased; the only noteworthy incident was the coronation of Conrad II in 1026. On the death of John XIX in 1032 the Papacy fell to Theophylact, the namesake of Benedict VIII, the nephew of the two preceding Popes, and the son of their brother Alberic, Count of Tusculum. Young at the time of his

---

[1] Fedele p. 408; Lane Poole *Brit. Acad.* VIII. 26.
[2] Lane Poole *Brit. Acad.* VIII. 27.

appointment, the pontificate of Benedict IX was a career of moral depravity and degradation, marked by at least one attempt on the part of the citizens of Rome to assassinate him, and ended finally by a financial arrangement with his godfather John Gratian, the arch-priest. Whether Gratian actually paid him a thousand pounds and a pension from the Peter's Pence of England is not clear, but he seems to have obtained money to enable him to marry his cousin. In the meantime, John, Bishop of Sabina, aided by bribery and the house of the Crescentii, had been chosen as anti-Pope, and took the name of Sylvester III (1044). So, when Gratian became Gregory VI in 1045, there were three Popes in existence at the same time. Two of them were involved in simony and one of them was immoral. Thus the Papacy itself reflected the scandalous condition of the Roman nobility, and indeed of the church in Italy. But a deliverer was at hand.

In 1039 died Conrad II, the first of the Salian line, an astute ruler, who had done much to reduce the unruly magnates of Germany to submission to the royal house, but who hindered the work of reforming bishops and abbots, and made use of the abbey revenues in the interests of his friends. Conrad by no means deserved the title ' Vicar of Christ ' applied to him at his coronation. He was succeeded by Henry III, who possessed more than his father's administrative and military capacity, and much of his grandfather's (Henry II) devotion to the church. Henry III was one of the great rulers of history, revealing the merits and the virtues, as well as some of the weaknesses of Charles the Great. Not so faithful in domestic life as William the Conqueror, he had much of that monarch's zeal for the welfare of the ecclesiastical organization and the purity of its administration. In 1046 he appeared in Italy in order to clear up the muddle around the papal chair.

On what grounds had he the right to intervene ? On

the old theory, dating from the time of Pippin and
Charles the Great, who had secured to the Papacy the
provinces around Rome and the exarchate of Ravenna
which was then connected with the City by a broad strip
of territory,[1] the Emperor possessed the right of consent
to a papal election, on the ground that the Patrician
dignity was a concomitant of the imperial state. The
Patriciate was the last vestige of the old Roman imperial
might in the City, and as the old Emperor had maintained
supervision over papal appointments, this function was
preserved in the person of the chief Roman citizen,
designated *Patricius*. Otto I had deposed John XII in
favour of Leo VIII in 963, but by the time of Otto III
the Crescentii had succeeded in regaining the Patrician
dignity for themselves, and this was the new theory
lying behind the grant of the Patriciate to Henry III by
the Roman citizens—not by the Pope—at his coronation
by Clement II on Christmas Day, 1046. The possession
of the Patriciate gave the German King the right to
consent to a papal election, although not to nominate.
But when Henry III came to Italy in the autumn of 1046
at the age of twenty-seven he was neither Emperor nor
Patricius. The imperial coronation had yet to take place,
but at the hands of which of three contending Popes ?
Hence, in addition to a sincere desire to reform the
Papacy, Henry had a strong personal reason for intervening in the affairs of the church at Rome. It is difficult to see what solution, short of the intervention of
the German King, could have been found.

For some two years, John Gratian had fulfilled the
functions of Pope. He had the support of some of the
leading clergy in Italy, and especially of Peter Damiani,
the hermit monk of the order of S. Romwald, and the
leading Italian publicist of the day. Gregory VI, wrote
Damiani, came as a dove with the olive branch to the

[1] *Cf.* R. Macaigne *L'Église Mérovingienne et l'État Pontificale* (1929)
pp. 194, 321.

ark of the church. But Gregory could make no head-way against rival Popes in the stalemate at Rome, and his financial dealings with Benedict IX, or the negotiations of rich relatives on his behalf,[1] had given him the character of a simonist in the eyes of some reformers, which made it impossible for him to attack one of the two great ecclesiastical evils of the time. Beside him was the young Hildebrand. To the end of his career Hildebrand was convinced of the integrity of Gratian's motives. When looking back in 1080, he did not hesitate to refer to him as the 'lord Pope'.[2] During the short pontificate of Gregory VI, Hildebrand, although holding no office, made his first acquaintance with papal administration. If Gregory VI was a simonist he had erred in order to remove the papal scandal of the day, and the first principles of reform, learned by Hildebrand, were received from his former master, during the two short years of his administration.

At the Synod of Pavia, held on October 25th, 1046, Henry III denounced simony. Already in Germany he had realized that the purchase of dignities by the clergy, and the payment of fees or gifts at investiture with the symbols of their office, was one of the chief causes of the prevailing decadence of church-life. He had already taken steps to uproot the evil in Germany. But Henry III was a sagacious man of business, and a generous judge of men, and it is not certain that in the interests of peace he might not have overlooked the simony of Gregory VI, when the motive was peace, and when men like Damiani approved of Gratian's elevation. But the quickest way to a solution of the confusion in Rome was to remove all three contending Popes, and make a new election. Moreover, Henry was probably convinced that he had better material in Germany for reform in Rome than any Italian could offer. Yet again, Henry had recently taken, as his second wife, Agnes of Poitou

---

[1] De Ord. Pont. (Lib. de Lite I. 10).   [2] Reg. VII. 14a.

—a marriage within the prohibited degrees—and Gregory VI may not have been able to consent to the union.   Another synod was held at Sutri (December 20th), and whether Henry now heard for the first time the details of Gratian's transaction with Benedict IX, or not, Gregory VI voluntarily resigned.   Three days later the other two Popes were removed at a synod in Rome. Benedict IX appears to have been deposed with a semblance of legal form, since he had been legally elected, and Sylvester III went into the monastery of Fruttuaria, perhaps without the form of deposition, since he had never been recognized by the proper authorities.   On Christmas Day Suidger, Bishop of Bamberg, was consecrated as Clement II, and on the same day placed the imperial crown on the head of Henry III and his Empress.   The new Papacy was short. and terminated with Clement's death in October (1047). In the first half of the year he had accompanied the Emperor to South Italy, but before starting had held a synod at Rome in January, at which simony was for the first time formally condemned by the first of the reforming Popes.   Clerks who had received ordination from a simonist bishop were allowed to retain their orders after a penance of forty days.

On his return to Germany in May, 1047, Henry took with him Gregory VI and Hildebrand.   The report that the Emperor was anxious to remove from Rome so staunch a supporter of the exiled Pope is probable enough, and we must accept Hildebrand's statement that he left Rome unwillingly.[1]   This also is probable if Hildebrand's zeal for papal reform had already been aroused.   An entirely new regime, under a German Pope, was commencing, and an interesting prospect opened out before a young and ardent mind.   But once on the journey, in the entourage of the Emperor, Hildebrand's regrets were obliterated by a young man's

[1] *Reg.* VII. 14a.

experience of his first foreign tour. Such an experience only comes once in a lifetime, and Hildebrand's entry into Germany in the cavalcade of the Emperor had something of the excitement of a military advance. There had been operations in South Italy, and Hildebrand liked to be with soldiers. Moreover, he was travelling with his friend and relative Gratian. The son of Benedict the Christian had already shown that he was likely to be one of the banker's heirs. Hildebrand always had a shrewd sense of the value of money, although his hands were never stained yellow. Did he at this time foresee the possibility of a legacy?

In Germany Hildebrand no doubt remained with his relative, probably at Köln, where ' I was nourished ' in the days of Archbishop Herman.[1] John Gratian died in 1048, and then Hildebrand's mind, already separated, by an interval of about a year, from the excitement of Rome, was able to devote itself seriously to one of two intellectual interests sustained throughout his life. Hildebrand was not a theologian or philosopher, either by taste or education. When his practical mind turned to study it was to subjects which offered equipment for the activity of life. So the canon law and the writings of Gregory the Great were eagerly investigated. His knowledge of the Bible was gathered later. While in Germany he may have visited Liège, and we know that he went to Worms. At Liège Wazo was propounding his theory of the relations of church and state.

Liège had been a centre of reform for over a hundred years. In contrast with the Cluniac movement which was confined to monastic houses, the Lorraine programme, which spread into Flanders and the Rhine districts of Germany, dealt with the reform of the parochial clergy, and was operated by the bishops. For this reason it covered less than half the ground, for more than half the churches were controlled by their pro-

[1] *Reg.* I. 79.

prietors, the territorial magnates.[1] But within these limits the Lorraine movement made a permanent contribution to the revival of discipline and morality among the clergy. The source of this movement was the monastery of Lobbes, which like many another Benedictine house, remained unaffected by Cluniac influence. Here Rather, successively Archbishop of Liège and Verona, who died at Namur in 974, was trained. He condemned the practice of lay election or appointment to ecclesiastical functions, and so struck at the theory and customs of the Germanic proprietary church system. Simony also, and connections between the clergy and women, were condemned. The episcopate must be freed from lay interference, it was subject to no civil court, and over the whole hierarchical system Rather set up the Papacy as the court of final appeal, and as the source of episcopal authority. The bishop's authority, while derived from the same divine origin as that of the King, is superior to it in range and character. Yet like Hincmar of Reims in the middle of the ninth century, he could not break away entirely from the habits of mind of Germanic church law, which allowed the King and lay magnates a decision in ecclesiastical affairs. If, as Rather saw, the primitive right of supervision in an episcopal election rests with the metropolitan, he allows also for the intervention of the King, and he congratulated Otto I on his appointment of Pope Leo VIII.[2]

Otto's action in deposing John XII was criticized by Thietmar of Merseberg early in the eleventh century,[3] and towards the middle of the century Wazo, Bishop of Liège (1041–1048), developed the theory of ecclesiastical independence a stage further. In the case of Widger, Patriarch of Ravenna (1044), Wazo informed Henry III that the Emperor was concerned only with

---

[1] Stutz Die Eigenkirche (1895); Scharnagl Der Begriff d. Investitur (Kirchenrechtliche Abhandlungen, Hft. 56. 1902).
[2] Fliche La Réforme Grégorienne I. (1924) 74 ff.
[3] Carlyle Polit. Theory in the West IV. (1922) 17.

the secular aspect of a bishop's action, and the Pope with its spiritual aspect. When Clement II died on October 9th, 1047, Wazo, who was consulted by Henry III on a new appointment, informed him that no appointment could take place while Gregory VI lived. He had examined the decretals of Roman bishops, and the canons of councils, and reported that no one had the right of judging the Pope. Then appeared a treatise, the *De Ordinando Pontifice auctor Gallicus*, written under the influence of Wazo towards the end of 1047. It contained the same criticism of Henry's treatment of Gregory VI, condemned the Emperor's marriage with Agnes, and took up Rather's condemnation of simony, together with his reassertion of the principles of free election to ecclesiastical offices by the clergy and people, and of the pre-eminence of the Papacy over all temporal authority. The Emperor might not place himself above a ruling of the canons. Yet, while the Lorraine reformers realized that no permanent improvement in ecclesiastical and moral life could come from imperial intervention, and while they reflected the independent spirit of Godfrey the Duke of Lorraine, a magnate who caused more uneasiness of mind to Henry III than the Bohemian or the Magyar, they managed to preserve a sense of feudal duty towards the civil authority.[1]

To Liège, according to Sackur,[2] Hildebrand came, but, whether he actually visited the Lorraine centre or not, the theories of Wazo and of the *De Ordinando Pontifice* were being widely discussed in the Rhine areas, and the practical-minded youth cannot have failed to absorb them, for Hildebrand was attracted by the new and growing study of the decrees of ancient councils and the decretals of Popes and bishops, a development destined in the next generation to produce a scientific formulation of the canon law. In the ninth century Hincmar of Reims had produced a lengthy work on

[1] Fliche I. 113 ff. [2] *Neues Archiv.* XVIII. (1893) 139.

the canons, and at Worms in the early years of the eleventh century Burchard had issued a collection of the same in twenty books, which was widely used, and formed in some measure a foundation for the work of Ivo of Chartres, as well as that of the many framers of smaller collections, which appeared in the middle of the eleventh century.[1]   At Worms the influence of Burchard was still strong, and to that city Hildebrand travelled in the company of Herman the Archbishop of Köln.   Here he attached himself to a Benedictine house, where leisure and instruction and materials for the study of the canons were amply provided.   Since the beginning of the century the Benedictine monasteries—not the Cluniac houses—were drawing students in all branches of knowledge away from the old cathedral centres.   Berengar's experience at Tours, where the scholars left him to attend the lectures of Lanfranc at the new Benedictine house at Bec, was not isolated.

While at Worms, Hildebrand had an opportunity of inquiring into the details and habits of the Benedictine life.   Some reports say that he took the cowl in Germany, but that probably occurred later.   During the few months spent at Worms, he had opportunities for the study of the canons, which never came again, yet the absorbing interest of those months was never forgotten, and in after years his practical mind turned to most fruitful results the impressions received during that period.   While he did not become a learned canonist, Hildebrand developed in Germany the habit of mind of a canon-lawyer.   The teachers and students of the canon law in France, Italy and Germany were forging new weapons for the reform of the church by tracing out the sources of ecclesiastical authority.   Their methods differed from those of the Lorraine school.   Leaving

[1] Before Burchard other collections of canons were in use—the *Hispana*, the *Dionysio-Hadriana*, and the False Decretals—drawn up from the seventh to the ninth centuries.   *Cf.* Z. N. Brooke *The English Church and the Papacy* (1931) p. 33.

for the time being the question of imperial authority and of imperial intervention in ecclesiastical affairs, they concentrated their attention upon the positive definition of episcopal and papal authority, and sharpened their definition of ecclesiastical authority by ever increasing systematization and definition. Thus first a barrier, and then an instrument of offence against the spreading influence of German ecclesiastical law was being formed. The theory of the proprietary church, which vested the rights of ownership and appointment in the territorial lord, whether great or small, was to be challenged by the revival of ancient ecclesiastical law, in which the bishop possessed the right to appoint to a spiritual charge, and was himself appointed to his diocese by the election of the cathedral chapter, confirmed by the archbishop, a rule strengthened soon by the practice of appeal to the Bishop of Rome as the final arbiter in cases of dispute. In Germany Hildebrand saw the rival proprietary church system at work, and in Germany he began those studies which prepared his mind for the coming conflict with the German secular power.

CHAPTER THREE

INITIATION (1049-1054)

HILDEBRAND attended the imperial Council of Worms in December, 1048. On August 9th Damasus II, the successor of Clement II, had died after a twenty-three days' rule. At Worms the Emperor nominated to the vacant Papacy his cousin Bruno, Bishop of Toul, and here Hildebrand met the man who fixed his destiny finally, and who began the effective work of reform to which his own life was to be dedicated. ' Yet unwillingly did I cross the mountains with my Lord Pope Gregory, but more unwillingly did I return with my Lord Pope Leo,' [1] said Hildebrand in later years when he had become an inveterate phrase-maker. The study of the canons had fastened down his attention for the time being; the leisure of a Benedictine house had pervaded his soul, and, if he had recently taken the cowl, the great peace of a new decision had descended upon him. But Bruno was gathering a company of assistants for the work to be done in Rome, and Hildebrand, ' a young man of noble character with a clear mind and sound piety ',[2] was persuaded to go back with him. The occasion was novel, and provided the student of the canons with an opportunity for seeing Lorraine principles put into practice, since Bruno, according to Damiani, was a student of the canons. Bruno accepted nomination to the Papacy from the Emperor without question, but he declined to regard his appointment as complete, or to assume any pontifical state, until it was confirmed in the old canonical manner by the formal

[1] *Reg.* VII. 14*a*.   [2] Watterich *Pont. Rom.* I. (1862) 96.

consent of the bishops and clergy of Rome.   So in the
garb of a humble pilgrim, with a small band of friends,
including Hildebrand, he set forth on the journey to
Rome.   The quickest route from Worms was down the
Rhine to the Simplon, but an early document used by
Bonizo reports that Bruno went through Besançon,[1] and
if he paid a final visit to his bishopric at Toul, he may
well have directed his steps to Grenoble and the Mont
Cenis.   From Besançon no great detour had to be made
in order to visit Cluny, and such a visit perhaps lies
behind the mere legend that Hildebrand, a young monk
of Cluny, was there first introduced to Bruno.   In the
course of his correspondence with Köln and Worms and
Venice in later years, Hildebrand lost no opportunity
of referring to his early acquaintance with these centres,
though in the many letters sent to Hugh, Abbot of
Cluny, he made no reference to an early sojourn at
that monastery ; but, if Bruno went on to Cluny from
Besançon, Hildebrand went with him.   He may have
broken his journey there again on the way to Tours in
1054 and to Anjou in 1055, for, if these fleeting visits
took place, they were the only occasions for which we
have a hint of any personal acquaintance between Hildebrand and Cluny.   They may well have occurred, and
Hildebrand's omission later in life to draw attention to
his visits may have been due to disappointment at
Hugh's half-hearted support in the contest with Henry
IV.   But Hildebrand was never a monk of Cluny, and
never made any prolonged stay there.[2]

The humble approach of Bruno to Rome, barefoot,
and unaccompanied by German troops, or escort of any
kind, raised the acclamation of the Roman clergy and
people, and on February 12th, 1049, he was consecrated
and took the title Leo IX.   Throughout the first year

[1] Watterich I. 101.
[2] *Cf.* L. M. Smith *E.H.R.* XXI. (1911); *The Early Hist. of the
Monastery of Cluny* (1920); *Cluny in the 11th and 12th Centuries* (1931),
for a full discussion of Hildebrand's relations with Cluny.

of his pontificate Hildebrand played a very minor part, and not for many years did he become a leading instrument among the reformers. He was scarcely twenty-five years of age, and, although at this time he decided finally to devote his life work to the church in Rome, he possessed so little influence in the papal counsels, that in March, 1049, Leo passed over his impulsive protest in favour of the Archbishop of Köln, against the appointment of Eberhard, Archbishop of Trier, the Pope's former Metropolitan, as Primate of Gallic Belgium.[1] Indeed, the ardent young man was not yet qualified for commissioned service, and Leo found his theological education so imperfect, that he placed him under instruction, when the Pope left the City for his first great pontifical tour in Gaul and Germany.

Another watchful eye was upon Hildebrand at this time. Peter Damiani warned him against the excessive use of leeks and onions, and, somewhat inconsistently with his own general principles, praised his zeal for the study of the poets and philosophers, an early, and perhaps transient interest which soon died away. Damiani sent him a mystical interpretation of the season of Lent,[2] and on another occasion a tractate on the Sabbath.[3] When Leo returned from Germany, he admitted Hildebrand to minor orders and to the sub-diaconate, thereby placing him in the ranks of the cardinals. About this time he was also appointed Treasurer of the Abbey of S. Paul and he may have fulfilled the office of Custodian of the altars of S. Peter's,[4] with the maintenance of their equipment. As Treasurer of the Abbey of S. Paul he must have been already a monk. Perhaps he took his vows at this appointment, whether or not he actually wore a monk's dress.[5]

---

[1] Reg. I. 79.   [2] Op. XXXII. (Migne 145, 543c, 545a).
[3] Ep. II. 5 (Migne, 145, 260b).   [4] Martens I. 16 f., II. 252 ff.
[5] Martens War Gregor VII Mönch? (1891) and Gregor VII, II. 254 ff. denies that Hildebrand was a monk, but this is contested by most modern authorities, among them Whitney E.H.R. (1919) 138 and Brooke C.M.H. V. 52 n. 1.

At S. Paul's, he assisted with the reform of monastic life.

The state of the Roman and Western Church required overhauling by an energetic and strong-minded pontiff. Such had now appeared in Leo IX. Supported by a sympathetic and devout Emperor, many of the hindrances to reform, which fettered the action of previous and succeeding Popes, were absent. Leo's policy of independent yet prudent papal intervention and supervision grounded the reform of the church in head and members on secure foundations, and from its moderation promised more success in the issue than the more dogmatic and headstrong policy of Gregory VII. It is significant that Leo IX was free to travel anywhere in the area of the Western Church, save in one small part of France, whereas Gregory VII never succeeded in crossing the Alps. The prisoner of the Vatican was already foreshadowed between the years 1076 and 1084.

In Italy we have seen that simony was one of the sins of the Papacy, and was found among all grades of the clergy from the cardinals downwards.[1] At Milan, the conditions were worse, almost the whole body of about a thousand clergy was affected. Tedald, the Bishop of Arezzo, said that he would give a thousand pounds for the Papacy, in order to cleanse the church from simony, so that Gregory VI was not alone in desiring to defeat the enemy by turning against him his own weapons. If in Germany the traffic in benefices was not so shamelessly pursued, that was partly due to the widespread existence of proprietary churches and abbeys. When appointments were made, the payment of dues or fees by the clergy to the landlords, was subject to regulation by German ecclesiastical legal theory. Yet the practice was open to abuse, and created an example for open simony in churches under the sole control of the bishops. In France the evil was rife, but it was due rather to local

[1] Cf. Damiani (Lib. de Lite I. 59).

influences, than to royal interference with ecclesiastical affairs.[1]   Guifred of Cerdagne, a boy ten years old, received the Archbishopric of Narbonne in 1016 after the payment of 100,000 solidi had been made by his relations. He held the see until 1079, and easily recouped himself and his relations for the purchase price from the revenues of the see.   It is reported that a bishop belonging to the ducal house of Gascony disposed of eight sees by will.[2] ' Let me make my profit out of him,' said Philip I (1060–1108) to a disappointed candidate for a bishopric, ' then you can try to get him degraded for simony, and afterwards we can see about satisfying you.' [3]   In England simony was probably less prevalent at the appointment to bishoprics ; it is rarely mentioned in the findings of Saxon church councils,[4] but it was practised by the parochial clergy in the performance of their spiritual functions.[5]   Simony was epidemic in the Western Church, and the decrees of the provincial councils show that it had been in existence for a thousand years.

The history of clerical marriage was entirely different in character.[6]   In primitive Christianity, there had been of course no prohibition, and marriage was the practice, even for bishops.   A change in ecclesiastical opinion was first introduced through Gnostic influence, by way of Montanism which came from Phrygia, that centre of Oriental ascetic fanaticism.   Then came the era of Monasticism, both eremetic and coenobitic, which set up celibacy as the standard of the most pious religious life. The Eastern Church both encouraged and checked the development of celibacy among the diocesan clergy. By proclaiming celibacy as the rule for bishops, it set up an ideal which the more logically-minded Latin Church would not fail to apply to the lower orders of the

---

[1] Whitney C.M.H. V. 26.   [2] Ibid. p. 10.   [3] Ibid. p. 9.
[4] Böhmer Die Falschungen des Erzbischof Lanfranks (1902) p. 31.
[5] Böhmer Kirche und Staat (1899) p. 71 (quoting William of Malmesbury).
[6] On the whole question cf. Mirbt Die Publizistik (1894) pp. 239 ff.

hierarchy. By permitting the parochial clergy to marry, the Eastern Church checked the advance of monastic practice into the ranks of secular church life, and for many centuries the Western Church permitted, although not without increasing protest from the Council of Elvira (305) onwards, the marriage of the clergy.

The practice led to evil results when the economic and domestic problems of the clerk's family became acute. For this feudalism was largely responsible. The grading of society according to the principles of feudal land tenure created a caste system throughout the West. A son was expected to follow the occupation, or to inherit the status of his father. So the clergy endeavoured to secure the succession of their offices to their sons or relatives, without regard to their fitness for the cure of souls, and clerical marriage even led to the alienation of church property on behalf of relations who did not wish to take orders. Political conditions hastened the growth of this abuse in the earlier centuries, when the break-up of the old Roman and Gallo-Roman city-life in Italy and Gaul took place, and when the Teutonic races broke into the Empire. The sons of the clergy could no longer find careers in the large towns.

Like simony, clerical marriage was universal in the Western Church in the eleventh century. The custom was so widespread in Italy that some bishops in conference with Damiani were doubtful whether regulations against it would meet with any success.[1] At Rome, as we have seen, Benedict IX was married, and in the time of Gregory VII the married clergy in the City still formed a problem. The same condition prevailed in the provinces around Rome. The clergy were openly married in Apulia in the south. To the north in Lombardy, the marriage of the clergy was the accepted practice, especially in Milan, and if in Milan the clergy were allowed to marry only once, they enjoyed more confi-

[1] Neukirch *Das Leben des Pet. Dam.* (1875) pp. 82 f.

dence and approval from the laity than the celibates. Indeed, the ample revenues of the Milanese Church made marriage with the clergy an attractive consideration for the heads of families with daughters on their hands. Nor were the married clergy of Milan less efficient in the discharge of their duties than their celibate brethren. Damiani had ' never seen such clergy ', he was impressed by their ' noble breeding, their fine appearance, and magnificent apparel, their probity of conduct and faithful devotion to the discharge of the details of business '.[1] Anselm of Lucca commented on their capacity in preaching.[2]   Yet Arnulf of Milan qualifies this picture,[3] and Landulf, whose testimony must be received with caution, regarded the clergy of Milan as degenerate.[4]   At Turin the marriage of the clergy was regulated by Cunibert the Bishop ; its secular details were supervised by a notary public ; and again Damiani expressed approval of the life of the Turin clergy.

In Germany and Hungary, clerical marriage was almost the rule, although the practice was not so frequent among the higher clergy.   In France, where there were frequent charges against the bishops and the cathedral clergy, marriage was common.   From the Synod of Bourges (1031) onwards, legislation was directed against the married clergy, sometimes in the face of protesting bishops, who approved the custom.   Even in Spain, the home of celibacy, marriage of the clergy was not unknown, and called forth synodal action.   In England the legislation of Lanfranc against the Saxon clergy testifies to the prevalence of the custom, although Lanfranc, at Winchester in 1076, wisely left alone those who were already married.[5]

Difficult though the marriage question was for the ecclesiastical authorities, in view of the unsuitable appointments, and the alienation of church property

---

[1] Arnulf (*M.G.H. SS.* VIII. 20 f.).   [2] *Ibid.* p. 76.
[3] *Ibid.* p. 21.   [4] *Ibid.* 73 f.   [5] *Cf.* my *Lanfranc* p. 105.

entailed by it, a far more distressing problem was
created by the prevalence of concubinage, and the resort
by the clergy to houses of ill-fame. No doubt this was
partly due to the low moral conditions existing in lay
society. But it was also an inevitable reaction against
the prohibition of clerical marriage. The rule of celibacy
proved too severe for a half-converted, semi-civilized
society, even when its members were immured in the
monastery, and some unsavoury tales are reported of
conditions at monastic centres, before the Cluniac and
Benedictine reform movement became widespread.
Peter Damiani's strictures in the *Liber Gemorrhianus* are
almost unreadable in the Latin, and untranslatable for
any vernacular. In another work he said that the
immorality of the clergy was public knowledge and so a
public scandal. The brothels to which they resorted
were known, and so were the names of their concubines.
As they passed through the streets they were subject to
tittering mockery and ribald jokes.[1]

Leo IX, in 1049, gave orders that prostitutes found in
Rome should be shut up in the Lateran to work as
domestics. Bishop Hugh of Langres (1049) and Mauger
of Reims (1055) were condemned for immorality, and
their cases were but symptomatic of the extent of that
evil in the Western Church.[2] Reform had been attempted
from time to time, for many decades, in the provincial
councils, but not until the Papacy undertook the work
was there any chance of success. However, the complete
eradication of the evil was rendered nugatory from the
beginning, by the adoption of an extreme policy—the
condemnation of marriage as well as irregular incon-
tinence. The medieval church was never cleared of the
latter abuse. Great though the loss of efficiency was
through the misuse of church property, and the appointment of unsuitable clergy, arising from the effect of
contemporary economic and feudal laws upon the mar-

[1] Migne 145, 380*c, f*.   [2] Mirbt pp. 239 ff.

ried clergy, these evils might have been slowly removed by a patient administration on the part of the bishops, supervised by a prudent and watchful Papacy. The condition of the married clergy of Milan and Turin, worldly and possibly luxurious, none the less indicated the avenue to a satisfactory solution of the whole problem. But the invasion of diocesan life by the monastic principle of celibacy rendered such a solution impossible. Yet the problem was attacked, and considerable improvement was achieved in the habits and life of the clergy, and conditions never again became quite so bad as they were when Leo IX summoned his first council in Rome.

The legislation against simony, commencing, as we have seen, with Clement II, was not new. It had been prohibited by the Roman civil code of the Christian Emperors, as well as by the canons of the church. But the old rules had been confined to the simonist himself, to the clerk or bishop who purchased his office. No legislation was passed against those who assisted in the transaction or at the consecration ; still less did it strike at the clergy ordained by simonists. Not until the second half of the eleventh century was simony in all its ramifications surveyed, defined and prohibited by conciliar action.[1] In the Roman Council held after Easter, 1049, Leo IX declared the ordination of clerks by simonist bishops to be invalid. But the opposition of the Council compelled the Pope to revert to the milder ruling of Clement II. Leo, however, persisted with his policy, and before September, 1050, he had re-ordained simonist bishops and clergy. Such appears to be the meaning of some obscure phraseology of Damiani, and it is confirmed by Berengar's account of the events of 1050.[2] No doubt after 1049 Leo's hand was strengthened, as Berengar says, by the influence of Humbert, the monk of

[1] Imbart de la Tour, *Les Élections Épis.* (1891) p. 378.
[2] *Cf.* my *Berengar* pp. 83 f. ; but also L. Saltet,*Les Réordinations* (1907).

Moyenmoutier, who was brought back by Leo from Mainz at the end of that year, and created Bishop of Selva Candida. Some years later Humbert published his celebrated work *Adversus Simoniacos*, in which the invalidity of simonist ordinations is proclaimed. The zeal of Humbert had little difficulty in reviving the inclination of Leo towards stringency, even after the Pope had been defeated in Council, but we hear of no further development of legislation against the simonists during his pontificate, although the general prohibition was repeated again and again, and bishops guilty of the offence were from time to time deposed.

At Reims (1049), as an additional check upon simony, a decree was passed prohibiting appointment to ecclesiastical office, without election by clergy and people. This was a revival of ancient canonical custom, current in the time before Meroving and Caroling kings and bishops intervened at ecclesiastical elections. Yet Leo's decree did not rule out lay election, provided that the canonical pre-requisites had been satisfied. Here was the first rumble of the coming storm, although it attracted little attention at the time.

Regulations were made against the marriage of the clergy at most of Leo's synods, and some glaring cases of immoral life were condemned. In Germany Adalbero, Archbishop of Mainz, attempted to carry out the decrees, but, although he ejected the wives of the clergy from the city, he failed to secure obedience in the diocese outside.

The pontificate of Leo was significant as much for its administration as for its legislation. Not until the time of Urban II did a Roman pontiff again make his influence so markedly felt, by ubiquitous travel throughout the West. Synods and councils were held, not only up and down Italy, but in France, Germany and even Hungary. The Papacy was kept informed of affairs in distant lands by the despatch of legates, and Adalbert of Hamburg-Bremen was appointed (1053) Papal Vicar for the

Baltic countries. No doubt that ambitious prelate, who aspired to a patriarchate, if not to a new papacy over North-Western Europe,[1] was largely responsible for this concession, but Adalbert's ambition happened to coincide with the policy of the reviving administration of the Curia. The College of Cardinals was created at Rome, and the papal Chancery was reorganized on the model of the imperial Chancery of Germany.[2] Leo's plans included the subjugation of the Normans of South Italy, and reunion with the Greek Church. A new archdiocese for Sicily was projected, and Humbert who possessed a knowledge of Greek, still spoken in cities of the south, was to be the first archbishop. When this plan fell through, Humbert was despatched to Constantinople, together with Frederick of Lorraine, the Chancellor, and Peter, Archbishop of Amalfi (January, 1054).

We hear little of Hildebrand throughout the time of Leo IX. The young Treasurer was busy with the affairs of the Abbey of S. Paul, observing the effects of the new regime on the papal treasury, nursing the support of his rich relatives, especially that of his cousin Leo, the son of Benedict, watching with growing excitement and emotion the preparations for the Eastern embassy. Already the young monk was thinking in terms of continents and patriarchates. His military instincts were re-awakened, and during the military preparations of the old soldier-bishop, Pope Leo, against the Normans, Hildebrand perhaps conceived his first idea of leading the host of Christendom against the infidel. But he was not allowed to accompany Leo on the campaign, which led to the Pope's defeat by the Normans at Civitate ; Hildebrand was despatched to France on some minor business, as they thought in Rome, business for which he was certainly competent by temperament, but quite unquali-

---

[1] *Cf.* Grunhagen *Adalbert Erzbischof von Hamburg und sein Idee eines nordischen Patriarchats* (1854).
[2] *Cf.* Lane Poole *Lectures on the History of the Papal Chancery* (1915) 98 f.

fied by knowledge. Yet it was the Treasurer's first
legatine commission. He was now about thirty years of
age. It was time to try out his capacity.

By one of those chances which accompany the affairs
of men, an obscure dispute in France became a turning-
point in the history of the Papacy and of European
civilization. While the practical reformers at Rome
were preoccupied with the abuses of simony, clerical
marriage and lay-election, one of their sympathizers in
the domains of Geoffrey Martel, Count of Anjou, was
attempting to draw attention to an important question
of church doctrine, which by implication involved the
whole dogmatic system of the Western Church. Such
has ever been the tendency of eucharistic controversy,
although conservative opinion has generally succeeded
in warding off re-statements of doctrine without revolutionary consequencs. But the negative effect of that
action has generally been disastrous in the long run.
Berengar of Tours had for some years past been criticiz-
ing the prevailing interpretation of eucharistic doctrine,
derived from Paschasius Radbert, and based upon the
realist statement of Ambrose, in favour of the symbolism
of S. Augustine. By reason of his actual or supposed
quotations from John the Scot, the philosophic-theo-
logian of the time of Charles the Bald, and whose views
had long been suspect, Berengar became involved in a
charge of heresy. He was regarded as a dangerous
innovator by moderate theologians like Lanfranc and by
zealots like Humbert. Yet Paschasius Radbert was himself the innovator, as Berengar readily showed, and
at the time when Radbert wrote his Book *De
Corpore et Sanguine Domini* in the middle of the ninth
century, the Augustinian tradition was still strong even
in the Benedictine monasteries.[1] The theories of Rad-

---

[1] *Cf.* my *Berengar* pp. 227 ff. and *Evangelical Doc. of Holy Com.* (1930)
pp. 88 ff. on the significance of the Berengarian controversy for the
future of the Western Church ; *cf. Berengar* pp. 103 ff. and 194 ff.

bert prevailed, and were the accepted interpretation of
sacramental teaching in the time of Leo IX.   Berengar
was twice condemned by that Pope at Rome and Vercelli
in the year 1050.   The accused was detained by Henry I
in France, and naturally he resented the excommunication
passed upon him in his absence, and continued to express
his views at Tours.

It is possible that Leo IX was compelled to take notice
of the controversy chiefly because of Berengar's connection with Henry I of France.   The King had prohibited Leo's Synod at Reims in 1049, and had prevented
many of the French bishops and abbots from attending.
If Berengar became a servant of Henry, a considerable
body of French and Angevine clergy, who had been
influenced by Berengar's theological views, might be
permanently alienated from the Pope.   The situation
seemed serious since Henry I and Geoffrey of Anjou were
now at peace.   So the young Hildebrand was sent in the
spring of 1054 to investigate the business, and to report
at Rome, bringing with him Berengar.   Berengar had
powerful friends in Anjou, among them Eusebius, Bishop
of Angers, and especially Count Geoffrey, who had used
him—so complicated were political and ecclesiastical
affairs in Gaul—as a tool against his rival and suzerain
Henry I.   Hildebrand's embassy was therefore expected
with high hopes, although with some anxiety in Tours.[1]

It is instructive to observe the effects of early training
at critical points in the later career of great men.   When
Napoleon turned suddenly and confronted the Revolution on October 5th, 1795, it was his artillery placed at
dominating points around the Tuileries which made him
master of France.   The young Corsican had learned
soldiership and the command of men with the guns.
So Hildebrand, fired by a novel situation, in which an

---

[1] *Cf.* The Epistle of Geoffrey Martel to Hildebrand, Sudendorf
Berengarius Turonensis (1850) pp. 215 ff., but probably written under
Berengar's influence.

acute theologian, and his own stubborn critics could carry the decision far above his own head, snatched a definite result from both sides, by an appeal to his early studies— the canons. There is a report of a preliminary interview with Berengar, when both men acquired respect for each other, but Hildebrand had the sense not to repeat this experiment when the watchful eyes of the gathering clergy were upon him. Then he assembled books, and marked certain passages in them, after the manner of a canonist, and had them ready for the Synod which met in the church of S. Maurice. Two alternatives were put before the assembled bishops. The teaching of Berengar might be examined in an open session of the Synod, in the light of the passages which Hildebrand had selected as a test ; or, after ascertaining Berengar's views by putting to him a plain question, the decision might be referred to Rome, and the Synod could, in the meantime, proceed to more general business of the church in Anjou. The bishops agreed to the substance of the second proposal. A private enquiry was conducted by the Archbishops of Lyons and Tours and the Bishop of Auxerre, at which Berengar was urged to state his belief in the Eucharist. ' The bread and wine of the altar, after the consecration, are the true body and blood of Christ,' replied the Archdeacon, and he repeated his statement in the Synod, when the sub-committee reported. Some of the clergy present objected that he did not mean what he said, but after persuasion by his friends, the Bishop of Anjou and the Abbot of Marmoutier, Berengar wrote down his statement, and confirmed it by an oath. Hildebrand was silent while the discussion took its course ; he did not rebuke an interrupter, who struck at Berengar by shouting that all should be excommunicated, who did not avow that the bread and wine ceased to be on the altar after consecration. But he was on the alert for vital points, especially when made by leading ecclesiastics. When the Abbot of S.

Aubin's asserted that they were not authorized to state how the body and blood of Christ came to be in the Eucharist, Hildebrand said that the point could not be left undecided, lest error were spread among the people. Finally he persuaded the Synod to accept Berengar's statement and oath, provided that he went back with the legate to Rome. Thus, without actually making use of his own collection of patristic statements, without actually bringing his own weapon into action, Hildebrand manipulated the Synod towards the very conclusion which he was charged at Rome to bring about. At the same time, the bishops were not going to be tied down to the interpretation of a legal-minded canonist who might rule out their theology ; but, under the threat of a decision to be made by one who obviously was not hostile to Berengar, they were compelled to adopt Hildebrand's other alternative.

The Synod then passed to other business, and, before it ended, the report arrived of Leo IX's death. That report neutralized all Hildebrand's policy. Berengar now declined to accompany him ; and the legate returned to Rome. Count Geoffrey, as well as Berengar and his friends, were acutely disappointed at the results of the Synod. In the very home of his friends the Archdeacon had expected to be able to win over the young legate. Hildebrand's coming had been anticipated as the advent of an ' angel of light ', yet it was alleged that he had done less than Pilate did. He was afraid to plead for Berengar, even though learned men at Angers upheld his opinions. Hildebrand had dissimulated.[1] We may pass over the complaints of this querulous disappointment. Hildebrand had fulfilled his instructions, and only the death of Leo IX prevented him from taking Berengar back with him to Rome.

[1] *Berengar* pp. 124 ff.

CHAPTER FOUR

LEGATE (1054-1061)

ON his return to Rome another legatine commission awaited Hildebrand. The report of his transaction at Tours must have given satisfaction. Yet it is improbable that Hildebrand would now have been sent to Germany if either Humbert or Frederick of Lorraine had been in the City. They had only recently reached Constantinople, and Boniface, Bishop of Albano, the other leading ecclesiastic at Rome, was required to watch the interests of the Papacy there. So Hildebrand was sent to Germany in order to request the appointment of Leo's successor by the Emperor Henry III. Only if Hildebrand was already the leading cardinal at Rome, already sure of his later policy, does this embassy present any difficulty. But he was still a subordinate at the Curia, and so merely carried out orders; and the question of Hildebrand's attitude, at this juncture, to the appointment of another Pope by Henry III, does not arise. Hildebrand had grown up with the new German tradition. The beneficial effect of Henry's two last appointments at Rome was too patent to permit now of a challenge on the ground of canonical rights vested in the Roman Church and clergy. Moreover, the political horizon in Italy was again full of clouds. Boniface of Tuscany, who had ruled Lombardy to the satisfaction of both Emperor and Papacy, was dead, and his wife Beatrix had married in this very year (1054) the rebel Godfrey of Lorraine. His brother Frederick was indeed a trusted leader at the Lateran, but that might not protect the Roman Church if Godfrey

regarded it as an ally of Henry III.   Moreover, the first
papal policy framed to meet the Norman menace from
the South, had ended with Leo's defeat, and had hastened
his death.   Henry's protection was needed in case the
Normans seized the opportunity of a vacant Papacy to
secure revenge for Leo's campaign.   Hildebrand was no
more than an agent of the Curia and the ambassador of
its policy, when he was despatched to the German
Court in the early summer of 1054, perhaps in time
for the coronation of the young Prince at Aachen in
July.

Born on November 11th, 1050, elected to the throne
in November, 1053, the child who was to become the
mighty wrecker of his schemes thirty years on was now
seen for the first time by Hildebrand.   That was the
only event big with presage for the future, experienced
by Hildebrand on that embassy.   If the young child was
already taking notice of his elders, handicapped by the
prejudice of all children for the mere external appearance
of a man, then the young Henry would see in Hildebrand
nothing strikingly noble to be riveted on an impulsive
child's imagination.   Small in stature and slight of
build, swarthy of countenance and somewhat deformed,
he possessed the figure, if not the physiognomy of his
cousins the Pierleoni.   His aspect was indeed redeemed
by a bright eye and piercing glance, but this was hardly
a feature to be noticed by a child, either now or when
Hildebrand came to Germany again a few years later.
If Hildebrand stayed in Germany until the new Pope
crossed the Alps, his sojourn lasted nearly a year, and
his intimacy with the imperial circle certainly increased.
The Emperor ' treated me with special honour at his
Court '.[1] Agnes in later days was his friend even against
her son.   Court life was simple then in Europe, and free
from Byzantine pomp and aloofness.   There may have
been some romps between the little prince and the

[1] *Reg.* I. 19.

4

Italian stranger—incidents when the little Henry expressed dislike of Hildebrand, and which lie behind the foolish stories of Saxo. Historians are apt to forget that the great men of former centuries were of flesh and blood, like ourselves, and the truthful core of many a legend is thrown away together with its wrappings. If all the legends, at any rate those of ordinary life, were pure invention, the novelist's art began long before Cervantes. Yet we have not a trace of unimpeachable information concerning this year in Hildebrand's early career. We may dismiss the suggestion that he contemplated the Benedictine life during these months. He was now a confidential emissary of the Papacy with a career before him, fixed firmly, and offering the most attractive possibilities. The only apparent outlet for his activity at this time lay in the further study of the canons, and perhaps of the views of the Lorraine publicists. Possibly a tremor of distrust at the existing method of imperial election to the Papacy may have moved in his mind, as the long months passed and no appointment was made. Shortly after his return to Italy, he wrote to Damiani, and emphasized the canonical rights of the Roman Church. We know of the matter only through a letter of Damiani to Victor II, and he reports Hildebrand vaguely. But Damiani's own letter represented to Victor II that the rights of the Empire passed to the Pope on the death of an Emperor.[1] The papal theory of independence was developing, and Hildebrand seems to have been investigating it in the canons. At length in the spring of 1055 an appointment was made, not one which could arouse much enthusiasm in Hildebrand, for the Emperor's choice fell upon Gebhard, Bishop of Eichstadt, who had prevented Leo IX from receiving German help against the Normans.[2] On April 13th, he was enthroned in Rome as Victor II, and was soon followed to Italy by Henry III.

[1] Whitney C.H.J. (1925) p. 241.   [2] Whitney C.M.H. V. 31.

An immediate transformation took place in Italian affairs. Godfrey of Lorraine fled across the Alps and allied himself with Baldwin of Flanders, Henry's Western enemy, leaving his wife Beatrix with her daughter Matilda to be placed under restraint in the train of the Emperor. Cardinal Frederick of Lorraine, who had returned from Constantinople with Humbert, fled to the Abbey of Monte Cassino. The Normans did not move even when Henry handed over Spoleto and Camerino to Victor II. The papal state now consisted of a compact territory in central Italy lying between Lombardy and the Norman lordships of the south. To heighten the Pope's prestige, as well as to guard him from attack, Victor II was nominated Imperial Vicar in Italy. The unity of interest and sympathy between Papacy and Emperor was never more completely indicated than during the short pontificate of Victor II.

On October 5th, 1056, Henry III died at the age of thirty-nine. Before the end came he adopted a policy of reconciliation with his enemies in the interest of his youthful son. The disputes with Baldwin and Godfrey were settled, and a reconciliation took place with Beatrix. In the spring of 1057 Beatrix and Godfrey returned to Italy to rule the great inheritance of Boniface in Lombardy, and to become the bulwark of the Papacy in the troublous years ahead. Victor II pursued the conciliatory policy of his dead master. He buried Henry at Speier on October 28th, 1056, and at Aachen placed the already crowned Henry IV on the royal chair. He confirmed the peace between Godfrey and the Regent Agnes. After a council held at Rome in Lent, 1057, Victor went south to Monte Cassino, and there again strengthened the alliance with Godfrey by appointing his brother, the Cardinal Frederick, as Abbot, a step which began a change in the attitude of the Papacy towards the Normans. In France the Pope continued Leo IX's work. At the time of his death (July 28th,

1057) he was on his way to hold a great council at Reims.

In the autumn of 1055 Hildebrand had been sent back to France as legate, and, together with Hugh of Cluny, convened synods at Tours, Chalons (February, 1056) and other centres, where the decrees against simony and clerical marriage were re-issued. At one of these councils a piece of drama occurred, such as Hildebrand staged more than once in later years. At this early period in his career he had realized the effect of a sudden dramatic appeal on excitable and emotional natures. A simonist bishop was confronted with the test applied by S. Peter to Ananias. When challenged suddenly in the council to state his belief in the Trinity, and especially in the Holy Ghost, the offender was unable to utter the sacred name of the Spirit, and fell in submissive prostration before the legate. At another of these councils the affairs of the church in Spain, and the relation of Ferdinand of Castile to Henry III were discussed. This business was probably the chief reason for the despatch of Hildebrand to Anjou in this year. Ferdinand was attempting to set up a new patriarchate at Compostella, and disputed the theory of Henry's imperial rights over Spain. The authority of both Pope and Emperor was being challenged. No reliable report of the proceedings has come down, but on that occasion Hildebrand's eyes were first drawn towards Spain.

Another result of this legation bearing upon Hildebrand's future was the development of his acquaintance with Hugh of Cluny. We have seen that a meeting probably took place between them when Hildebrand accompanied Bruno of Toul to Rome in 1049, and it is reported that he broke his journey at Cluny on the way to Tours in 1054. The Abbot Hugh, godfather of Henry IV and the friend of Agnes, never became a whole-hearted supporter of Hildebrand's later policy, but the two men conceived a respect for each other, which became especially strong on the side of Hildebrand, and developed into a friendship unaffected by divergent views.

The prestige of Hildebrand was growing. For a time, under Victor II, he was papal Chancellor. Together with Humbert and some other Italian bishops his name was mentioned as a possible successor to Victor. Although not yet thirty-five he was not much younger than the late Pope, but in the presence of leading cardinals like Frederick of Lorraine and Humbert the elevation of Hildebrand was not yet seriously considered, and not for two pontificates to come was he in any sense the dominating personality at the Curia. Frederick was elected as Stephen IX on August 2nd, 1057, largely through the support of Humbert. An ex-canon of Liège, he was acquainted with the anti-imperial tendencies of Wazo, and with the growing desire among churchmen to liberate ecclesiastical appointments from lay interference. Shortly before his death he warned the Romans to uphold an election based on the authority of the canons. He was the first of the reforming Popes who had taken the cowl, and the principles of monastic reform were now more closely associated with the Papacy. Peter Damiani, the reforming monk of Fonte-Avellana, was made Cardinal-Bishop of Ostia in November (1057).

The method of Stephen's appointment was of radical significance for the future relations of the Papacy and Empire. He was elected by the cardinals and clergy of Rome without reference to the imperial court. In this transaction Hildebrand had no share, since he was absent at Arezzo, where Victor II had died. But he was selected, no doubt on account of his previous knowledge of the German Court, to announce the election to the Empress Agnes (November, 1057). With him went Anselm, Bishop of Lucca, another rising Italian ecclesiastic, and, before the envoys left Rome, Hildebrand secured from the Pope a privilege for the Church of

Lucca. On the way they tarried at Milan. In the absence of Archbishop Guido in Germany, Ariald the deacon had been sent by the Milanese reforming party to Stephen IX, praying for a papal embassy to give support against the reactionary but dominant clerical party in the city, who were almost without exception married and guilty of simony. Hildebrand's mission made no permanent impression at Milan, but the reforming party there were now definitely taken under the wing of the Papacy.

In Germany the election of Stephen IX caused alarm. Not only was it a challenge to a custom of more than ten years duration, observed at the appointment of four successive Popes, whereby the Emperor nominated directly to the vacant chair ; in addition, the consecration of Frederick of Lorraine elevated the brother of Godfrey, an imperial rival in Italian affairs. Yet Hildebrand's diplomacy was successful, and the Empress-Regent gave her consent to the appointment. In the meantime Stephen, in a letter to the Archbishop of Reims, postponed a decision concerning the affairs of the Archbishop of Bourges until Hildebrand's return from Germany. Gervase, Bishop of Reims, and formerly Bishop of the Angevine see of Le Mans, was involved in the business, and, as the Pope said, Hildebrand had special knowledge of the details—the result of his embassies in 1054 and 1055 to Anjou. Finally, before his death in March 29th, 1058, Stephen urged the Romans not to proceed to a new election until Hildebrand's return.

The warning of the dying Pope produced no effect upon the Roman nobility. The opportunity to reassert their old influence was too good to be allowed to slide. No swift advance of a German army across the Alps need be feared, and the leading cardinals were away from Rome. Humbert fled from Florence, where the Pope died, to Benevento, and thence to Monte Cassino, where he consecrated Desiderius Abbot, in accordance

with the late Pope's wishes. Damiani fled to Fonte-
Avellana. Hildebrand was still in Germany. The
Curia, for the time being, was without a guiding hand.
The families of Galeria, Tusculum and the Crescentii
buried their old rivalries, and breaking into the City on
the night of April 5th, elected John Mincius, the Cardinal-
Bishop of Velletri, as Benedict X. This latest thrust of
the Roman aristocracy was carried out with considerable
astuteness—except perhaps when they allowed the new
Pope to take the old, ill-favoured name of Benedict—
for the College of Cardinals might be divided by selecting
one of their number as the patriotic Roman candidate.
But they had forgotten the new commercial community in
the Trastevere, headed by the banker Leo, son of Benedict the Christian, an uncle by marriage of Hildebrand.
A deputation was sent to the Empress at Augsburg
protesting against the violent proceedings in Rome.[1]
The commercial community clearly looked to the
German Court, to give security against the barons of
Rome. Here is revealed a hint of the political need
of medieval Italy, a need similar to that of the trading
community in every other Western land.

By the end of the spring Hildebrand, still only Sub-
Deacon, was back in Tuscany at Florence, where
Stephen IX had died. Here he found the late Pope's
brother, Duke Godfrey, and Cardinals Humbert and
Damiani. The scattered Roman clergy were gathering
in the Tuscan city. A month before he fled from Rome,
Damiani had been discussing Hildebrand with Hugh,
Abbot of Cluny, who was in Rome in March, 1058.
The effusive hermit had been pained by Hildebrand's
cool attitude to his advances. Hugh attempted to
console him by saying ' Hildebrand does not know that
you have so deep a love for him, otherwise he would
certainly return it '. Now in Florence, the tireless
letter-writer wrote to Hildebrand thanking him for his

[1] *Cf.* Whitney *C.M.H.* V. 35.

praises at the imperial Court, and then complaining of
an incident which occurred immediately after Hildebrand's return to Florence. ᛫ A vassal of the Florentine
Count Guido, had objected to Hildebrand that Damiani
had allowed a cloister to be built on his land. Without
further inquiry Hildebrand believed the story. Damiani
says that he will not bear resentment, and prays that
their friendship may continue. Yet at the end of the
year he complained that Hildebrand's treatment of him
was partly that of a tyrant, and partly that of a friend.
Damiani's effusiveness no doubt bored Hildebrand, but
he could not shut his eyes to the piety and genuine
friendship of the older man.

Events moved slowly. Godfrey of Lorraine was the
only territorial magnate who could supply the cardinals
with armed help at short notice. His support was
forthcoming, since the election of Benedict X contravened the expressed wishes of his brother, the late Pope.
But Godfrey, so recently reconciled with the German
Court, would not risk a new breach by hastily intervening
in the papal election. Moreover, Hildebrand, who had
just returned from Germany, where he had witnessed
the misgiving caused by the election of Stephen IX,
would not favour a step which alarmed the Court again,
especially in the presence of a powerful hostile combination at Rome. The reformers were not yet in a
position to dispense with the aid of the German Crown.
Among the cardinals the lead in the new election at
Florence appears to have been taken by Humbert. A
countryman [1] of his, Gerard the Burgundian, Bishop of
Florence, was nominated, with the approval of Godfrey.
Gerard was also a relative of Godfrey's wife, Beatrix of
Tuscany, who zealously supported his elevation.
Damiani greeted the nomination with joyful verses. A
delegation was sent to Augsburg in June, to secure the

[1] Humbert was a Burgundian, not a Lotharingian as Lanfranc alleged;
cf. Berengar p. 156.

consent of the Court,[1] not to invite it to nominate. So the policy of the reformers, and of Humbert especially, was being upheld. Here the submissive tone of the deputation from the Trastevere had already created a good impression. The Court gave its consent to Gerard's election, and Godfrey was authorized to conduct Gerard to Rome. In the meantime, Hildebrand, who managed the political details of the election, was active with preparations for the advance on Rome. Towards the end of the year Gerard's election was confirmed at Siena, and the Pope-elect with his supporters, accompanied by Godfrey and five hundred horsemen, went on to Sutri, two days' march from Rome. Here appeared the newly appointed Imperial Chancellor, Guibert of Parma, another relative of Beatrix of Tuscany. Sentence of excommunication and deposition was proclaimed against Benedict X. Hildebrand was in communication with his relatives in the Trastevere, on the northern bank of the Tiber. At the turn of the year the cavalcade of Godfrey rode in ; the island of Lycaonia was seized, and the two regions of the City on either bank were at war.

The Prefect Peter, in the region of S. Angelo, the papal stronghold, was displaced by John Tiniosus, a follower of Hildebrand in the Trastevere, and Benedict X was forced to surrender the Lateran and fly from the City. Without unsheathing the sword himself, Hildebrand no doubt played a part in the direction of the military operations, although the presence of an experienced soldier like Godfrey, with an efficient body of horsemen, left little doubt as to the issue of the turmoil. On January 24th, 1059, Gerard was enthroned, and at the suggestion of Humbert and Hildebrand [2] took the name of Nicholas II, after the great Pope, who in the middle of the ninth century developed and extended the influence of the

[1] Meyer von Knonau I. 92. Martens I. 23 f. thinks that the Court was not notified until after the election, but the two statements are not irreconcilable.

[2] *Cf.* Meyer von Knonau I. 120.

Papacy,[1] although Humbert did not refer to Nicholas I by name in the *Adversus Simoniacos*, published in 1058.

But it was many months before Benedict X was finally suppressed. He took refuge with the Crescentian Regetellus, in the castle of Passarano, a few miles from Rome. From here he fled by night to Count Gerard at Galeria. There the indefatigable Hildebrand drew new enemies around him. We have seen that Victor II reversed the hostile policy of Leo IX against the Normans, and whether or not Stephen IX attempted to form an alliance against them with the Eastern Emperor, his nomination of Desiderius as Abbot of Monte Cassino placed at the head of this hitherto strongly anti-Norman centre a conciliatory negotiator. When the Norman Richard of Capua and his son, Jordan of Capua, at war with Adenulf, the Duke of Gaeta, guaranteed on November 12th, 1058, the possession of the fortress abbey of Monte Cassino, Desiderius was able to secure liberal terms for Adenulf. Hildebrand seized the opportunity presented by this favourable turn of politics in the south, and, on the very day that Nicholas II was enthroned, left Rome and sought out Richard of Capua. Again, through the mediation of Desiderius, an alliance was concluded. Hildebrand recognized Richard and Jordan as Princes of Capua ; secured from them an oath of fidelity to Nicholas II and the Roman church ; and returned with three hundred horsemen to Rome. The cavalcade of Godfrey and Beatrix had already left the City. No further help was needed to suppress the supporters of Benedict in the neighbourhood of Rome. Hildebrand's Norman force united with the papal troops, and rapidly reduced Tusculum, Palestrina and Mentana, strongholds of the Roman nobility on the southern bank of the Tiber. At last the martial Sub-Deacon was personally sharing in the direction of a campaign. But after passing through Rome, and devastating the ter-

[1] *Cf.* Imbart de la Tour pp. 148, 160.

ritory of Count Gerard, the combined papal and Norman force was baffled by the strength of Galeria, and the Normans returned home, leaving Benedict still in possession of the fortress. For his share in the Norman alliance, Desiderius was made Cardinal-Priest, and his appointment as Abbot was formally confirmed by Nicholas II (March, 1059).

Meanwhile, the great pontificate of Nicholas II had begun. A notable victory was achieved by the Papacy in Milan. There was more than one reason why the Papacy should try out its strength here. Milan had been the most independent of the provincial Italian churches since the days of Ambrose. It regarded with jealous zeal any interference from the Bishops of Rome. Yet internal division had already compelled each party at Milan to appeal for papal assistance against the other, and the opportunity for securing the recognition of Roman suzerainty was not allowed to pass by the Curia. Yet the Papacy had definite reforming aims in view, and did not merely play off one party against another.

The ecclesiastical dispute at Milan threatened to become a social revolution. On the one side were the clergy, headed by Archbishop Guido, married, self-respecting, conscientious men, but lacking spiritual zeal and tainted with simony. Few appointments were made without the payment of money. Yet they stood for age-long custom and local tradition, and for law and order. They had the support of the vavasours, the lesser Milanese nobility, whose daughters many of them had married. The charge of widespread shamelessness of life seems ungrounded. Opposed to them were the city populace, always ready to criticize the clergy, headed by Ariald the Deacon, a vavasour by birth and a canonist, and by Landulf and Herlembald, the former in minor orders, members of the noble family of Cotta, all men of eloquence, who set fire to the envious discontent of the populace, by fusing it with the aims of the ecclesiastical movement. War was declared against the marriage and simony of the Milanese clergy. Ariald preached in the villages around Milan, and Landulf and Herlembald addressed the people of the city. Their supporters received the name ' Pataria ' or ' Ragamuffins.'

In the early part of 1059 the popular party were compelled to appeal again to Rome for assistance. There was a danger lest the nobility should come to the aid of the clergy of Milan, in the interests of ordered society. Peter Damiani, and Anselm of Lucca, who was acquainted with local conditions, were despatched from Rome. It was a trial of strength by the reforming Papacy against the strongest centre of reaction in Italy. The clerical party perceived the threat to Milanese independence, and exploited it among the people, by raising the cry that the liberties of Milan were in danger. When the Synod began in the Archbishop's palace, Damiani caused an uproar by placing Anselm on his right hand, and the Archbishop Guido on the left. For some moments the legate's life was in danger ; even Landulf thought of abandoning the Pataria, and of taking refuge in a monastery. But Guido weakly allowed the opportunity to pass. In order to save bloodshed, he agreed to sit at the legate's feet, and Damiani mounted a rostrum to quell the disturbance. His bold yet diplomatic eloquence did the rest. He paid full honour to S. Ambrose, and the prestige of Milan, but alleged that the Church of Milan was the daughter of the Church of Rome, to whom she owed her birth. The clergy of Milan were all guilty of simony, and there must be no more of it in future. But they should retain their office after performing penance. Guido swore amendment for himself and the clergy, and promised that clerks of all ranks should separate from their wives. The oath was written down and subscribed, and the Synod adjourned to the cathedral where the oath was read out at the high altar to the assembled laity. Penances ranging from five to seven years were imposed, involving pilgrimages to Rome, Tours, and, for the Archbishop, to Compostella.

The Milanese question was not settled, nor would it be for many a year. Other and more powerful influences from across the Alps intervened at later stages. But from that day the papal grasp on Milan was never relaxed. The genius of Damiani combined with the moderation of Clement II's ruling on simony secured permanent results for the Roman hegemony in Milan. Nicholas II upheld the policy of Damiani. The legate reported his success to Hildebrand, who was acting as Archdeacon of Rome, although Mancinus was still in office. It was in this report that Damiani expressed regret that he had not followed Hildebrand's repeated suggestion to search the canons and decrees of the Popes, in order to draw up a practical manual on the precedents for the authority of the Roman see. Hildebrand was seeking to promote the study of the canons, and as at Tours to turn it to political use. No doubt he hoped also to counteract Damiani's own views, which at this period laid great emphasis upon imperial authority in ecclesiastical affairs.

Archbishop Guido and seven of his suffragans followed Damiani back to Rome, and were favourably received by Nicholas. At the great Roman Council of one hundred and thirteen bishops, which assembled about the middle of April, Guido was placed on the right hand of the Pope. In the chief transactions of the Synod Hildebrand took no leading part. The ' eyes of the Papacy ' at this time were Humbert, and Boniface Bishop of Albano. Hildebrand was occupied with the political relations of the Curia, watching for an opportunity to bring Benedict X to submission. Up to 1059 Hildebrand signed only four bulls while Humbert signed thirty-six. The great achievement of the Roman Council of 1059 was the passing of the Election Decree, defining the process of future papal elections. This was inspired mainly by

Humbert, not by Hildebrand.[1] In his work *Adversus Simoniacos*, published the year before, Humbert distinctly protested against lay election and investiture,[2] and thereby supplemented Leo IX's decree at Reims. If he confined his discussion to church politics rather than the wider question of the relation of the spiritual to the civil power,[3] he clearly objected to the interference of the German imperial authority in ecclesiastical questions.[4] So he developed the theory of Wazo of Liège. He protested against the right of intervention in ecclesiastical business claimed by the Ottos, and concluded that current evils began with them.[5] Yet together with all the leading clergy of the day he could not avoid paying a tribute to the good work done by Henry III for the church.[6] Three of his principles were embodied in the election decree of 1059. Humbert complained that the order of election to church office, which gave precedence to the secular authority over the ecclesiastical, was inverted. He allowed that a candidate might be selected from another diocese, in the absence of one qualified in the vacant bishopric. Only kings, and princes who had the right of confirming an appointment made by clergy and people, were to take part in an election. These principles were embodied in the decree of the Council.[7]

The initiation and control of a papal election were placed in the hands of the cardinal-bishops, who were authorized to nominate the new pontiff. The cardinal-clergy and the rest of the Roman clergy and people confirmed the nomination. The election was now complete except for the consent of the German King. If a qualified candidate could not be found among the

---

[1] *Cf.* Martens I. 25 ff.; Fliche, *La Réforme Grégorienne* I. (1924) 281 and 324; Voosen *Papauté et Pouvoir Civil à l'époque de Grégoire* VII. (1927) p. 102.
[2] Halfmann *Cardinal Humbert* (1883) p. 69 f.   [3] *Ibid.* 78.
[4] *Ibid.* 66 f.   [5] *Ibid.* 72.   [6] *Ibid.* 73.
[7] Meyer von Knonau I. 134 ff., and *Excursus* VII. For a comparison between Humbert's statements and those of the Decree *cf.* Martens I. 27.

Roman clergy, a member from another church might be selected ; if conditions prevented an election being made in Rome, it might be made elsewhere ; when necessary the new Pope might fulfil his functions before enthronement had taken place. Thus the procedure followed in Benedict X's election was nullified, and deficiencies in that of Nicholas II were made good.

Formerly a ' canonical election ', especially in the decrees of Stephen II (769) and Stephen IV (862–863), had been vested in the hands of the whole Roman Church—procedure which was recognized by Otto I, although Otto prohibited consecration before the oath of allegiance to the Emperor had been taken.[1] Now the cardinals were placed in a predominating position. While a saving clause was inserted in favour of the imperial dignity, thus reducing to very small proportions the imperial rights conserved by Otto I, the new decree, although embodying ancient ecclesiastical tradition, which had been growing under the influence of the reformers of the Lorraine school during the last two decades, struck at an equally venerable and well-established imperial tradition,[2] and still more at the custom of imperial intervention in a papal election, re-established by Henry III in 1046. Since the days of the Carolings —except for occasional measures like those of Stephen II and Stephen IV—the Curia, save when the initiative was taken from its hands by secular Roman or Italian influences, had allowed the Frankish and German Kings a definite voice in papal elections in return for protection offered to the Papacy, a privilege which was assumed on their side, in the light of Germanic ecclesiastical theory, as a proprietary right.[3] Before the intervention of Pippin and Charles the Great, the imperial right of consent had been exercised by the Eastern Emperors,[4]

[1] Whitney *C.M.H.* V. 36. [2] Carlyle IV. 66.
[3] Stutz *Die Eigenkirche* (1895) pp. 37 ff.
[4] *Cf.* Macaigne p. 335.

and was formulated in the ecclesiastical law of the sixth century.[1] In theory it was current even when distance from Rome and preoccupation with other business made impossible more than a merely nominal assent to a Pope already chosen. Only by going back behind this long period of historical precedent and custom could the Council of 1059 find authority for its decree—apart from current needs and the minority in Germany—in the primitive liberty of the Roman Church; a liberty which was shared by every church in Christendom, in the era before the relationship with the state was established, and long before feudal duty had bound every see to the royal or imperial allegiance. These matters become of prime significance in estimating the relationship of Henry IV to Gregory VII in coming years.

The next important business of the Council was the settlement of the Berengarian dispute in France. Berengar had not rested after the Synod of Tours in 1054, and he and his friends were still smarting from the failure of Hildebrand to justify him on that occasion. They now made another appeal to Hildebrand to make good the lapse in his support of Berengar at Tours. In a letter despatched by Geoffrey Martel to Hildebrand, but inspired by Berengar, Hildebrand was urged to use all his influence for the vindication of Berengar, who was coming to the Council in response to a letter received from Hildebrand. Now must Hildebrand act with magnanimity in his defence, since his behaviour at Tours had amounted to base neglect, ' Behold now is a convenient time—now you have Berengar in the presence of the Pope—take care that you do not surrender your honour.' [2] But at Rome in 1059 Hildebrand had no share in the condemnation of Berengar managed by Humbert and Lanfranc. At Tours he had certainly been impressed by the Archdeacon's personality, and was not convinced that his teaching was heretical, but he did not

[1] Imbart de la Tour p. 72.　　　　[2] Cf. *Berengar* pp. 124 ff.

feel competent to deal with a high doctrinal problem, and made no effort to express his own opinion. No doubt, also, his moderate policy at Tours, had alarmed the zealous Humbert, so that he may have been deliberately prevented from taking part in the discussion. Lanfranc's support of the Curia in the affair of Berengar was rewarded by the grant of absolution for William of Normandy. His wife, Matilda, the daughter of Count Baldwin of Flanders, was a distant relative.

A decree was passed enforcing celibacy, and the laity were prohibited from attending Mass said by an incontinent priest. Laymen were forbidden to appoint clergy to their benefices, even though no payment was received ; nor might they try a clerk for his offences, or expel him from the church. An indication of Hildebrand's intervention at this stage of the proceedings is revealed by an eleventh-century manuscript on the mode of life of the secular canons. Hildebrand said :

' Some of the clerical rank, influenced by the Holy Spirit with the fire of perfect love, long ago in this Roman Church and in the provinces . . . are known to have embraced the common life by the example of the primitive church, so that they declined to reserve any of their property for themselves, and distributed it to the poor or to their neighbours, when they did not hand it over to the church. But some of them afterwards, both young and old, resumed this property, which at their own or their parent's desire they had relinquished, and in defence of their conduct they appealed to certain chapters in the rule concerning (secular) canons, originating with the Emperor Louis the Pious, compiled by an unknown writer. This document, after directing, according to ancient canons, that the property of the church should be shared only by those who surrendered their own property, proceeded to contradict this principle.'

Then Hildebrand urged the Council to reform the abuse, and to uphold the ancient custom of the Roman Church whereby secular canons were to live by a common rule.

Hildebrand's interest in ancient precedents was clearly producing results. Nicholas replied that this matter had repeatedly been brought before his attention, and he urged the Council to remove indiscipline in the life of the secular or cathedral canons, and to restore the primitive conditions. Two anonymous works were then produced—possibly by Hildebrand, following his procedure at Tours—one concerned with the lives of the parochial clergy and secular canons, and the other with the life of nuns ; and appear to have been drawn up by the Synod of Aachen (817) in the time of Louis the Pious. The Council raised objection to the contradictory statements in these books, which reflected, if they had not caused, the abuses condemned by Hildebrand. It was alleged that such customs were not to be found in Asia, Africa, or Europe, save in a small corner of Germany. They reversed the Gospel rule, so that it appeared that ' unless a man *retain* all that he possesses he cannot be my disciple '. Louis the Pious, it was urged, had no power to change the rule without the authority of the Roman Church and papal see, especially as his innovation was against the tradition of Gregory the Great—one of Hildebrand's favourite arguments—and the assembly was provoked to indignation by the statement which allowed to each canon or nun four pounds of bread a day and six cups of wine, no doubt, it was alleged, for the support of spouses and children, or for their harlots—a regulation which issued, said some, from the Church of Reims or one of the other French churches.[1] This hit at the French clergy came from the German representatives in the Council. Our document here breaks off, but such regulations as Hildebrand wished were passed, strengthening the discipline of the secular canons, especially since it aimed

[1] A. Werminghoff *Neues Archiv.* Bd. 27 (1901–1902) 669 ff. But Werminghoff is wrong in thinking that he printed the MS. for the first time. It was first printed by Mabillon, *Annales* IV. Appendix LXXVII.

at extending the reforming programme in Germany and France.

Throughout the long sessions of the Easter Council Hildebrand had been waiting for an opportunity to complete the downfall of Benedict. The withdrawal of Godfrey's troops in January, before the first attack upon Galeria commenced, made known to the Curia that no further military aid was forthcoming from Godfrey for the time being. From June to the middle of September Godfrey was occupied with operations against Ancona. The Curia, therefore, was compelled to turn again for assistance to the Normans, but the event showed that bigger schemes than the mere reduction of the anti-Pope were being woven at Rome, schemes of large political import for the future, grounded in a knowlege of the events of the distant past. On June 24th, the Pope was at Monte Cassino, and its Abbot, the negotiator Desiderius, together with Humbert and Hildebrand, accompanied him to Melfi, where a council was held on August 23rd. Here Nicholas invested Robert Guiscard with the duchies of Apulia, Calabria and Sicily, and Richard with the principality of Capua. So was the policy of Leo IX completely reversed.

Robert Guiscard, son of the Norman Tancred de Hauteville, near Coutances, had arrived in South Italy in 1046. He was tall, with broad shoulders, a fresh healthy complexion, blond hair, and beard the colour of flax, with quick and piercing eyes. His war-cry roused terror in the enemy, and his eloquence could thrill a multitude.[1] Although one of the latest of the Normans to arrive in South Italy, he rapidly became the leading chieftain among them. For the weal and woe of the Papacy and of Rome this extraordinary man was now drawn into an alliance with the Curia. In return for his investiture with the largest inheritance in South Italy,

[1] Heon *Les Normands d'Italie* (1866) p. 12, derived from the account of Anna Comnena.

he promised to pay an annual tribute to the Papacy, and swore fealty to the Pope and the Roman Church. As the ally of the holy Roman Church he would help her to obtain and uphold the rights of S. Peter and his dominions. He would never plunder the papal territories, especially the principality of Benevento. The churches and their possessions in his domains he would hand over to the Papacy, and he would maintain the election decree of the Easter Council. Richard of Capua, the descendant of an earlier Norman adventurer, probably took a similar oath, though it has not been preserved.

Sicily had not yet been captured from the Saracen, yet the Papacy had granted it away as a fief to Guiscard. Who was the negotiator of this mighty gesture of papal authority ? The actual negotiator was, no doubt, Desiderius, who had already won the confidence of Richard and his son Jordan. But deep political craft and a far-seeing political ambition lay behind the programme, coupled with some knowledge of the ancient claims of the Papacy. The grant of Sicily to the Normans was based upon the old forged Donation of Constantine, which assigned to the Papacy, among other territories, the islands of the sea—a forgery not yet exposed by historical science. Two men at Rome were acquainted with the earlier privileges of the papal see, Humbert and Hildebrand. No doubt Humbert's knowledge of the canons and decretals was more complete than that of Hildebrand, who had urged Damiani to produce a manual for general use, and Humbert was more expert in ecclesiastical policy and theory. Thus if Hildebrand had secured his knowledge of the Donation from Humbert's work the *Adversus Simoniacos*—a book littered with quotations from the canons [1]—that does not lessen the courage and vigour of his action when he applied the ideas of the Donation to the practical

[1] *Cf.* Halfmann pp. 34 ff.

policy of the day. If the Normans wanted conquest they should pay for it; they and their conquests should be swept into the papal dominion. Not only should they be made to guard the Roman Church, but, lest they should be tempted to attack her, their gaze should be permanently directed across the Straits of Messina; and in his ambitious stride Hildebrand also secured assistance for the final attack on Benedict X.

In the autumn a Norman force followed Nicholas to Galeria. Count Gerard's support weakened. Benedict ascended the walls and declared that he had been made Pope against his will. Under a safe-conduct for life and limb, and for the occupation of his property in Rome, he surrendered and abandoned his pontifical robes.

Hildebrand's services were now recognized by the Curia. For some time he had been fulfilling the functions of Archdeacon of Rome, and this designation appears in some early documents against his name, although Mancinus the Archdeacon was still living. Mancinus alone signed the Election Decree as Archdeacon, followed by Hildebrand who subscribed as Sub-Deacon, and at the beginning of August he again signed as Sub-Deacon. Now he was officially appointed Archdeacon of the Roman Church, and signed a document on October 14th in that capacity.[1] On November 7th he assisted at the consecration of the Church of S. Felicitas at Florence.

The Roman Synod of 1060 began on April 9th. For some thirty days past Benedict X had stayed in his own house with his mother, near the church of Santa Maria Maggiore. So for about seven months his safe-custody was respected. Hildebrand, who realized that popular sympathy for him was growing, now caused him to be seized by force, and led before the Synod in the Lateran church, arrayed in pontifical robes. At the high altar

[1] Meyer von Knonau I. 170 f. and n. 93.

his robes were torn from him, and a writing containing an account of his misdeeds was thrust into his hand. In spite of lamentations and cries and the presence of his relatives, he was compelled to read the document, while his mother stood by weeping, with dishevelled hair and bared breast. This woman's tears might turn the hearts of the volatile Romans as some later incidents showed. Hildebrand had ever a swift eye for the influence of melodrama upon human action, and knew that it must be countered by melodrama. He seized the critical moment and cried, ' Ho ! Romans, hear the deeds of the Pope whom ye crowned,' and at the order of the Archdeacon, the papal robes and insignia were torn off Benedict. But he was not degraded from his orders. For a time he was imprisoned in the church of S. Agnes, and prohibited from performing any ecclesiastical function. Later on, at the request of the confessor of Nicholas, he was allowed to read the Epistle, and then the Gospel, in the Church of Santa Maria Maggiore, but never again might he celebrate Mass, for fear of his supporters within and without the City, and he continued to live quietly in his own house in Rome, so that the terms of his safe-conduct were substantially fulfilled. The official deposition staged by Hildebrand was a necessary step in order to vindicate fully the appointment of Nicholas II, and to secure the Election Decree against future misuse by the Roman nobles. Events in the next pontificate showed the wisdom of his action.

Legislation during this period is indistinct. The universal practice of some of the evils against which it was directed made a vigorous policy almost impossible to fulfil. Nicholas II, like Leo IX, had to give way to milder measures. He appears to have decreed that clergy already ordained by simonist bishops, provided they had not been guilty of the offence themselves, should retain their orders. However, for the future, anyone allowing himself to be ordained by a simonist bishop would be deposed together with the bishop. Apart from the Election Decree, the short pontificate of Nicholas was occupied with administration rather than legislation. The reform programme was vigorously promoted in areas distant from Rome. The decrees against simony and clerical marriage were proclaimed at Melfi in South Italy. Cardinal Stephen was sent to France, with a legatine commission, and issued similar prohibitions at Vienne and Tours (1060). In 1061 Stephen went on to the German Court, which had been alienated by the new papal alliance with the Normans. The legate was refused an audience, and at the instigation of Anno of Köln, the name of Nicholas II was no longer recited at Mass. On July 27th, the Pope died. In the months before his death the Roman nobility in the country outside the City were again becoming turbulent. Tostig, the brother of Harold of England, and Aldred, the Archbishop of York, were robbed by Gerard the Count of Galeria, when on a visit to Rome.

The Election Decree of the Lateran Council of 1059 was confirmed at the Easter Synods of 1060 and 1061. This was the last service rendered by Humbert to the course of reform and the development of papal supremacy. On May 5th, 1061, the great Cardinal died. Censorious, sometimes almost to fanaticism, there were occasions when his action compromised papal policy, as when he compelled Berengar to read the gross statement on Transubstantiation at the Council of 1059—a statement which Roman theologians henceforth deplored. Yet Humbert had been the ecclesiastical statesman of the Curia for more than ten years, drafting its policy, no doubt in collaboration with Hildebrand, although with more attention to papal theory than that manipulator of men and money was able, at this era, to give. The contrast between them was that of statesman and politician. With much of Damiani's zeal, but with a restraint in small matters, which saved him from the endless letter-writing of that more emotional man, Humbert's work on the new papal constitution preserved the Papacy during the months after his death, and twelve years later placed Hildebrand on the papal throne.

CHAPTER FIVE

MILES ECCLESIÆ (1061–1073)

THE two years which followed the death of Nicholas II were a time of critical negotiation and anxious conflict for the supporters of the Election Decree, and more than once it seemed on the point of being torn to pieces. Now that Humbert was dead, no rival remained at Rome to share the administration with Hildebrand. Damiani went on with his letter writing, and was soon to involve the Curia in vexation by his impulsive missives. It was fortunate for the Papacy that the last of the able band of clergy brought to Rome by Leo IX was still comparatively young. At every election since his death Leo's cardinals had saved the Papacy from becoming again the victim of Roman selfishness and German policy. Hildebrand was now alone to uphold the new tradition of papal freedom, and if, as indeed occurred, there was a weakening in curial policy during the next two years, that was due not so much to the absence of Hildebrand's older collaborators, as to the enormous odds which now gathered against him. If his hand weakened it was not because it was no longer sure, since others were not there to strengthen it ; still less was it because of any weakening of Hildebrand's aim ; it was due rather to the influence of political movements in Germany, Lombardy and South Italy.

Soon after the death of Nicholas, Hildebrand gathered the cardinals and leading churchmen together in Rome in order to prevent dissension among them. So the first step towards fulfilling the terms of the decree of

63

1059 was taken. In the meantime the Roman nobility, repeating the action taken after the death of Stephen IX, but with more circumspection and a wiser policy, had despatched to Germany Gerard of Galeria and the Abbot of S. Gregory, with the emblems of the Patriciate—the green mantle, ring and gold crown. Hildebrand acted more promptly. He went to Lucca and returned to Rome with Anselm, the associate of Damiani at Milan in 1059, and persuaded him to accept election. So the second condition in the decree of 1059 was fulfilled—the election took place at Rome. Then, through Leo de Benedicto and his relatives in the Trastevere, Hildebrand secured a sum of money, which he sent to Richard of Capua, through Desiderius of Monte Cassino, and, by the aid of Richard's Norman force, Anselm was enthroned as Alexander II at the end of September (1061). The Normans were never again to be of so great assistance to the Papacy until Guiscard's advance drove Henry IV from the City in 1084.

The new Pope, like Nicholas II, was the friend of Godfrey and Beatrix, and was chosen in order to secure their support. It was needed, for Richard of Capua left the City immediately after his consecration, at a time when the Lombard bishops, opponents of the reform movement, were conspiring with the Roman nobles. At the instigation of the Imperial Chancellor, Guibert, they demanded an Italian Pope from the German Court, and sent Guibert to Germany. The Regency, most willing to re-assert the old authority of Henry III, and flattered by the subservience of the Roman nobles and Lombard bishops, felt that it had the position in hand. The insignia of the Patrician were in its possession, and, waiving the custom of appointing a German pontiff, and seeking to gratify the Italians, Henry IV, a boy of eleven, not yet girded with the sword of knighthood, donned the Patrician's insignia, and nominated Cadalus, Bishop

of Parma, to the Papacy.   Cadalus assumed the title of
Honorius II.

This event took place at Basel on October 28th, and it
was almost all that the German Court ever did for Cadalus.
The Empress had no troops to despatch with him to
Italy, and not a royal squadron ever crossed the Alps
on his behalf.   Yet for two years, supported by his own
riches and by the Roman bannerets, he placed corps after
corps in the field, until with the last three hundred
pounds of silver, he purchased his flight from Rome.
It was the spring of 1062 before Cadalus was able to
approach Rome.   Hildebrand was eagerly looking
around for armed assistance—sanctioned by the Roman
Synod of 1060—in defence of the papal candidate
approved by the cardinals.   Richard of Capua and
Robert Guiscard were engaged with the conquest of
Sicily—in the coming years their eyes were usually gaz-
ing across to Messina or eastward to Constantinople,
while the Papacy expected their assistance under the
terms of the Treaty of Melfi.   Godfrey was not in Italy.
He also played for his own hand throughout these two
hectic years, and never gave the Papacy more than intermittent support.   His wife Beatrix, on the contrary, did
what she could, and hindered the passage of Cadalus
across the Apennines for the whole winter, assisted by
a war between Milan and Pavia, which deflected troops
from the army of Cadalus.   But in the spring he was
on the outskirts of Rome.   Now arrived Benzo the
Bishop of Alba, whose tawdry puns were to dominate
the Roman mob.   He came charged by the German
Court to lead Cadalus into Rome, and well-supplied
with money.   He effected a junction with the troops
of the Roman nobles on the heights to the west of the
Trastevere, Hildebrand's stronghold, and passed into
Rome across the Tiber bridge accompanied by Guibert,
the Imperial Chancellor.   He addressed the Roman mob
in a circus, and easily silenced Hildebrand and Alexander,

ridiculing them under the epithets ' Asinandellus and his
stall-keeper Prandellus '. Beatrix, occupied with the
Lombard forces nearer home, could do nothing in
defence of Alexander II.

Yet Benzo was uncertain of movements in the south.
In order to check a Norman advance he opened communications with Constantinople, and sought the aid of
the Emperor Constantine X, against the princes of the
south.   Meanwhile, he and Cadalus distributed money
in Rome.   But that was a measure which Hildebrand
understood.   We have a vivid picture of him during
these active days riding about the Trastevere with his
friends, clothed as a horseman.   On the night of April
14th–15th, Hildebrand raised fresh forces for Alexander.
He went out among the people, not like the spearmen
to make them ' humbly bring pieces of silver ', but to
scatter the gold of his banker cousin and the gifts of
Beatrix of Tuscany.   On the next day the troops of
Cadalus won a hard fought battle on the Neronian Field,
and captured the Leonine quarter of the City, but his
army withdrew to Tusculum in order to recruit fresh
support from the nobles of the Campagna.   Both sides
took breath.   Damiani flung two angry letters at Cadalus, in one of which he prophesied the latter's death
within a year—an example not lost upon Hildebrand.
A false report of the death of Alexander II caused
Cadalus to think that the victory was his, but help was
at hand for the other side.   Hildebrand had not been
able to concentrate enough military force to secure a
final decision, yet he had held the Trastevere long enough
to enable assistance from an unexpected quarter to arrive,
and the gold of Leo de Benedicto lasted longer than the
gold of Cadalus.   Godfrey of Lorraine, who could
hardly allow the Lombard bishops, enemies of the house
of Tuscany, to triumph in Rome, and who was always
eager to hold a balance between forces which might
some time be hostile to himself, descended upon Rome.

Cadalus was put to flight, and both Popes were ordered to retire to their respective bishoprics—Lucca and Parma —to await the decision of Henry IV and the Empress Agnes. This was never made, for a revolution at the German Court transferred the settlement of the Italian question to other hands.

On the death of Henry III, when his successor was barely six years old, the Regency fell to Agnes, a woman renowned for her beauty and piety, but lacking in the capacity for government, or even for the training of the young King. With Pope Victor II she lost an adviser who might have guided her safely through some of the difficulties of the coming years. The appointment of Stephen IX and Nicholas II by the Curia reflected against the prestige of the Regency in Italy, and, although the Empress recognized both these elections, her confidence in the Papacy was shaken by the Election Decree of 1059, and by the Treaty of Melfi with the Normans. In Germany the break-up of the central authority of the throne so jealously built up by Henry III, began. Swabia was bestowed on Duke Rudolf (1057), who had eloped with Agnes' daughter, and Bavaria on Count Otto (1061), and these magnates began to assert their power against the Crown. Among the bishops, rivalry and jealousy existed between Archbishop Anno II of Köln, Siegfried of Mainz and Adalbert of Bremen, who was seeking by mission work and negotiation to build up a great north German patriarchate which was to include Scandinavia and some of the western Slavs. These great prince-bishops were also jealous of the influence at the Court of Bishops Henry of Augsburg and Gunther of Bamberg.

Amid these intricate political and ecclesiastical intrigues, the education of the young King was being neglected. This formed an excuse for the plot which came to a head at Easter, 1062. The chief agent was Anno, appointed Archbishop of Köln by Henry III in 1052, against the wishes of the people. He was a trust-

worthy follower of Henry III, energetic, able in administration, and a supporter of religious reforms, but without the thoroughgoing zeal of the Italian school. Although canonized after his death, he was a politician—
certainly not a saint—dominated by a love of power, and
sharing with Adalbert of Bremen a great ambition.
Together with Otto of Nordheim, Ekbert of Brunswick
—both Saxons—and possibly with the knowledge of
Godfrey, at that time in Lorraine, Anno planned the
abduction of the young King from his mother. At
Easter (1062) the prince was enticed to Kaiserswerth,
then an island in the Rhine, and was persuaded to go on
board the Archbishop's finely appointed barge. Immediately the ropes were slipped, and the oars flashed
in the water. The King flung himself overboard, but
was rescued by Count Ekbert with some difficulty. He
was taken to Köln and there became the prisoner of
Anno, who assumed the Regency. Thus, at less than
twelve years of age, Henry IV was torn from the side
of a mother to whom he was attached, and fell under the
control of a guardian whom he never ceased to dislike.

A change of policy towards the Papacy was now
instituted. Hitherto Anno had agreed to the support
given by the German Court to Cadalus, but at the
Council of Augsburg, held in October and attended by
the young Henry IV, he secured a decision so far in
favour of Alexander II, that the latter was directed to
return from Lucca to Rome, to await a final decision
to be made by a German bishop at a synod in Italy.
Whether or not Damiani's work, the *Disceptio Synodalis*,
had already appeared, and so influenced opinion at Augsburg, this work shows that the supporters of Alexander
had not retracted from the attitude adopted at the
Roman Council of 1059. Damiani put forth high papal
claims to superiority over the royal authority, although
the Empress's right of approval was maintained. Damiani was moving away from the imperialism of his earlier

years, although he never completely surrendered it. In January, 1063, Burchard, Bishop of Halberstadt, nephew of Anno, arrived in Italy, with powers conferred on him at the Council of Augsburg, and pronounced a decision in favour of Alexander II, who was then led by Godfrey of Lorraine back to Rome. In a letter of thanks, which accompanied the pallium, to Burchard, Alexander recognized the assistance rendered by Henry IV to the Papacy. The shadow of illegality resting upon his pontificate had indeed been removed, and, on the other hand, the saving clause of the Election Decree was at length implemented. Anno's services were acknowledged by his appointment as Arch-Chancellor of the Roman Church, and his friend Gunther of Bamberg received the pallium, a detail which suggests that Hildebrand had little voice in these affairs, since, according to his view, the pallium must be received in Rome in person.

At the Easter Synod of 1063 Cadalus was formally condemned and the Election Decree of 1059 was confirmed, but it was really no time for practical *Te Deums* of this kind. A Synod of the Lombard bishops at Parma hurled back Alexander's anathema, while Cadalus collected money for a new campaign. His cause was by no means lost in Rome, where his supporters held the Leonine city and the castle of S. Angelo, besides the south bank of the Tiber. Godfrey and Hildebrand, aided by the gold of the Trastevere, called up a Norman force, and set it to attack the castle of S. Paolo which was threatening Alexander II in the Lateran.

Godfrey's action was as usual ineffective, until a critical moment arrived. He left Rome, but allowed Beatrix to guard the passes of the Apennines against Cadalus. This she did successfully for a time. But the gold of Cadalus won fresh supporters among the Roman nobility, and, crossing the mountains one night, he appeared in the Leonine city, accompanied by Benzo, and secured S. Peter's Church. The next morning he was compelled to take refuge with Cencius in S. Angelo. Hildebrand was again in sole charge of the operations in Rome. His distress was acute. The work of the past three years was undone, but throughout his life he never recognized defeat. Three days he spent in prayer and then called upon the Norman force for a supreme effort against his enemies. In the fight, which extended from the southern bank of the Tiber across the river to S. Angelo, the Normans were worsted, and they did nothing for a month. Then two months were consumed with skirmishing in which the Normans made no serious stand. They were finally defeated by a device which in three years time was to win for their kinsman so great a victory elsewhere. Cadalus persuaded the Roman nobles to feign flight. The Normans rode out of the Lateran and were overwhelmed near the baths of Constantine. To save themselves they agreed to leave Rome. The God of battles does not always answer the prayers of his servants, certainly not in the manner they desire. Hildebrand's money was able to keep his Roman force intact around the Lateran, although he could not persuade the stricken Norman force to return. At the critical moment Godfrey came back to Rome, and restored the balance of the opposing forces by securing the aid of another Norman force. Fighting now concentrated at the Appian Gate and around the castle of S. Paolo. Cadalus was again driven to apply for help to Germany and Constantinople. The summer heat of Rome distressed his northern supporters, and, as his money became less, the Roman nobility began to fall away. The last months of Cadalus in Rome were embittered by the knowledge that his patroness, the Empress Agnes, who had appointed him to the Papacy at Basel three years before, had gone over to his enemies. Perhaps the greatest service ever done by Damiani for the Papacy, certainly for the future of Hildebrand, was to persuade the unhappy woman to pass some months in Rome and to take the veil at Fruttuaria. At the Papal Chancery Guibert, the supporter of Cadalus, was displaced by Gregory, Bishop of Vercelli, an appointment doubtless influenced by Hildebrand, who appears to have devoted much of his attention to the Chancery when the fighting in Rome was over, and at a later stage in Alexander's pontificate may have acted as Chancellor himself.

So soon as the fighting was over, the direction of the broad features of papal policy passed out of the hands of Hildebrand, as events in North Italy were soon to reveal. Alexander II assumed direction of affairs himself [1] and no Pope since Victor II pursued so indefatigable a policy, although a definitive turn, at the moment of execution, was sometimes effected by Hildebrand. [2]

During his sojourn in Rome, while practically a prisoner in S. Angelo, Cadalus attempted to take advantage of the growing discontent against Anno's regime in Germany, by applying for assistance to Henry IV and to Adalbert of Bremen, who was the rising hope of the German malcontents, whom Anno had been compelled to associate with himself in the Regency. About this time another letter arrived in Germany which far outweighed that of Cadalus in its effects. While on an embassy to France and Burgundy in the summer of 1063, Damiani wrote to Anno of Köln, and with characteristic impulsiveness suggested that he should hold a synod in Italy, in order to decide definitely between the claims of Alexander II and Cadalus. Adopting the tone of his earlier relations with Henry III, he paid a high tribute to the German kingship in its relation to papal affairs. The whole case of the Papacy since the decree of 1059 was given away, and a tart message of remonstrance reached Damiani from Alexander II and Hildebrand, which Damiani attempted to mollify in the spring of

[1] *Reg.* VII. 24, VIII. 42.   [2] *Cf. Reg.* II. 77.

6

1064, by a communication in which he addressed Hildebrand as ' his holy Satan '. But the damage was done,
and Anno did not lose the opportunity of making an
attempt to re-establish his waning influence at the German Court, by securing in the King's name a notable
victory in Italian affairs.

With trouble threatening in North Italy the Curia
turned its eyes again to the South. Towards the end
of 1063 a consecrated banner was sent by Alexander II
to the Norman Roger, who had won a victory over the
Saracens at Cerami in Sicily. By the despatch of this
emblem the Papacy sought to indicate its spiritual hegemony over the land yet to be conquered, and endeavoured
to retain its claim to the future service of the Normans.
Again and again, a consecrated banner was sent from
Rome to great Captains at the beginning of a campaign,
in circumstances when the hand of Hildebrand is clearly
indicated. So the warlike gesture in favour of Roger
was no doubt urged by him. Alexander's nature was
more peaceable.

At Whitsuntide, 1064, Anno appeared in Italy and
convened a Synod at Mantua on May 31st, to which
Alexander II and Cadalus were summoned. Alexander,
probably without the approval of Hildebrand, alone
attended. Damiani also declined Alexander's invitation
to go with him, and remained at Fonte-Avellana.
Cadalus, who had left Rome one dark night at the beginning of the year, remained at Aqua Nigra near Cremona,
but sent three hundred armed men to protect his supporters, the Lombard bishops, headed by Archbishop
Guido of Milan, who was still hopeful of making headway
against the reforming Papacy, by snatching a victory
for Cadalus, and so bringing to an end the Patarine movement in Milan and the whole reform programme. Yet,
if Anno staged an attack on Alexander, in the name of
the King, and charged him with simony and the Norman alliance, he was at heart a reformer, and when

Alexander, denying the charge of simony, and evading the Norman question, held out the promise of Henry's imperial coronation at Rome, Anno readily assented to the condemnation of Cadalus which Alexander pronounced on the next day. The armed followers of the anti-Pope rushed into the cathedral with the object of reversing the decision of the Synod. They were ejected by the forces of Beatrix, and Alexander went back to Rome. Anno returned with the promise of the imperial coronation to Germany, but found himself completely displaced at the Court. The Empress Agnes was again in Germany and had joined the party of Adalbert. In the following year, when Henry was girded with the sword, the young King attempted to plunge it into the body of Anno, and was only restrained by his mother and Archbishop Adalbert. The change in the Regency was disastrous for Henry's training. If under Anno's care he had been protected from youthful favourites, no impression had been made upon his character by the Archbishop of Köln. Now, under the slack supervision of Adalbert, whose attractive personality won the King's regard, but whose very indulgence to the faults of a growing youth spelled trouble to the Empire in the future, the final stage in an apprenticeship of folly, indiscipline and indulgence was reached. Henry IV, a youth of splendid physique with certain fine qualities of mind, had some of the weaknesses of Robert of Normandy. These were encouraged by the experiences of his early years, and remained unchecked by any of his preceptors. The later disasters of the Empire were partly due to his early training.

In the long history of the Roman anti-Popes no more extraordinary figure than Cadalus appeared. Throughout the pontificate of Alexander II he maintained a hydra-headed opposition. So soon as he was condemned at one synod—his armed men scattered, his cause repressed —he appeared again, and by bribes and machinations stirred up powerful movements against the Papacy. In the early part of 1065 his emissary Benzo was at the German Court, and succeeded in suggesting to the mind of Henry and his advisers the necessity for the King to appear in Italy for his coronation at Rome; for the suppression of the Normans; and, of course, for yet another decision between Alexander and Cadalus. Hildebrand was kept informed of German movements by Anno, and succeeded, in spite of Duke Godfrey's approval of the journey, in procuring the postponement of the King's visit from month to month, although the royal army was ready to move into Italy at Whitsuntide.

At this stage the policy of the Curia was again compromised by another letter of Damiani addressed to Henry IV, urging him to hasten his visit for the suppression of Cadalus, and the vindication of the Roman Church. He quoted the services of previous Emperors —Nerva, Constantine and Theodosius—to the church. Let him follow the example of his father Henry III and come to the rescue of the church. Let him come as a second Constantine against a second Arius—against Cadalus. But in the eyes of Alexander and of Hildebrand, the case of Cadalus was already decided, and, although the Curia would welcome any support that Anno and Godfrey might lend, it could not be welcome in the form in which it had been revealed at Mantua. The political ineptitude of Damiani's letter was bound to cause estrangement between him and Hildebrand, and this is reflected in a letter of Damiani to Alexander II, in which he complains that his mind begins to grow cold towards the Pope.

Meanwhile, the report of Henry's coming visit to Italy had stirred up Cadalus and his supporters to renewed efforts in the province of Milan. Here they were joined by Hugh the White, one of the company of able clergy brought to Rome by Leo IX from Lorraine, and the only cardinal who deserted to Cadalus. Landulf, the democratic Captain of the Pataria, died of consumption after his wound at Piacenza. The Milanese clergy again became active. But Ariald persuaded Herlembald, Landulf's brother, newly returned from Jerusalem, to take the lead of the Patarine party. ' A lean, red-bearded man with flashing eyes ',[1] splendidly arrayed, Herlembald moved about the city with an imposing bodyguard, and by persuasive oratory played the rôle of an idolized Patrician democrat, while Ariald appealed to plebeian sentiments by acts of obsequious though sincere deference to the poor. During Herlembald's visit to Rome in 1065, Alexander in the presence of Hildebrand symbolically took the new Milanese leader and his cause under the special protection of the Roman Church, by handing to Herlembald a consecrated banner. This extension of papal influence, instituted with the grant of a consecrated banner to Roger of Sicily the year before, served in the year following as a precedent for extending it over yet another island of the sea. Duke William of Normandy sent Gilbert, Archdeacon of Lisieux, to Rome to secure the Pope's blessing on the coming invasion of England. But the indifferent support given to the Curia after the Treaty of Melfi, the growing power of the Normans in the South of Italy, the complications with the German Court, created by the Norman alliance, raised opposition at Rome towards any new entanglement with the Norman race. Yet William had already won the approval of the Papacy by his prompt fulfilment of the terms of his absolution in 1059. He had built and endowed the monasteries of S. Stephen and Holy Trinity at Caen, and his measures for the reform of the church in Normandy promised a similar extension of the reforming programme, in the event of a successful conquest of England. Hildebrand regarded the enterprise in the light of a crusade. His own martial

[1] Previté-Orton *C.M.H.* V. 219.

spirit, rightly or wrongly, never shrank from an appeal to the sword. Much of the old Lombard fierceness remained in his breast. The opponents of William's scheme in the Curia were over-ruled by Hildebrand's voice, though with much difficulty, and, drawing upon himself the murmuring comments of his critics and complaints amounting almost to infamy, Hildebrand secured the Pontiff's approval for William's plans, and Alexander II sent to the Duke a consecrated banner. On this occasion Hildebrand's belligerent attitude was entirely justified by the event. When the conquest of England was completed, Lanfranc, the Abbot of S. Stephen at Caen, and the former Prior of Bec, became Archbishop of Canterbury. The dioceses and monasteries of England were entirely overhauled. From the abbeys of Normandy and France, monks trained in the new reforming principles were brought over, and filled the English bishoprics and abbacies. A series of great councils extended the movement to the parishes of England.[1] Fliche's contention that the practical reform movement in the Western Church sprang entirely from Lorraine [2] cannot be substantiated in the case of England, nor even of Normandy. In both areas the reform of diocesan life was effected by bishops and clergy drawn from the Benedictine abbeys of Normandy and France, not always indeed framed on the Cluniac model, but all influenced by the example of Cluny, and in many cases directly allied with her.[3] Even the intense activity in the field of canon law—the research devoted to the resolutions of ancient councils and the decrees of former pontiffs ; the issue of collection after collection of canons, in compact form, ready for the use of the Popes and their legates—which Fournier confines to Italy and Southern France during this period, was being carried

[1] *Cf.* my *Lanfranc* (1926) p. 95 f.
[2] Fliche *La Réforme Grégorienne* I. (1924).
[3] Böhmer *Kirche und Staat* 106 ff.

on first in Normandy, and then in England, under the impetus supplied by Lanfranc, the ex-lawyer of Pavia. A manuscript at Trinity College, Cambridge (No. 405), proves that before he came to England Lanfranc was promoting the study of the canons at Bec, and Mr. Z. N. Brooke has shown that the inquiry was being pursued all over England under Lanfranc's influence.[1] In this era there flourished a distinctive school of Norman and English reformers, indirectly influenced by Cluny, but owing more to Lanfranc and his Norman collaborators.

In spite of Herlembald's vigorous measures at Milan, the northern archbishopric continued to be a source of anxiety to the Papacy. The agents of Cadalus ceaselessly carried on their machinations. On the other hand Archbishop Guido was threatened with excommunication by Alexander II, and Ariald infuriated the Milanese clergy by attempting to introduce the Roman Liturgy. The Patarines joined in the uproar, and Milan became a mass of seething confusion. Guido issued an interdict and Ariald left the city, and was soon afterwards mysteriously murdered.

The Normans of the South were also giving trouble in this year (1066). Richard of Capua invaded the papal territories, and advanced towards Rome—a menace which produced vacillation in the papal policy towards the German Court. Letters were despatched to Henry IV begging his assistance against the Normans, and the imperial visit which two years before had been vigorously opposed by the Curia was now encouraged. However, the Papacy was saved from German interference by the arrival of Godfrey in Italy (1067) with an armed force, contrary to the wishes of Henry IV and the German princes, who desired an imperial advance to Rome. Accompanied by Alexander and the cardinals, Godfrey proceeded to the south, but, after some indecisive opera-

[1] *The English Church and the Papacy* (1931).

tions, concluded peace with Richard of Capua. Godfrey was pursuing his usual policy of maintaining the balance between the Normans and the Curia, and, although he delivered the papal territory, for the time being, from Norman aggression, the result of his campaign was so inconclusive for the Papacy, that in July Alexander II and Hildebrand returned to Apulia, and renewed the treaty of alliance with the Normans concluded by Nicholas II at Melfi. The policy of securing aid from Germany was abandoned. In this manœuvre the hand of Hildebrand is indicated.

The Curia was now strong enough to intervene again at Milan. In August Mainard, the Cardinal-Bishop of Selva Candida, and John, the Cardinal-Priest, were sent from Rome, and order was restored on the basis of Damiani's settlement of 1059. Archbishop Guido was again recognized by the Papacy.

In the first week of 1068, a royal embassy crossed the Alps, headed by Anno of Köln, Henry, Bishop of Trent, and Duke Otto of Bavaria. On the way to Rome they visited Cadalus and Benzo, and conveyed to the anti-Pope the good wishes of the King. For this slight upon Alexander's dignity full satisfaction was obtained at Rome, and Anno had to make it. Barefooted, and walking beside the martinet Beatrix, the proud German patriarch was compelled to enter the City, protesting that this was not the way to treat a royal ambassador. At the Synod he was faced by his enemy Abbot Stablo, and received a papal order to do justice in the affair of Malmedy, when he returned home. A charge of simony, lodged by Anno two years before against Udo, the new Archbishop of Trier, was now publicly refuted, and Udo received the pallium. Finally, Anno was deprived of the papal archchancellorship. The tables of Mantua were completely turned.

In the spring of 1068 Godfrey became involved in a dispute with the Papacy. A quarrel had arisen between

the monastery of Vallambrosa and Peter, the Bishop of
Florence, who was charged with simony.   At Rome the
Abbot of Vallambrosa challenged the Bishop to the
ordeal by fire, and was vigorously supported by Hildebrand.   Alexander, Damiani and Godfrey were in favour
of lenient measures, but Hildebrand, assisted by the
Countess Beatrix—had they arranged the humiliation of
Anno ?—secured the ordeal, to which Peter succumbed,
and was declared deposed.   So Godfrey and his wife,
like his son and Beatrix's daughter on a later occasion,
found themselves on opposite sides in their relations
with the Curia.   Godfrey was then charged by Damiani
with negotiations with Cadalus.   Alexander imposed on
him as a penance separation from Beatrix, until he undertook a vow to build a monastery.   The growing strength
of the Papacy is also indicated in the desertion of Cadalus
by Hugh the White, who returned to Rome and received
the pardon of the Curia.   Hugh was sent as papal
legate to Spain, where he published the reforming
decrees, especially against simony, and persuaded some
of the churches to adopt the Roman order for the
Mass.

A still more striking victory for the papal power was
obtained in Germany in 1069.   In 1066, at the age of
sixteen, Henry IV had married his ten-years affianced
bride Bertha, the daughter of Odo of Turin and Adelheid of Susa, but in pursuit of wild courses, the King
refused to live with his wife, and at the Council of
Worms, with the approval of Siegfried, Archbishop of
Mainz, sought a divorce from her.   The project was
opposed by the German nobles, but the King was
encouraged by the rapid suppression of the rebellion of
the Margrave Dedi.   In the autumn Damiani appeared
at the Council of Frankfurt, and threatened Henry with
excommunication, and the refusal of the imperial crown.
The King gave way and some months later was reconciled with Bertha, who retained his affection to the end

of his life.   On December 24th, Godfrey of Lorraine
died and was buried at Verdun.

In the last years of Alexander's pontificate the prestige
of the Papacy in distant lands was growing.   Anno's
condemnation at Rome in 1068 was repeated in 1070
when he, together with Siegfried of Mainz and Herman
of Bamberg, was summoned to answer charges of
simony.   Their appearance at the Curia testified to a
genuine respect for the principles of the reform movement among the leading ecclesiastics of Germany,
especially since this visit of the German bishops was
not connected with imperial relations with Rome.   At
the Synod of Mainz in 1071, convened by the Pope's
order, Archbishop Siegfried was commanded to settle
a dispute at Constance in the presence of the two papal
legates, the Archbishops of Trier and Salzburg.   The
King wished this case to be settled at Rome, but the
Pope over-ruled the royal request.

Lanfranc, the new Archbishop of Canterbury, asked
that the pallium might be sent to him.   There were
many ancient and some modern precedents for the grant
without his appearance in Rome.   Hildebrand replied
with a tactful letter.   He regretted the trouble of the
long journey which Lanfranc must undertake.   If it had
been possible the pallium would certainly have been sent
to a dignitary of Lanfranc's eminence.   In 1071 Lanfranc came to Rome, and was received with unusual
honour by his old pupil, the reigning Pontiff, and the
settlement of the dispute between Canterbury and York
was referred back to Lanfranc, in collaboration with the
English bishops and abbots.[1]

In October (1071) a great gathering of bishops and
lay-magnates attended by Alexander, Hildebrand and
the other cardinals, was held at Monte Cassino, where
the splendid church, built by Abbot Desiderius during

---

[1] *Cf. Lanfranc* p. 84.   For a discussion of the forgery question *cf.* the
Appendices, and *Journal of Theological Studies* (Oct., 1930).

the last five years, was consecrated. Only Robert Guiscard and Count Roger were absent, engaged on the conquest of Italy. Recent quarrels among the Norman and South Lombard princes were composed, and the influence of the Papacy over the Normans was confirmed and strengthened.

The only quarter where the predominance of the Curia was still violently disputed was Milan. After the Roman embassy of 1067, Archbishop Guido contemplated resignation. A scheme was now unfolded by Hildebrand which was destined to contribute to the many causes of dispute in later years between him and Henry IV. By ancient custom the King of Italy had nominated the archbishops of Milan. If Henry IV had already been crowned with the iron crown of Milan, this right would have fallen to him. Hildebrand now proposed to Herlembald that the only possible solution for the troubles in Milan lay in a canonical election, after the resignation of Guido, confirmed by the Roman Church. In the absence of a formally crowned Italian king there was some reason in Hildebrand's view, although the right of the Papacy to intervene in the question had not been established. Guido thought he could check the proposal by secretly resigning, and sending Henry a nominee, his Sub-Deacon Godfrey, for appointment to the vacant see. Godfrey was invested with the ring and staff at the imperial court, but was driven out of Milan by the Patarines, enraged by the charge of simony which their leader had astutely brought against him. In Lent (1071) half the city was destroyed by fire. Guido withdrew and died on August 23rd. In January, 1062, Herlembald secured the election of Atto, a young cathedral clerk, in the presence of the legate Cardinal Bernard. On the very day of his election Atto was carried into the cathedral, and forced to swear that he would never allow himself to be enthroned. But Herlembald held his ground, and Hildebrand took up Atto's cause at

Rome. He obtained the confirmation of his election, and the excommunication of Godfrey [1] at an assembly of the Roman clergy, headed by Alexander, and sent off a courier and a large sum of money to Herlembald, releasing Atto from his oath. Thus, when the dispute between the Papacy and the imperial court, created by Cadalus, had ended with the death of the anti-Pope at the turn of the year 1071–1072, a fresh cause of dissension, started by a local difficulty, took its place, and was already a cause of burning mutual recrimination between Rome and Germany, before it supplied fuel to the great conflagration of the next pontificate. Almost immediately another source of contention was started at Ravenna, where Guibert the ex-Chancellor, supported by Agnes and Anno, who had regained the King's favour on the death of Adalbert (March 16th, 1072) was created by Henry IV Archbishop of Ravenna. Guibert himself was to take the place of Cadalus in the next pontificate, but, long before that occurred, Henry's appointment of Guibert without consulting the Curia, became one of the cardinal points at issue between them.

The royal intervention at Milan was at once challenged by Alexander II in a letter of warning sent to Henry IV. Similar admonitions, both by letter and messenger, were despatched by Hildebrand to the young king.[2] The warnings were disregarded. No doubt Anno's advice upheld the King's action. He was not the man, when smarting under the indignities to which he had been submitted at Rome in 1068 and 1070, to lose this opportunity of revenge. Yet Henry was now nearly twenty-three, and had already shown that his independent mind reacted stubbornly against dictation from baron and bishop alike. Nor was the legality of the claim of the Curia to interfere with ancient imperial and royal rights at all clear, save on the ground that, as Henry was not

---

[1] *Reg.* I. 15.   [2] *Reg.* IV. 1 and *Ep. Coll.* 14.

yet either German Emperor or Italian King, his reliance upon ancient precedent was weak. The Papacy was on safe ground in claiming a free canonical election at Milan, according to old custom, which preceded the rights of the Italian King in that city. But it had no precedent for intervening in the election against the wishes of the Milanese clergy. Henry sent an embassy to the bishops of the province of Milan, ordering them to consecrate Godfrey. This took place at Novara. Yet the Curia acted with caution. At the Lenten Synod of 1073 no retaliation was adopted against Henry, although his counsellors and those of the Empress were excommunicated, and Count Eberhard of Nellenburg was mentioned by name. Cardinal Hugh the White succeeded in rebutting a charge of simony brought against him by the monks of Cluny, and Guibert, the new Archbishop of Ravenna, was consecrated, against the wishes of Alexander, who warned Hildebrand against him. Hildebrand, although a man of action, was strangely unable to judge character. At this Synod, by allowing the attitude of Hugh the White and Guibert to pass without challenge, he laid up trouble for himself in future days.

On April 21st, Alexander II died. His pontificate epitomized the story of the Papacy during the past forty years. The storms of Benedict IX's era had gradually given place to the power and confidence of Leo IX. So when Cadalus was finally turned out of Rome Alexander took up again the programme of reform. Exciting incidents and dangerous complications occurred from time to time, but they were overcome by the fighting spirit of Hildebrand. The last six years of Alexander's life were accompanied by a gradual but sure extension of papal influence throughout Italy and the West, and yearly synods at Rome became the rule ; embassies and legations were despatched to distant princes and metropolitans ; archbishops were summoned to the Lateran, and the oversight of the provincial churches, formerly left almost entirely to the metropolitans, was increasingly assumed by the Papacy. In one respect there was a contrast with the pontificates of Leo IX and Victor II —Alexander was not able to travel to synods outside Italy. Under Alexander II the papal administration became more centralized and more Roman. Leo IX had introduced imperial methods into the Chancery ; Alexander reintroduced the Roman scrinium and the old curial hand, and the old local usages were not finally excluded from the Chancery [1] until the beginning of the twelfth century, when the Popes, for a time, were again elected from the trans-Alpine churches. No doubt the Papacy, in this period, was favoured by the minority in Germany. If Henry III had lived, and if he had trained his gifted son in the ways of strong and prudent administration, the development of the papal hegemony must have been indefinitely postponed. Perhaps a reformed Papacy might have learned to confine itself to spiritual matters—the reform of clerical life, the guardianship of lay morality, the administration of purely ecclesiastical affairs—protected and encouraged by an enlightened imperial rule. But the weakness of the Regency encouraged, if it did not make necessary, the intervention of the Papacy in the sphere of civil affairs, although usually at points where the two administrations crossed. Such being the case, a clash of opposing principles was bound sooner or later to occur, although it is remarkable that it came so soon. A really great administrator on the papal throne, in the days of Gregory VII, would have outmanœuvred a young and headstrong German monarch, who had lost the confidence and support of half a kingdom, but how that opportunity was missed is the tale we have yet to tell.

When Alexander died, Hildebrand alone, of all the great cardinals who had struggled for reform since the

---

[1] Lane Poole *Papal Chancery* pp. 70, 98 f.

time of Leo IX, remained to carry on the tradition. Peter Damiani had passed away on February 22nd (1073). Yet how unsuited was Hildebrand's past experience for the mighty opportunities now opening before him. Statesmanship garbed with moderation, policy clear and undeviating, a philosophic grasp of both sides of the great principles at issue, above all, sympathy with the laymen's standpoint—such were some of the qualifications necessary in the successor of Alexander II. Hildebrand with all his fearless devotion to duty, his vision of high spiritual requirements, his long service in the Curia, had not received the mental and psychological training needed for his task, His one practical intellectual interest had been abandoned amid the press of business, and, although he took it up again, he never had time to study the canons exhaustively. If his knowledge of the Bible and of Gregory the Great remained as an abiding equipment for the motions of his mind, that was too thin an intellectual endowment for the founder of the new European statecraft. There was a curious similarity between the early training of Henry IV and of Hildebrand. Neither of them was moulded in circumstances which corresponded with the promise of their characters, or with the great offices to which they were called. For thirteen years, from some standpoints the most critical period of his life, Hildebrand, covered by archidiaconal consequence, had yet been occupied with the harassing and sordid duties attached to the control, equipment and payment of the little armies which were called in to establish and defend Pope after Pope in the Lateran. Such a man, like a military commander, becomes self-centred and unsympathetic ; but Hildebrand was without the saving opportunities provided to a great Captain by broad fields of vision, which create a certain hard nobility, supply conditions for wide success, and prevent mere pettiness and fanaticism. Blessing papal banners for Norman commanders was

but showman's work—as the failure of the Treaty of
Melfi showed—which would have been cured by six
months on the staff of either Roger or William as chaplain to the Duke.　Although he had seen much fighting, Hildebrand had never seen war in all its grandeur,
and in all its horror ; otherwise he would have hesitated
to encourage half Germany to make war upon its youthful King, or, if that was really inevitable, he would have
supported Rudolf and the Saxons with something more
than pious aspiration.　Hildebrand, indeed, was meant
to be a man of action, but his training operations were
conducted on too limited and petty a field.　He was now
called to be a man of policies and big combinations behind the scene of action.　He emerges from time to
time into a more active theatre.　But after his elevation
to the Papacy, he becomes in the main the personality
behind the scenes.　Such is the fate of all who reach
the pinnacle of human greatness and are refused the
executive reserve of the sword-handle.　Yet, if shrouded
from active life, they become those who direct the ideas
and manipulate the thoughts of others ; and what a
sequence of self-repeating movement Gregory VII set
going in the great world of Germany and Italy, and in
every country and diocese of Europe !　His couriers set
armies in motion which he did not control, and his
legates convened innumerable councils which he did.
The thunder of his anathema reverberated from kingdom
to kingdom and church to church, but, apart from his
portrait stamped in the letters, he is the figure behind the
scenes, moving onwards to a doom which he cannot see,
and which bursts upon him from a quarter never expected,
and rolls him again into the white light of action when,
broken in health, though not yet full of years, he was
past assuming the reins of control, as in earlier days when
he rode forth among the bankers and the soldiery of
the Trastevere.　Indeed, that early training ruined him.
He attempted to manipulate Henry IV and Rudolf of

Swabia as he had controlled Leo de Benedicto Christiano and the squadron-commanders of Norman horse in Rome. He attempted to rule an Empire with the gestures of an Archdeacon.

CHAPTER SIX

ELECTION (1073)

ON the third Sunday after Easter, as the Vesper bell was ringing, Alexander passed away. In a brief pathetic sentence, repeated to at least three correspondents, Hildebrand expressed his sense of loss. ' Our Lord Pope Alexander is dead.' These simple words bring him close to the heart of every mourner who has taken up the pen to announce a great emotion in an unemotional way. Then his feelings for a moment gushed forth. ' His death overwhelmed me and disturbed me inwardly, dashing all my bowels together.' Even the turbulent city mob was sobered by the news. ' At his death the Roman people, contrary to its custom, was quiet, and left the reins of counsel to my hand ; so that it would clearly appear that this happened by the mercy of God.' Was Hildebrand becoming weary of guiding the Popes through turmoil to the tiara ? Anxiously he watched the movements in the City as Alexander lay dying, and with great relief of mind at the unwonted calm, took counsel with the cardinals, and arranged a three days' fast with litanies and prayer and almsgiving, that, ' supported by the divine aid ', they might arrange for the election of the new Pontiff. But less than twenty-four hours later the hope of a quiet and orderly canonical election was rudely shattered in the midst of the funeral ceremonies. That restless soul, Hugh the White, had been at work, and in the crowded church of the Lateran his agents began to shout ' Hildebrand for our Bishop ! ' The cry was taken up by the throng of clergy, laymen and women, until it became a tumult. They surged around the Archdeacon, as he made his way to the pulpit, in an effort to quell the uproar. But Hugh was before him, and harangued the multitude, reminding them of Hildebrand's long service to the Roman Church and City, ' Let us elect him, a man ordained in our own Church, known to us all, and in all things a tried man.' ' With violent hands ' they seized him and bore him to S. Peter's, where the formal election was hurriedly carried through by the cardinal clergy, amid the assenting throng of bishops and abbots, clerks and monks, and lay folk.[1] Still unwilling, and still only in Deacon's orders, he was then enthroned.

These events took place on April 22nd. They were followed by several hours of extreme exhaustion, when Gregory was too fatigued and troubled in mind even to dictate letters. Yet the next day he was busy with the scribes. Letters were despatched to a number of friends, and correspondents, some of whose couriers were perhaps awaiting replies to communications already received by the Curia. The despatches sent out by Gregory between April 23rd [2] and 30th were all more or less written in the same terms, and at least five of them were copied from the same exemplar. Gregory announced his election, declared his unwillingness for the high office thrust upon him, his unfitness in view of the serious problems before the Roman Church, and begged for the prayers and support of his friends— sentiments quite compatible even with a voluntary acceptance of the office, if a considered invitation to it had been offered to him. The list of people addressed is interesting. Desiderius, Abbot of Monte Cassino and Gisulf, Prince of Salerno, were urged to come to Rome,

---

[1] I have given a summary of the statements of Gregory (*Reg.* I. 1), Bonitho and the *Commentarius* (*Reg.* I. 1*), and of the conflicting accounts of Meyer von Knonau and Martens. The account in the text is substantially that of Mr. Brooke (*C.M.H.* V. 51). Fliche II. (1925) 74 refused the account of the part played by Hugh the White as mendacious.

[2] Following Caspar's chronology.

and a message of greeting was conveyed to the Empress
Agnes, at that time in South Italy. Robert Guiscard
was back in Apulia and his movements were causing
anxiety at the Curia. Guibert of Ravenna was invited to
send frequent messengers to Rome—so Alexander's
warning was now being observed. The loyalty of
Beatrix of Tuscany Gregory had already tested in dealing
with Anno of Köln. Hugh of Cluny was Henry IV's
godfather. Two letters, sent to Denmark and Spain,
prove that Gregory's idea of the universal range of the
papal sway was already conceived in the first days of his
pontificate. Since Adalbert of Bremen's death the year
before, no more was heard of a North European patriarchate, but the letter to Svein of Denmark indicates
that the Curia had taken over the direction of ecclesiastical
affairs in that land, although the tenor of Gregory's
communication on this occasion is unknown. But his
attitude to Spain is completely unfolded. In a letter to
the legate in Gaul, Gregory announced that he was
sending to Spain Cardinal Hugh the White as ecclesiastical
adviser to Count Ebulo of Roucy near Reims, who was
conducting, under the ægis of the Papacy, military
operations against the Saracens in Spain. The legate
Gerald was to restore friendly relations between the
Cardinal and Hugh of Cluny, since the former had given
satisfaction at Rome for his behaviour in Spain during
the time of Alexander. But trustworthy monks of
Cluny were to accompany Hugh the White on his
embassy, to assist in reforming the Spanish churches
elsewhere, and to watch the fulfilment of Ebulo's compact with the Curia.[1] In his letter of April 30th Gregory
tells the princes of Spain that the kingdom had been the
property of the Roman Church from ancient times, and
although it had been conquered by the Saracens, the
rights of the apostolic see were not affected, ' for what
had once, by God's providence, become partly the

[1] Reg. I. 6.

property of the church, remained with it, and could not be torn from it without lawful concession, either by custom or law, or the lapse of time.' Whatever parts of Spain, therefore, Count Ebulo conquered from the Saracens, should be held by him as a grant from the Roman Church, under the conditions of the compact made by him with the apostolic see. The Spanish princes were free to assist the Count in his enterprise, but if any of them wished to conduct separate operations, they might do so, yet, unless they were ready to uphold the rights of Peter ' by a similar pact ', he opposed such undertaking.[1]

This amazing claim, based no doubt on the forged Donation of Constantine to Pope Sylvester I, illuminates the nature of Gregory's ambitions towards Sicily and England. Regions of Europe, recently conquered or yet to be conquered from non-Christian rulers, were to be held as fiefs of the church, on the theory that all pagan Europe was the property of the Roman Church. It was but a logical step to apply to the rest of Europe, and to Germany especially, another implication of the Donation of Constantine—the theory that the hegemony over the whole of the West had been awarded to the Papacy by Constantine. Whether or not Gregory at this date contemplated the expansion of this vast claim to the German kingdom, the tendency of his later pretensions is clearly revealed in his extraordinary letters to the Spanish princes, and, through the operation of a mind more logical than statesmanlike, was almost bound to be applied, sooner or later, to practical politics.

He was certainly anxious about Germany. Its political conditions, especially in Saxony, were seething with discontent. Its bishops were partly hostile to the Papacy, but Henry, so far, had engaged in no act of hostility to Gregory. Soon after his election Gregory had sent off an ambassador to the German Court, in order to fulfil

[1] *Reg.* I. 7.

the terms of the decree of 1059,[1] and to secure the royal consent to his appointment. This can hardly have been received before May 6th, when he sent a letter to Godfrey the Younger of Tuscany, the son of Godfrey the Bearded, the collaborator with Hildebrand against Benedict X and Cadalus. The younger Godfrey had married Matilda, the daughter of Beatrix, in 1069. By this marriage, which in due course would make him master of the Tuscan principality of Beatrix, Godfrey the Younger inherited the function of his father, as protector of the Roman Church. He had expressed his joy at Gregory's election, so Gregory compliments him on his faith and courtesy, and expresses confidence in him as ' a beloved son of S. Peter '.

' Concerning the King—no one can be more solicitous or more desirous for his present and future glory. Moreover, it is our will, at the first opportunity, to confer with him in paternal love and admonition, by our legates, upon those things which we think belong to the advantage of the church and the honour of the royal dignity. If he shall hear us we shall rejoice in his welfare as well as our own, for then certainly he will be able to profit himself, if in maintaining righteousness he shall acquiesce in our warnings and counsel. But if—which we desire may not be—he shall unfairly return hatred for our love, and shall return to almighty God, by deceiving His righteousness, contempt for the great honour conferred on him, the threat contained in the words, " Cursed is the man who withholdeth his sword from blood," shall not in the providence of God come upon us. Nor indeed are we free, because of favour to anyone, to put aside the law of God, or to draw back from the path of rectitude, on account of human favour, for the apostle says " If I wished to please men, I should not be a servant of God ".'[2]

On May 22nd, still waiting for a royal embassy from Germany, Gregory was ordained priest, and a month

---

[1] The decree of Nicholas II was not strictly followed. *Cf.* Fliche II. 77 f. and Voosen *Papauté et Pouvoir Civil à l'époque de Grégoire* VII. p. 99.
[2] *Reg.* I. 9.

later on June 24th, when he must have heard that the embassy was on its way, even if it had not already arrived in Rome, the Pope-elect, in a letter to Beatrix and Matilda, again hinted at drastic measures to be adopted against Henry.

'Concerning the King, as you have already received in our letter (no doubt the epistle to Godfrey) it is our will to send to him religious men, by whose warnings, through the inspiration of God, we may be able to recall him to the love of the holy Roman Church, our mother and his, and to instruct and furnish him for the worthy conduct of the imperial coronation.   But if—and we desire it may not be —he should refuse to hear us, we cannot and ought not, God guiding us, to deviate from our mother, the Roman Church, who nourished us, and who has often from the blood of her sons brought forth other sons.   And certainly it is safer for us, by defending truth for his own salvation, to resist him even to our own blood, than, by consenting to wickedness for the fulfilment of his will, to rush with him —God forbid—into ruin.' [1]

Gregory also warned the Countess to avoid communication with the Lombard bishops who had dared to consecrate the simoniacal and excommunicated heretic Godfrey, Archbishop of Milan.   In this affair he was allowing a purely local incident to become a cause of dispute between the Curia and the German King, without waiting to ascertain whether any change of policy would be adopted by Henry now that a new pontificate had begun.   In both letters he makes it clear that he is prepared for bloodshed in order to enforce his will. Possibly he accurately anticipated the royal attitude in the affair of Milan, but what chance had Henry of securing a settlement with honour against a pontiff whose mind was so obviously biased against him ?

It is reported that the Imperial Chancellor of Italy, Gregory, Bishop of Vercelli, who over twenty years ago

[1] *Reg.* I. 11.

had been condemned for a moral offence at Vercelli,[1] and pardoned by Leo IX, attempted to persuade the King to refuse consent to Gregory's election, and that some of the German bishops gave the same advice. If so, Henry generously brushed the suggestion aside, and sent the Chancellor himself to convey to Gregory the royal assent to his election, and to represent the King at the consecration. If this report is true, Henry appears at this stage of their relationships in a more magnanimous frame of mind than Gregory, for the King might, with equal justification, have expressed chagrin over the state of affairs at Milan. He had already been threatened with excommunication for conduct which could be justified by a long historical tradition.[2] When a strong mind plays with resentment, it is apt to lose opportunities suddenly presented for the removal of its cause, and the resulting complications may make retractation impossible at a later stage. By refusing, at this juncture, to sever in his mind the connection between Henry and the appointment of Godfrey of Milan—a mere political blunder in diplomacy —the Pope-elect was encumbering his own mind with an unnecessary prejudice, which made it difficult, if not impossible, for him to estimate fairly new acts of offence which Henry was soon to commit. No admonition was needed from Abbot Walo to gird the sword on his thigh against his enemies in Germany, in order to win the blessing of the Lord. The hard-minded Pontiff, like Charles I, could never retract once he had felt personal chagrin at the conduct of another, and, like the Stuart King, he sought to justify his intransigeance by a lofty but cold appeal to principle. In both cases it was ' our mother the church ' for whom the stiff unbending policy was unrolled, and in both cases for our mother the

---

[1] Walo, Abbot of Metz, who sent this information to Gregory, describes him as ' that devil of Vercelli ', and refers to his *flagitia*. This opinion of him was general, *cf.* Meyer von Knonau II. 219 n. 53.

[2] But *cf. supra* p. 82.

church her misguided advocates died. But were they martyrs ? [1]

On Saturday, June 29th, the festival of S. Peter, the apostle to whom he always paid particular honour, Gregory was consecrated. The date is fixed by the passage in the Gospel, ' Whomsoever ye shall bless, shall be blessed, and whomsoever ye shall bind upon earth, shall be bound in heaven ', which Gregory himself stated was read on that day. [2] The consecration was performed by the Cardinal-Bishops of Albano and Porto, and by the representative of Gerald, the Cardinal-Bishop of Ostia, who was himself returning to Rome from his legation in Gaul. The Empress Agnes and the Countess Beatrix, together with the Bishop of Vercelli, the Italian Chancellor, represented the civil authorities of Germany and Italy. But a Norman prince was not present. On the same day a letter was despatched to William, Bishop of Pavia, urging him to give his assistance to the ' Milanese Catholics ' in their fight against the excommunicated Godfrey and his supporters among the Lombard bishops. [3] No reference is made to Henry. These weighty matters of the King were not, in their inception, to be discussed with mere diocesan bishops. Behind the Milanese business lay the Spanish dream, and with it the militancy of spirit which that enterprise encouraged in the martial breast of the Pontiff. Two days after the letter to William of Pavia, Gregory issued a pastoral letter to the churches in Lombardy, describing the consecration of Godfrey to the see of S. Ambrose as a prostitution of the bride of Christ to the devil. ' We command that in no way shall you agree to this heretic—but resist him by every possible means.' Apart from the violence of the terminology, this monition was reasonable. The papal

---

[1] It is difficult to follow Fliche's argument that at the beginning of his pontificate Gregory's attitude to Henry was one of conciliation (cf. II. 88, 99, 204), especially since he allows that by 1075 it was clear that the Pope ' would break those who did not obey him ' (cf. p. 178).
[2] Ep. Coll. 18.   [3] Reg. I. 12.

candidate, the canonist Atto, elected by the reform party in Milan, was entitled to papal support. But Gregory could not keep his mind free from the idea of an appeal to the sword : ' Cursed is he who withholds his sword from blood '. This metaphor taken from Jeremiah, was equivalent to a direct incitement to the use of force, and the hint was given in the name of ' your mother, the holy Roman Church, the mistress of Christendom '.[1]

And mistress of Christendom he meant her to be, from the beginning of his pontificate. The day after his consecration, he ordered, by ' the apostolical authority ', Manasseh, Archbishop of Reims, not to encroach upon the rights of the Abbot of S. Remi, nor to intrude anyone in place of the Abbot in a manner contrary to the canons.[2] Hugh of Cluny was authorized on the same date to send a messenger to Reims in support of this demand, and to report the Archbishop's action to the Curia.[3] The legate Gerald of Ostia was rebuked for not returning with a report on a synod held in Spain, but Gregory agreed that the offence of holding communication with persons under the ban of the church was not sufficient, unless clearly indictable crimes were proved against them, for the deposition of two bishops. So there was one law for the bishops of Spain and another for the bishops of Lombardy ; yet, in this very letter, he enunciates the principle that the same causes are to be judged by the same laws.[4]

A dispute in Bohemia was inherited from the time of Alexander II, and Gregory began a correspondence which went on for many years. The bishopric of Prague was founded c. 975 by Otto II. In the following year, it was placed under the supervision of the Metropolitan of Mainz, but from the beginning the Papacy had watched its development. Brâtizlav in 1068 appointed a layman, his brother Jaromir, Bishop. In 1071 Jaromir attacked and grossly ill-used John, the Bishop of the revived

[1] *Reg.* I. 15.　　[2] *Reg.* I. 13.　　[3] *Reg.* I. 14.　　[4] *Reg.* I. 16.

Moravian see of Olmütz. Brâtizlav referred the dispute to Alexander II for settlement (1073), and he sent legates for investigation. In a letter of July 8th, when already on his way to South Italy, Gregory cast blame upon the action of his predecessors, for not sending legates frequently enough to Bohemia ; and upon Brâtizlav's forebears for not asking for the same. The result was, he said, that the legates were now treated with contempt. He overlooked the fact that only during the pontificate of Alexander had the reformed Papacy been able to get the legatine system into operation, and made no allowance for the inevitable weakness of the papal administration in past days. Brâtizlav and the legates were ordered to convene a synod, and, if Jaromir would not then submit to the legates nor appeal to Rome, Gregory would confirm the sentence of suspension already passed by the legates upon him, and would ' unsheathe the sword of apostolic indignation to his destruction '.[1] Within ten days of Gregory's consecration even the spiritual discipline of the church was threatened in the belligerent and provocative terms sometimes used by an angry temporal suzerain, terms justified perhaps in the case of a semi-barbarian like Jaromir, but, when read with the letters to the Tuscan family and the Lombards, indicating a fixed idea, quite foreign to the broad statemanship of his predecessor Leo IX or his successor Urban II.

Of happier augury for the peace of Christendom was the letter dated the next day from Albano to Constantinople. Constantine X had been in correspondence with Cadalus and his supporters, with the object of sending them assistance against Alexander II and Hildebrand. Now his successor, the Emperor Michael VII, sent an embassy of two monks with congratulations to Gregory on his election, and the Pope despatched to Constantinople, Dominicus, the Patriarch of Venice, to discuss

[1] *Reg.* I. 17.

with Michael some matters raised by the embassy. The Pope desires to renew the ancient concord between the Churches of Rome and Constantinople, and so far as possible ' to have peace with all men '. If the ancient concord between the Popes and the Eastern Emperors had been of so great profit to the apostolic see and to the Empire, no less had been the damage to both, resulting from the chilling of their love. Yet Gregory writes in a high papal tone, and claims the Church of Constantinople as the daughter of the Roman Church.[1]

In the early part of the year war had broken out between Robert Guiscard and Richard of Capua. Robert's victorious career had driven Richard back into Capua, but was brought to a standstill by Robert's illness in the spring. A report of his death was published and reached Gregory, who sent a consolatory message to his widow, Sigilgaita, offering to invest their son Roger with his father's territories, if she would send him to Rome. But Guiscard recovered and was so gratified by the Pope's embassy that he promised him ' loyal service '. Gregory determined to improve this favourable turn of events by a visit to the south. He invited Robert Guiscard to meet him at San Germano, and the Normans advanced with an imposing force to Rapolla. Possibly this movement alarmed Gregory, for he took refuge in Monte Cassino and Benevento, and sent Desiderius to invite Robert to meet him there. The Norman arrived outside the walls with a large force, but, suspecting the intentions of the citizens, he declined to enter the town, and asked Gregory to come out to him and to trust to his fidelity. This, in turn, Gregory was afraid to do, and angry recriminations followed. Gregory, who now began to show his limitations as a diplomatist when his hand was completely free, thoroughly antagonized Guiscard by making independent treaties with Landulf, the Lombard Prince of Benevento,

[1] *Reg.* I. 18.

and with Richard of Capua, with whom Guiscard was still nominally at war. No effort was made to resort to the diplomacy of Desiderius, who found himself compelled to sign the astonishing agreement drawn up on August 12th between Gregory and Landulf.

'If from this hour the Prince is unfaithful to the holy Roman Church, to its Pope and his successors—if he seeks in any way to diminish the public good of Benevento or to grant any investiture to anyone without the consent of the Pope or without his order—if he shall have planned to make or receive an oath or promote dissension in any enterprise with any man in Benevento or outside—if either through himself or anyone suborned in Benevento or outside he tries, by any method or with any intention, to revenge evil usage, or to damage any of the faithful of the holy Roman Church, in matters which have pertained to fidelity to the Roman Church down to the present time—if he is not able to defend himself before the Lord Pope when called upon—let him lose his principality (*honor*) by the present instrument.' [1]

This formidable list of prohibitions, unrelieved by a single positive clause in favour of Landulf, can only have been directed against Robert Guiscard and accepted by the Lombard magnate in fear of the Norman duke. On Gregory's side it reveals a curious lack of statecraft.

The Pope then went on to Capua, and on September 14th obtained another oath of fealty from Richard.

'I Richard, by the grace of God and of S. Peter Prince of Capua, henceforth from this hour will be faithful to the holy Roman Church, and to the apostolic chair, and to thee my lord Gregory, universal Pope, I will have no share in plan or action, by which thou mayest lose life or members, or be seized by violent arrest. Counsel which thou mayest impart to me, and forbid me to reveal, I will not knowingly reveal to thy loss. I will aid the holy Roman Church and thee in acquiring, holding and defending the regalia of S. Peter and his possessions with true faith against all men,

[1] *Reg.* I. 18*a*.

and I will assist thee to hold securely and honourably the Roman Papacy. The land and principate of S. Peter I will seek neither to invade nor acquire, nor will I presume to despoil them without thy certain license, or that of thy successors, who shall have entered into the possessions of S. Peter, beyond that which thou or thy successors shall concede to me. The payment from the land of S. Peter which I hold or shall hold, right faithfully will I strive that the holy Roman Church may receive annually as arranged. Also all churches which exist within my rule, with their possessions, will I commit into thy power, and I will be their defender in fealty to the holy Roman Church. To King Henry, when advised by thee or by thy successors, I will swear fealty, saving fealty to the holy Roman Church. And if thou or thy successors shall depart this life before me, I will assist, as I shall be advised by the chief cardinals and Roman clergy and people, in the election and consecration of a Pope to the possessions of S. Peter. All these things written above, I will maintain with a true faith to the holy Roman Church and to thee, and this fealty I will maintain to thy successors consecrated to the possessions of S. Peter, if they are willing to confirm to me the investiture conceded by thee to me.' [1]

This oath clearly resembles the oath taken by Guiscard to Nicholas II in 1059, and by Richard to Alexander II in 1061, both drawn up, no doubt, under Hildebrand's influence. It contains an additional clause in favour of Henry IV, but dependent upon the Pope's discretion. The suspicious attitude of Gregory's mind, always expecting attacks upon life and liberty, introduced this unstatesmanlike gesture in a document of high diplomacy. It suggested and helped to create the very atmosphere it sought to dissipate. However fearless he may have been when swords were flashing, Gregory was not dauntless in diplomacy. His demands were frequently excessive because he was afraid. He over-reached himself at Melfi, he over-reached himself at Capua. No wonder

[1] *Reg.* I. 21a.

that his treaties were nearly always torn to ribbons.
The effect of this one upon Robert Guiscard was immediate. While Gregory stayed on at Capua till the middle
of November, Robert called up his brother Roger, who
had come over from Sicily, and now burst into the
principality of Capua, carrying fire and sword from the
Garigliano to Aquino. Meanwhile Roger seized Amalfi
in the territory of Gisulf of Salerno. Monte Cassino
was left untouched, and Robert sent to Desiderius five
hundred pieces of gold.

None knew better than Gregory the value of money
and the power of finance. Without the wealth of
Benedict the Christian and of his son Leo, the anti-Popes
would not have been defeated after the death of Henry III,
and the reforming Popes would not have been set up.
If troops were required to defend the principles of free
election and reform, the troops must be paid. Now
that he was Pope, Gregory knew that the contingency
might arise again, and in any case, the expenses of the
Papacy were increasing. So into the treaty. with the
Normans he inserted the clause for an annual tribute.
This demand was not uninfluenced by a desire to make
the papal hegemony effective in practice as well as in
theory, and it laid the foundation for the financial system
of the later Popes. As the conflict with the Empire
developed, more and more money was required, and the
bishoprics of all Western lands were raked for contri-
butions. The spiritual power was grounded on the
chicanery, injustice and extortion of the papal collectors,
upon whose rapacity no check existed save the needy
voice of the distant Curia.

CHAPTER SEVEN

POPE *v.* KING (1073)

GREGORY'S cautious provision for the interests of the German King in the Treaty of Capua was partly the result of a letter from Henry which arrived at Capua shortly before the middle of September (1073). The relations between Henry IV and the Papacy had already become strained towards the end of Alexander II's pontificate. Reports of the King's irregular life were being received in Rome, although, after his reconciliation with Bertha in 1069, they were without foundation. Henry was now conscientiously devoting his attention to the civil and ecclesiastical administration of Germany. But this in itself led to further difficulty with the Curia. In 1070 he appointed Charles, the Provost of Harzburg, to the bishopric of Constance. In overriding the wishes of the Chapter, who elected another candiate, the King was only following the example of his father Henry III, and his predecessors. In the same year he appointed Meginhard, Prior of Hildesheim, to the vacant Abbey of Reichenau. But Meginhard's promotion was stained with simony, and he resigned in order to pacify the monks. In his place Henry appointed Robert, Abbot of Bamberg, a promotion even more glaringly simoniacal. But the simony was not the act of the King.

The tension between Henry and the Papacy became critical when in the same year Henry invested Godfrey with the see of Milan. Warning messages were sent by Alexander II and by Hildebrand, then Archdeacon, and Henry proved himself amenable to advice. In the

presence of the legates he withdrew his support from
Charles in 1071, and from Robert in 1072. Yet the
King received no consideration from the Curia for these
concessions. He did indeed allow the excommunicated
courtiers, who had been concerned with an appointment
at Hersfeld, to remain in his presence, and this was
interpreted as a sign of dispute between the King and
the Papacy, but Gregory had already admitted to Gerald
of Ostia, the legate in Gaul, that conduct of this kind
did not in itself constitute a reason for drastic action.
The case of Godfrey at Milan was more serious, but
Henry had already shown that he was susceptible to
diplomatic handling ; and he had offered no challenge
to Hildebrand's election to 'the papal chair.

In the meantime the Pope had sent his despatches to
the Tuscan Court, anticipating continued difficulty with
Henry. The demands of the Papacy were growing.
Gregory was determined not only to suppress simony,
in all its many forms, but to transform the intermittent
prohibitions against lay election, which from time to
time had issued from the Curia, into a fixed and strict
policy, with no allowance for exceptional cases where
ancient custom recognized lay control. This was bound
to complicate relations with the German King. But
events were taking place in Germany which opened
up the opportunity for a complete reconciliation with
Henry.

At home Henry was faced with the necessity of
re-establishing the royal power—which had suffered
grievous loss of prestige during his minority—and of
defeating the separatist tendency of the great magnates,
which had begun to undo the effects of the centralizing
policy of Henry III before that monarch died. The
problem was most acute in Saxony where local custom
attached a vigorous and independent people more closely
to local magnates than anywhere else in Germany.
Saxony had never been so loyal to the royal house since

8

it had ceased to supply it with a line of kings. ' It was a bold policy for a young king to attempt, at the beginning of his reign, to grasp the Saxon nettle.' [1] The deposition of the Saxon Otto of Nordheim caused the rebellion of the Saxon Billungs. This was suppressed in 1071, and Henry placed Eberhard of Nellenburg with a garrison at Luneberg, the chief Billung stronghold. Castles were being built in other parts of Saxony. In the same year Henry recognized Godfrey as Archbishop of Milan, but withdrew his candidates at Constance, and the next year at Reichenau. In 1073 Saxony again broke into revolt, and Henry was compelled to fly from the Harzburg. He was now to reap the tares of his harvest of 1071. When he attempted to lead an army, destined for Poland, against Saxony, the German princes, alarmed by the King's success two years previously, declined to move until October. Moreover, Rudolf of Rheinfelden, Duke of Swabia, who had married Matilda, Henry's sister, at the end of 1059, and on her death in 1060, Adelheid, Henry's sister-in-law, wrote to the Pope. Rudolf was already taking the lead among the German princes, although until the end of 1075 he remained loyal to the King. He seems to have had a genuine desire to promote the welfare of Germany, but his letters to Gregory at this time may not have been uninfluenced by the desire to secure the goodwill of the Pontiff in the event of strained relations with the King. His letter has not survived, but from Gregory's reply it is clear that it was framed in most friendly terms towards the Pope, and it seems to have suggested proposals for the good administration of Germany and the promotion of ecclesiastical reforms, by means of an amicable understanding between church and kingdom.

Gregory replied to this letter on September 1st at Capua. Damiani had already compared church and state to two swords, and the Pope, following Rudolf's

[1] Brooke, *C.M.H.* V. 127.

hint concerning the relations between church and state, compared the two dignities to the two eyes of the human body, but his phraseology was theocratic, the *sacerdotium*—mentioned first—and the *imperium* are the two eyes which rule and give light to the body of the church. No specific reference was made in this passage to the empire. Gregory appears to think of church and empire as one whole, an ecclesiastico-political unity in which the stress is laid upon the *sacerdotium*. At any rate he expressed a sacerdotal view of the relations between church and state. But he then added some cordial remarks about the King.

' We wish your nobility to know, not only in respect of King Henry—whose debtor I think I am from the fact that I recognized him as King, and because his father of glorious memory, the Emperor Henry, treated me with special honour above all Italians at his Court, and, when dying, commended his son to the Roman Church, through Pope Victor of venerable memory—that I do not possess any ill-feeling, and I do not wish, by the help of God, to show malice towards any Christian man.'

Yet, the concord between church and empire must not be artificial, it must be sincere, and Gregory suggested a conference in Rome with Rudolf, the Empress Agnes, Countess Beatrix, Rainald, Bishop of Como, and others, at which his proposals might be accepted or amended.[1]

No doubt the hostility of Robert Guiscard disposed the Pope to show to the King a less determined attitude than when he communicated with Godfrey the Younger and Beatrix in June, but he did not propose to include Henry in the conference, he wished to secure the support of Rudolf before divulging his plans to the King, from whom he anticipated opposition. So that, although his attitude was for the time being conciliatory, his purpose was not modified. This rigidity of mind towards the

[1] *Reg.* I. 19.

King is further illustrated by a letter to Rainald, Bishop of Como, dated on the same day.   Rainald had apparently raised the question of the royal intervention at Milan. Gregory replied that his attitude to Henry had already been made known to the Bishop and to the Empress Agnes, who like Rainald had long been a friend of the Roman Church and of himself.   Both of them knew very well that he desired the King ' who is the head of the laity and shall, by God's will, be Emperor of Rome ', to excel private individuals and the princes in good behaviour, life and religion ; to love religion and to increase and defend the church ; to avoid the advice of evil men like poison ; to agree to the counsel of the good.   Rainald was free to take steps which might strengthen the concord between the Roman Church and the King.   Duke Rudolf was coming to Lombardy in September, and in the interest of the Papacy, and on behalf of its relations with Henry, Rainald must bring about this visit to Rome without delay.   He must come himself, and they would discuss and make plans for concord between the Roman Church and the King, together with the Empress and Beatrix, who had laboured much and often for the same thing.   Then Rainald might send an embassy to Henry, to announce that, if he came to Italy, he would find everything at peace.   The Bishop was also granted permission to discuss the matter verbally with the Lombard bishops, but not otherwise.[1]

The theocratic note is again struck.   Henry is the ' head of the laity ' and the Pope is the judge of his private and public behaviour.   ' I wish ', ' I desire ', that he does this and that.   Once again, before he will grant an interview to Henry, the Pope and his friends are to make sure of their ground.   Then Henry may be notified that the Pope will meet him, but the announcement is left to be made by an obscure Italian bishop.   That is the most

[1] *Reg.* I. 20.

striking passage in the letter. It shows clearly either
that the leading cardinals were not yet in Gregory's
confidence concerning the policy to be adopted towards
Henry, or that they disapproved of it at this stage. It
also shows that the Pope was not yet quite sure of his
hand, so he avoided addressing the King personally.
On the other hand, the King's presence in Italy might
be useful against Guiscard, and the Pope ventilates the
suggestion for a royal visit, but his agent is to avoid
negotiations in writing.

A third letter, dated on the same day, sent to Anselm
II, the Bishop-elect of Lucca, reveals what was rankling
in Gregory's mind—Henry had not severed relations
with excommunicated persons. Anselm was warned
not to accept investiture at Henry's hands, until the
King had given ample satisfaction, and was at peace with
the Pope. This matter was to be discussed by Agnes,
Beatrix and her daughter Matilda, and by Rudolf, whose
counsel Gregory could not and ought not to spurn.[1]

But there was no evidence that the King had broken
the peace with the Pope since Gregory's election and
consecration. Gregory was simply carrying forward the
status quo ante of the time of Alexander II, when royal
communication with courtiers under the ban of the
church was indeed in dispute. So far from exacerbating
his relations with the Papacy, Henry in September despatched to Gregory a submissive letter, which reached
the Pope at Capua, possibly at the end of the month,
and certainly stiffened his attitude to Robert Guiscard.

No doubt the King's letter was written under the
influence of the royal reverses in Germany. Saxony was
in revolt and the princes with the army destined for
Poland refused to march against it. Enemies and
enmities were threatening on all sides. In September
came a ray of cheer from across the Alps. Rudolf,
Henry's brother-in-law, had received a letter from

[1] *Reg.* I. 21.

Gregory in which the King was mentioned in kindly terms, and concord between *sacerdotium* and *regnum* was proposed. It is improbable that the contents of this letter were not made known to Henry. Moreover, it is even possible that the Bishop of Como, making a large use of the permission ' to make any arrangement you can between the Roman Church and the King, provided it is useful to both ', may have sent a messenger to Henry, in which, again, the Pope's well-disposed tone to the King was handed on, and the hope of ' concord ' between the Roman Church and Henry was held out. It is in any case remarkable that Henry opens his letter with a prolonged reference to the relations of the *regnum* and *sacerdotium*, and of the union which should exist between them—the very matter emphasized at the beginning of the Pope's letter to Rudolf. The King says :

' While the kingdom and the priesthood, in order that they may continue rightly administered in Christ, need always the viceregents (*vicaria*) of His power, it is especially necessary, my Lord and most-beloved father, that they disagree with each other as little as possible, but that they may rather cohere indissolubly to each other, entirely joined together in the bond of Christ, for so and no otherwise the concord of Christian unity and the state of formal (*ecclesiasticæ*) religion are preserved in the bond of perfect charity and peace. But we who, by the will of God, have for some time now enjoyed the ministration of the kingdom, have not shown as was necessary justice and due honour in everything to the priesthood. Indeed we have carried the sword, not without cause, in vindication of the power given to us by God, but we have not always done it, as was right, against evil-doers, as a judicial sentence. But now to some extent, stung by the divine mercy, and returned to ourselves, we confess our former sins, by accusing ourselves to your paternal indulgence, hoping from you in the Lord that, absolved by your apostolic authority, we may merit justification.

Alas ! criminal and unhappy, partly from the instinct of amiable youth, partly from the liberty of our potent and imperious power, partly by the seductive deception of those whose alluring counsels we have too readily followed, we have sinned against Heaven and before you, and are no more worthy to be called your son.   We have not only trespassed on ecclesiastical affairs, but we have sold the very churches to certain unworthy persons, embittered with the gall of simony, not coming in at the door, but otherwise, and have not defended them as we ought.

But now, since we are not able by ourselves without your authority to correct the churches, we seek strenuously both your counsel and assistance, on these things and in all our affairs, and we shall carefully observe your commands in all things.   And first of all, concerning the Church of Milan, which by our fault is in error, we beg that it may be canonically corrected by your apostolic labour, and then may the judgment of your authority proceed to the correction of other churches.   We shall not be wanting to you by the will of God in anything, humbly begging the same of your paternity, that it may be speedily and kindly with us in all things.   You will shortly receive a letter from us by trustworthy messengers, from whom you shall hear more fully, God granting it, what we have still to say to you.' [1]

This letter was hardly composed by Henry himself. It resounds with the phrases of one well-acquainted with the papal estimate of the King and his policy.   It was framed by an ecclesiastic who well knew how to approach the masterful Pontiff at Rome.   It reflects the attitude of Siegfried of Mainz, who at the last moment always surrendered rather than face a conflict, especially if his own interests were not involved.   Or it may have been inspired by Anno of Köln, who fully understood, from his own experiences at Rome in 1068 and 1070, what was required in the way of submission, and whose counsel was being sought by Henry in the latter half of 1073. The clever handling of the *regnum* and *sacerdotium* at the

[1] *Reg.* I. 29a.

beginning of the letter, meeting Gregory on the very ground selected by him in his letter to Rudolf, shows tact in selecting the term ' *regnum* ' in place of *imperium*, for Henry was not yet Emperor.   In justice to the King, only passing reference is made to his youthful irregularities.   They had ceased, but were still being discussed at Rome, and so they are mentioned.   The question of Henry's relations with courtiers under the ban of the church is not dealt with, but Gregory's attitude in this matter may not have been appreciated.   Even the Pope was not consistent on this point.   But simony and the affair of Milan are fully emphasized.

One wonders whether the King was entirely aware of the terms of the letter—a question which obtrudes itself when we read the compact made by Landulf of Benevento and Richard of Capua.   But, on the assumption that it was properly explained to him, and that he agreed to it, there is no need to accuse him—as has been done frequently—of deep dissimulation, and a calculating postponement of his dispute with the Pope, in order to clear the ground for action in Germany.   So far there had been no dispute with Gregory ; still less was there any widespread enthusiasm among the German bishops on behalf of the reform policy, which compelled the King to seek their support by humiliating himself to the Pope.   Henry was certainly impulsive.   He was in deep dejection of mind at the turn of events in Germany. He felt the need of a powerful but friendly counsellor. The report had arrived of Gregory's friendly sentiments towards himself.   Responding with inexperienced ardour and a characteristic impulse, the King appealed to one of the bishops to draft a letter to the Pope, in the most placable terms possible, and, without consideration, despatched it to Gregory.

But he had committed himself, and placed himself within Gregory's grasp.   Whatever may be said in favour of the King's simple motives before the letter

was written, after the event he could not withdraw or
modify or explain away any of its terms should an
unbending and ungenerous adversary tie him down to
them, even though incidents occurred—as they did—
to cause him to qualify his opinion of the phraseology
used by Gregory in the letters to Rudolf and the Bishop
of Como, if that prelate had written to the King.
Whether he knew it or not, Canossa for Henry took
place in September, 1073, not in January, 1077, and the
King must be held responsible for his own humiliation.

While Henry's courier was on the way to Rome,
Gregory was dealing with the affairs of the church in
Africa. On September 15th a letter was registered
which had been sent to the Church in Carthage. In
words breathing the language of S. Paul—he quotes the
apostle nine times—the Pope sought to encourage the
Christians of Carthage who were living in fear of ill-
treatment by their Saracen rulers. But a terrible offence
had been committed by some of them. They had
accused their Archbishop Cyriac before a Saracen
tribunal, and he had been scourged. Gregory says that
but for the long and dangerous sea voyage he would
come to judge this offence in person, but, as it was
impossible to adjudicate upon so sad and malicious a
case at a distance, he warned them to do justice against
the offenders themselves, under the threat of striking
them with ' the sword of anathema ', and of his own
' malediction '.[1] To Cyriac he also sent a letter of con-
dolence upon the double affliction which he had endured
—the treachery of the Christians and the persecution of
the Saracens. To break the law of God by demeaning
the *sacerdotium* before the *imperium* of worldly power in
this manner was equivalent to denying the faith. Cyriac
had been ordered by the Saracen authorities to conduct
ordinations contrary to the canons, and rather than obey
he had suffered torments. But it would be much· more

[1] *Reg.* I. 22.

precious if, after the blows which he had sustained, he could bring his persecutors to a different frame of mind, by preaching to them the Christian religion, even though he had been compelled to sever some from the church. They must pray that almighty God would revive the long-afflicted and badly-shaken Church of Africa.[1]

On September 24th King Henry's courier had not yet reached Capua. By that date a letter was sent by Gregory to Bruno, Archbishop of Verona, declining to award him the pallium unless he received it in person at Rome. The Pope says that he is anxious to make known to Bruno personally how much he cares for the royal welfare, and desires to guard the King's honour before God and the world, provided that Henry will perform the honour due to God, and, giving up puerile interests, will imitate the example of holy kings.[2] The allusion to the King's youthful faults would hardly have been made if the royal letter had already reached Gregory. The Pope's epistle to Bruno shows the same desire to keep Lombard opinion in a neutral condition, in view of a coming conference, as the letter to Rainald of Como.

The immediate result of Henry's letter was to strengthen the papal policy towards Milan. Soon after Gregory's election, Atto, Herlembald's nominee in the see of Milan, had gone to Rome, where he was kindly received by Gregory, and his drooping courage was revived. Godfrey, nominee of the late Archbishop and of the King, with difficulty maintained himself at Brebbia, while Herlembald with a free hand upheld the Patarine cause in Milan, and ravaged the supporters of Godfrey with fire and sword. On September 27th Gregory wrote with enthusiasm to Herlembald, reporting the receipt of the King's letter.

' May thy prudence know that, by the mercy of God, we have sojourned at Capua well and happy and not without

[1] *Reg.* I. 23.   [2] *Reg.* I. 24.

great benefit to holy church ; for the Normans, who to the
confusion and danger of the public good and of holy church
were contemplating an alliance, persisted in the commotion
in which we found them, and would not in any way have
peace, unless we had been willing.   If indeed, our discretion
had approved it as beneficial to holy church, they would
already have submitted themselves to us, and shewn their
customary reverence.

Moreover, you are to know that King Henry has sent to
us words full of sweetness and obedience, and such as we
cannot recollect either he or his predecessors have ever sent
to the Roman Bishops.   Indeed certain of his more important
supporters promise to us, on his behalf, that he will without
doubt obey our counsel concerning the cause of the Milanese
Church.   How far we may be able to be of use to him, or
how far, if we withdraw the helping hand, to injure him, we
hope you will speedily and freely perceive, and will clearly
realize, that God is with us and works with us.   We think
that there is no manner of doubt but that the Countess
Beatrix, and her daughter Matilda, are faithful to us in those
things which pertain to God and the religion of holy church.
Do you therefore, trusting in the Lord and in thy mother the
Roman Church, act manfully, strengthened in the Lord and
in the power of His might, knowing that the more heavily
the tempest of disturbance now rises against you, the more
happily afterwards, by the favour of God, will peace smile.' [1]

Gregory was looking at the Normans through the
rosy glass of the King's letter.   So far as they concern
Robert Guiscard, his words were only a pious aspiration,
for even amid the exhilaration caused by the royal letter
the Pope could hardly have persuaded himself that
Guiscard would submit.   There was neither peace nor
submission in the heart of the Norman captain.

The rest of the letter is patently clear.   The Pope felt
that his policy had the King in hand, and he had received
promises of co-operation not only from Rudolf, but
from other German princes.   Even the thorny Milanese

---

[1] *Reg.* I. 25.

problem could now be grasped, without fear of Henry's interference, so he counsels Herlembald, ' the Milanese knight ',[1] to go actively forward with his operations. Furthermore, he felt secure enough to be generous. On October 9th he wrote again to the ' Milanese knight ', who indeed, on his return to Milan in 1065, had contemplated taking up the warfare of the cowl. The Pope says that, being occupied with other matters, he can reply to only a few of Herlembald's many questions. He commits to Herlembald's discretion the treatment of the supporters of Godfrey, who had been bribed to return to Herlembald—the fathers of disloyal sons, or the sons of disloyal fathers—and of those whom Herlembald wished to correct without bribing them, but he must show clemency to any who desired to join his following. All who are penitent, and wish to offer compensation by returning to the party of reform, should realize that they would be kindly received and mercifully treated. Herlembald need not greatly fear the bishops who attempt to show enmity, so long as Beatrix and Matilda wholly support the Roman Church, and while certain of the German magnates labour to unite firmly the minds of the Pope and King, against whom Gregory ought not, and does not, wish to show any malice, unless the King himself opposed holy religion. The princes were confident that the King would satisfy the Pope in other ecclesiastical matters, and especially did they approve of Herlembald's attitude to Gregory. He is to be careful to conciliate Gregory, Bishop of Vercelli, by any honest agreement that was possible, since the Bishop had promised fully to obey the Pope's orders.[2]

On October 13th, Gregory wrote to Albert, the Bishop-elect of Aqui, saying that he had been reassured

---

[1] *Miles*, but Herlembald belonged to the class of *capitani* or barons, the leaders of North Italian communal life. The *secundi milites*, or *valvassores minores*, formed a secondary class of knights and esquires (*cf.* Previté-Orton *C.M.H.* V. 217, 219).

[2] *Reg.* I. 26.

concerning reports of Albert's presence at the consecration of Godfrey. He must direct his efforts against the 'heresy' of simony and clerical marriage, especially at Milan, where he must give assistance to ' that strenuous knight of Christ' Herlembald.[1]

Perhaps Gregory was never more justified by the favourable trend of events, in seeking to extend the temporal power of papal rule, than in the early autumn of 1073. He now extended the policy of claiming for the Papacy territory which was or had been recently under Saracen occupation. The island of Sardinia was overrun by the Saracens in 1007. Nine years later the Pisans re-conquered it, and had established five magistracies or judicatures (*judices*) on the north Italian model. To them Gregory addressed a letter (October 14th) :

' To you and to all who reverence Christ it is known that the Roman Church is the mother of all Christians. But since, through the negligence of our predecessors, that love, which in former times existed between the Roman Church and your race, has grown cold, you have to such an extent made yourselves more foreign towards us than people who are at the other side of the world, that the Christian religion among you has suffered the greatest loss. Whence it is very necessary for you that you should now think more carefully for the health of your souls, and should recognize your mother, the Roman Church, as lawful sons ; and should show that devotion which your ancient fathers showed to us. Our desire is, not only to be careful for the liberation of your souls, but to watch over the salvation of your country.'

If they did not cordially respond to the Pope's overtures it would be their fault if any disaster occurred to their country.[2]

Gregory was cautiously feeling his way. He does not yet definitely lay a claim to hegemony over Sardinia on the basis of Constantine's Donation, which had already

---

[1] *Reg.* I. 27.   [2] *Reg.* I. 29.

been asserted over Spain, but his intention is clear enough, and in due course was made plain.

The conference with Rudolf and the Tuscan family did not take place. The Swabian Duke was kept in Germany by a conference of greater import for the German monarchy and for the papal ambitions. At Cappel in August the princes had compelled the King to postpone his advance against the Saxons until October 5th, on the ground that they wished to make larger preparations for their contingents than a Polish campaign demanded. A week later Siegfried of Mainz, in negotiation with Otto of Nordheim, the Saxon leader, without the King's knowledge, arranged for a conference with Henry and his supporters at Gerstungen on October 20th.

Siegfried of Mainz had been Archbishop since 1060. Less able than Anno of Köln or Adalbert of Bremen, he exerted almost as great an influence upon the destiny of the King, and with equally disastrous results. An incurable paralysis, which from time to time laid him low, caused him to shrink from bloodshed,[1] and was partly responsible for his inconsistent and deviating handling of affairs. The one persistent interest in his changeable policy was the Thuringian tithe question. By an ancient practice the royal tithes in Thuringia were paid to the Archbishop of Mainz, but Siegfried struggled for ten years before his right to them was formally admitted. In 1067 he attempted to bribe Hildebrand in order to secure a favourable judgment from Alexander II. His letter, of course, remained unanswered.[2] Finally at the Synod of Erfurt in 1073, Henry IV agreed to the settlement of the Thuringian tithes on Siegfried. But the question had become involved in the Saxon dispute. The Thuringians joined the Saxons in revolt, and it was with the object of making sure of the tithes that Siegfried

---

[1] Gustav Schmidt *Erzbischof Siegfried I von Mainz* (1917) p. 21.
[2] *Ibid.* p. 25.

came to terms with Otto of Nordheim and arranged the conference of Gerstungen.

The King declined to attend the conference, but little knowing what he was doing, sent as his representatives Archbishops Siegfried and Anno, Bishops Herman of Metz and Herman of Bamberg, Duke Godfrey the Younger of Lorraine, Rudolf of Swabia and Berthold of Carinthia. The royal representatives agreed to the demands of the Saxons. Their rebellion was to be forgotten ; their ancient rights were to be restored. If Henry declined these proposals the princes would withdraw their support from him. The royal consent was demanded by Christmas, and Henry unwillingly gave it. At this point any possibility that he might be persuaded of the wisdom of the princes' attitude to Saxony was ruined by the scandalous report of Reginger, a royal counsellor. Reginger swore that Henry had plotted the murder of the leading magnates, including Rudolf. The King publicly denied the charge, and went to Regensburg in Bavaria. Siegfried summoned a meeting of the princes at Mainz, where it was not impossible that steps might be taken for Henry's deposition. In an attempt to check the rapidly growing disaffection, the King retired towards the Rhine, but was overcome by a serious illness, and his death was expected as a solution of the political tangle. Early in December he recovered, and was enthusiastically received by the citizens of Worms. On January 18th (1074) he rewarded them by a grant which heralded the civic liberties of the towns of north-western Europe. Worms received its freedom by royal charter, and for the rest of his stormy career Henry IV had the support of the Rhine towns. For the present, his reviving cause ruined Siegfried's council at Mainz.

Gregory, still at Capua, was watching events in Germany and in Apulia. For a month no letter was registered, partly on account of the difficulty of finding couriers in South Italy. When he wrote to Gebhard, Bishop of Salzburg (Austria), on November 15th, the Pope complained of the absence of messengers going across the Alps. But Gregory now began to deal again with the domestic affairs of the churches in many lands. Gebhard was warned to put into operation the decrees of a Roman synod enforcing the celibacy of the clergy:[1] On November 20th, at Monte Cassino, he urged Lanfranc, Archbishop of Canterbury, to check the encroachment of Herfast, Bishop of Elmham, upon the Abbey of S. Edmundsbury.[2] The Benedictine abbeys at this period were establishing, in all Western lands, their freedom from episcopal control, and the Curia bound their allegiance to the Papacy, by jealously supporting them. Yet there was frequently good reason for this intervention, against the interference of a tyrannical bishop. Lanfranc was admonished to warn King William ' the best-beloved and unique son of the holy Roman Church ' not to demean his ' singular wisdom ' by listening to Herfast's persuasive tale. But the chief interest of the letter lies in the wide claim made by Gregory to intervene in the affairs of local churches, on the ground of divine right, and especially to consecrate churches, priests and bishops, without the licence of any other authority, particularly when requested to do so by petitioners at Rome. The foundation of the vast appellate jurisdiction of the medieval church was being laid down, and in this case Lanfranc was ordered to refer the dispute to Rome, in the event of being unable to settle it himself.

In his policy towards Henry IV there was no gradual increment in the papal demands, commensurable with an increasing recalcitrance on the part of the King. Gregory would have the whole ecclesiastical reform programme observed, at once and undiminished. The only development in papal policy was concerned with the penalties pronounced against Henry at later stages

[1] *Reg.* I. 30.　　　　[2] *Reg.* I. 31 ; *cf. Lanfranc* pp. 119 ff.

of the controversy.   On the ecclesiastical points at issue, the Pope's mind was made up from the beginning.   A letter concerning Philip I of France, dated December 4th, is of decisive significance at this juncture.   Philip, who succeeded Henry I in 1060, was an unblushing simonist in the eyes of the Curia—a charge never fully proved against Henry IV, in spite of the histrionic admission in his letter to Gregory.   Philip had accepted the candidate elected by the Chapter for the vacant see of Mâcon, but demanded a gift before he confirmed the appointment. This was no more than the ancient custom of proprietary church usage, but, although the Papacy does not appear ever to have discussed the theory of German church law, it was in open contest with all the effects of the theory, whether in the royal churches or in those founded and controlled by local proprietors.   So Gregory charges Philip with being the worst of all the royal offenders in dissipating the church's property and treading her underfoot, like a hired woman.   The oppression of the French churches had reached the highest possible point.   This was the more offensive in that kingdom, because it had always shown devotion towards the Roman Church. Philip had, however, promised amendment by his Chamberlain, the Knight Alberic, but if he did not surrender ' the base traffic of simoniacal heresy ', Gregory would strike the whole of France with ' the sword of a general anathema '.[1]

The misdeeds of the youthful Henry did not generate the thunders hurled by Gregory against him in later years.   They proceeded from the Pope's own principles, from his preference for clearing the atmosphere by the aid of a flash of lightning, rather than by the gentle rain of reasonable discussion.   When Leo IX found half the French Bishops withheld from the Synod of Reims by Henry I, he did not retaliate with a threat of anathema, and, when Urban II excommunicated Philip for adultery

[1] *Reg.* I. 35.

9

with Bertrada, the wife of Fulk of Anjou, he did not involve his subjects in the sentence. If Gregory had not become involved with Henry IV, he would have found some other outlet for his dominating temperament, which required an atmosphere of conflict for the expression of inward impulse.

CHAPTER EIGHT

DREAMS (1074)

THE dispute in Germany between the King on the one hand, and the Saxons and the princes on the other, was the opening phase in the great medieval contest between the monarchy and the baronage. If ordered government was to be established, if the commerce and crafts of the towns were to have freedom for development, and the quiet life of the peasant security for rural occupations, the rule of the nobles in the country-side, and of the bishops in the towns, had to be made subservient to the royal executive. Without knowing it Henry was fighting for European freedom, although his grant of a charter to Worms shows how large his contribution might have been, had he inherited a more orderly realm. For the rest, the dispute in Germany was a domestic affair, unconnected with political developments across the Rhine or the North Sea, and in reality equally independent of ambitions and policies south of the Alps. There was the *damnosa hereditas* of a ceremonial march to Rome for the imperial crown, but that was an affair of the palace, and had little to do with the Rhine towns or the Saxon or Swabian villages ; and it was only the affair of the Papacy as a pawn in papal politics, and as an ecclesiastical tradition. Yet on the theory of a fixed relation between Papacy and Empire Gregory chose now to intervene in Germany, inspired by his own temperament and inclination for dominant action, and by the desire to seize a favourable moment in German politics, to further the interests of the Papacy. Up to the present time he had left the political development of Germany alone, and, except for some directions sent to a few bishoprics, he had not even divulged his ecclesiastical policy to the King. He had not written to him at all, but had confided his private opinion of Henry to Rudolf, one of Henry's subjects. Now he began to set himself up as arbitrator in the domestic affairs of the German peoples.

By adopting this policy the Pope was shackling his hands for future action. The time came when he no longer desired the responsibility of judging between Henry and Rudolf and the Saxons, when he would anxiously hope that a decisive battle would settle the dispute. But, as we shall see, each of them held him fast to his original intention, and accused him of prevarication and dissimulation when he repeatedly put them off. Gregory in a few years was to realize the full wisdom of the saying ' My kingdom is not of this world ', and well had it been if he had left politics to the warfare of the Gentile and the Jew.

At Christmas-time (1073) Henry was gathering forces at Worms for a new trial of strength with the Saxons, and, if it came to it, for his first passage of arms with the princes. On December 20th, Gregory addressed a letter to Werner, Bishop of Magdeburg, Burchard, Bishop of Halberstadt, the Margrave Dedi, and other Saxon princes. Among his many anxieties he was greatly solicitous concerning the discord and enmity which had arisen between the Saxons and their lord, King Henry, resulting in slaughter and fire, the robbery of the churches, and the miserable ravaging of the poor. He had sent ambassadors to the King urging him by pontifical authority to stop the war, until papal legates should arrive to enquire into the causes of the dispute, and by God's will to arrange peace and concord. By the same authority, he warned the Saxons to remain quiet, and wait until a stable agreement could be drawn up ; whichever side had unjustly suffered violence should have the papal favour and assistance.[1]

Gregory's attempt to bring about peace in Germany met with the reception which he might have foreseen. All parties quietly disregarded it. During the first week of the year 1074 Henry gathered a small army of Bavarians, Swabians and French, and towards the end of the month marched away from Worms to the North, in order to succour his garrisons in Saxony and Thuringia. He was opposed by the levies of the Saxon people. The winter was one of exceptional cold, the rivers were frozen and the corn could not be ground. Neither side appeared to have much stomach for the fight. After some manœuvring, a peace was arranged at Gerstungen on February 2nd. The Saxons were pardoned and submitted to Henry's rule, on condition that he administered their country by the advice of Saxons only. Both sides agreed to demolish the castles. It was a local negotiation in which the magnates of the rest of Germany had no share. Yet the King had scored a success by dividing opinion in Germany. The South German duchies did not forget that the Saxons had made peace without consulting them. For the rest, the Treaty of Gerstungen was soon shattered. Henry faithfully observed its terms by destroying his fortifications in Saxony, but he left the church and other buildings at the Harzburg standing. Without the consent of their leaders, in the middle of March the Saxon peasantry broke into the town and left not a stone standing ; the church was burned and the bodies of the King's brother and son were flung out of their graves. Henry refused to accept the protests of the Saxon leaders that the outrage was committed without their knowledge, and called upon the rest of Germany to avenge it.

On the same day that Henry agreed to the terms of Gerstungen, Gregory commenced some negotiations

[1] *Reg.* I. 39.

which might have altered the whole course of medieval history. His restless energy was not content with forming and maturing policies within the Lateran. He had not been back in Rome six weeks before he was scheming to place himself at the head of a vast enterprise which would take him away from the City, across the sea, and perhaps entail an absence of some years. The manipulation of armed forces on a small scale had in earlier years been one of the most successful of his activities, and when he became Pontiff he could not check the military ardour which, like the passion for righteousness, was a consuming force in his nature. If his zeal for the reform of the church was a more abiding stimulus to his policy, there were times when the prospect of stronger and more effective action called him away from the true mission of his life. Gregory VII was the first of the Crusaders, and although he never got further than Benevento, *en route* for a South Italian port, that was not due to any failure of his own zeal, or change in his own policy. The genesis of the enterprise was the letter received from the Emperor Michael VII in 1073.

In the time of Alexander II an oath had been obtained from certain Burgundian princes before the tomb of S. Peter, in the presence of a large assembly of bishops and abbots, that, whenever called upon, they would come with armed forces to defend the Roman Church. No doubt in those days the object in view was the protection of the church against attacks like that of Cadalus and his Roman supporters, and perhaps the Normans of the South. Gregory never allowed an oath or a treaty made on behalf of the church to remain inoperative, and he now planned to make use, on a wider sphere, of what he regarded as a sworn reserve of the Roman church-militant, and at the same time to use it to overcome the Normans of the South. On February 2nd he wrote to William of Burgundy reminding him of his undertaking, and urging him to mobilize his forces and to be ready to

march to the succour of the Roman Church.   He was
to warn Raymond of Saint-Gilles—the father-in-law of
Richard of Capua, and later Count of Toulouse—Amadeus
of Savoy, the son of Adalheid of Susa, and others who
had shared in the oath, to do the same.   The Tuscan
house, Beatrix, Matilda and Duke Geoffrey the Younger,
were labouring on behalf of the enterprise, and this was
the object of the summons of Beatrix and Matilda to
Rome on January 5th.   This ' great army ' was not to be
used for shedding Christian blood, but it would have
the effect of overawing any of the enemies of the church
at home, so that they would ' submit more readily to
justice '.   Having reduced the Normans to passivity in
this way, the army would cross to Constantinople, to
aid the Christians against the attacks of the Saracens.[1]

This ambitious scheme was not a mere attempt to
overwhelm Robert Guiscard and his brother by the aid
of a great Burgundian army, although the Pope rightly
drew attention to the beneficial effect which such an
armament would have upon the Normans, especially
when united with the forces of Lorraine and Tuscany.
At the close of the letter he says that the papal forces in
Italy were quite sufficient to deal with the ' Norman
rebels ', and no doubt he had in mind the troops of
Beatrix, Landulf of Benevento and Richard of Capua,
although the Tuscan force was detailed in the scheme
for the larger enterprise.   On March 1st he issued an
appeal to Christendom, by the hand of an envoy who
had come from Constantinople with the report of
Saracen depredations almost to the walls of the city, in
which ' many thousands of Christians had been slain
like cattle ', calling upon Christians to arm for the
defence of the Eastern Empire, and to notify the Pope
of their preparations.[2]

Probably in the spring of the year, when Gregory's
mind was occupied with large schemes for the extension

[1] *Reg.* I. 46.   [2] *Reg.* I. 49.

of papal influence, a letter was despatched to Turlogh O'Brien, an Irish King, and to the archbishops, bishops, nobles and the faithful of Ireland, claiming papal suzerainty over that land.

'The authority of Christ has founded His church on a solid rock, and has committed His rights to the blessed Peter, which church He had likewise constituted over all kingdoms of the world. To this church He has subjected the principalities, powers and everything else which is sublime upon earth.'

Gregory claims obedience and reverence to himself as the successor of Peter from the whole world.[1]

On January 25th the Pope had informed the bishops of the province of Milan that the Curia had for some time past established the practice of holding annual synods in Rome.[2] Citations for the Lenten Synod of 1074 were already going out. It assembled on March 10th. Its decrees have been lost, and the findings collected by Héfélé from the German correspondence have been

---

[1] M. J. Brennan *An Eccles. Hist. of Ireland* (1864). (*Cf.* H. Mann *Hist. of the Popes* VII. (1910) 182.) Jaffé *Reg. Pont.* I. (1885) 624 dated this letter 1083, on the ground that the Pope was not at Sutri, 30 miles north of Rome, where the letter was dated on February 24th, in any other year. But in the spring of 1083 after retiring from South Italy, Gregory was anticipating Henry's appearance at Rome, and the King may have been there by February (Meyer von Knonau III. 470 n. 2). There appears to be no reason for discarding the addressee Turlogh as Jaffé proposes. Turlogh's dates were 1072–1078. Weiland (*Zeitschrift für Kirchengesch.* XVIII. 451) suggests 1074, 1076, or 1078 as dates for this letter, on the ground that in 1075 and 1077 the Pope could not have been at Sutri in February. But it is improbable that he was there on February 24th in 1076 or 1078. The Lent Synods began in those years on February 14th and February 27th respectively. In 1074 the Lent Synod did not begin until March 10th, so that the Pope could easily have been at Sutri on February 24th in that year. The absence of the letter from the *Register* certainly agrees with Jaffé's date (1083), when the Chancellery was disorganized, but, as the *Register* is not a complete record, this objection is not sufficient to outweigh the presence of Turlogh's name. There is no reason why a letter in 1074 should not also be missing from the *Register*.

[2] *Reg.* I. 43.

shown by Mr. Brooke to belong to the Synod of 1075. Gregory's mind was preoccupied by the Eastern Crusade and the Normans, and in Lent 1074 he was content to reaffirm the decrees of his predecessors against simony and clerical marriage. At the beginning of the year Robert Guiscard had renewed his attacks upon the papal allies in South Italy. On February 7th Pandulf, the son of Landulf of Benevento, was slain in a battle near Monte Sarchio. Gregory was now compelled publicly to tear up the Treaty of Monte Cassino by the formal excommunication of Guiscard in the Synod. Other matters discussed at this assembly are indicated in the letters which issued from the Chancery during the next fortnight.

On March 19th, Alfonso VI of Leon and Sanche II of Catalonia were urged to re-introduce the Roman order of the Mass into their churches, and to cease using the liturgy of Toledo, and other Mozarabic forms in use in Spain.[1] Immediately after this letter was despatched, a communication was received from Sanche saying that this had been done. He was promptly commended for his zeal, and for his desire to maintain the friendship which previous kings of Spain had shown to the bishops of Rome. Nothing more was said of the expedition of Ebulo, but the Catalonian King was reminded that Christ had granted all the kingdoms of the world to S. Peter.[2]

Hungary is mentioned for the first time in the *Register*. Salomon, the brother-in-law of Henry IV, had been driven out of Hungary by his cousin Géza, and took refuge in Germany, where he swore fealty to Henry for the Hungarian kingdom. There was an ancient connection between the kingdom of Hungary and the Papacy,[3] and Géza now sought the assistance of Gregory. On March 17th the Pope acknowledged Salomon's assurance of loyalty to the apostolic see, and urged him to communicate his cause to him through the Italian

[1] *Reg.* I. 64.   [2] *Reg.* I. 63.   [3] *Cf. infra* p. 136.

Azzo, Marquis of Este, at the same time taking care not
to compromise his future action. He addressed Géza as
' Duke ' not ' King '.[1]

Siegfried of Mainz had written to Gregory protesting
against the intervention of the legates in Bohemia, since
the bishopric of Prague was within the jurisdiction of
Mainz. On March 18th [2] Gregory energetically contra-
dicted Siegfried's interpretation of the canons and of the
decrees of the Fathers. Siegfried had arrogantly objected
to the appeal of John, Bishop of Olmütz, to Rome.
No patriarch or primate had the right to interfere with
a papal judgment. Only the clemency of the Roman
Church prevented him from being deposed for his
interference.

To William of England the Pope sent, on April 4th,
an affectionate acknowledgment of his letter of con-
gratulation on Gregory's appointment to the Papacy.
He repeatedly addresses him as a ' beloved son ' who
loves the Scriptures more than any other King. In reply
to William's inquiry as to his welfare, Gregory says that
the Roman Church is like a ship tossed on stormy seas
amid hidden rocks, ' So we live and so by God's help
we shall live.' He grants William's request for a
privilege for S. Stephen at Caen, and commits the
collection of papal dues in England to the King's
liberality. The Pope does not request military support
for the Crusade. He was aware that William required
all his forces in England and Normandy, and his own
experience of Norman troops did not yet encourage him
to seek their aid again.[3] To this period may belong a
letter to Lanfranc [4] which Jaffé assigns to the year 1073.
It reflects more accurately the depression which began
to cloud Gregory's mind in April, 1074. He complains
that the princes seek only the fulfilment of their own
desires, the bishops go after the glory of the world and
the delights of the flesh. He warns the English Arch-

[1] *Reg.* I. 58.   [2] *Reg.* I. 60.   [3] *Reg.* I. 70.   [4] *Ep. Coll.* I.

bishop to check the wrong-doing of the Irish, who not only deserted their wives, but sold them, and to restrain the same offence in England if he discovered it there.

Gregory's grand scheme for the Eastern Crusade was going awry. Duke Godfrey the Younger, whose relations with Matilda were strained, was absent in Lorraine, occupied with German politics. He had made no attempt to send his contingent to the papal army of the East. As Gregory based his hopes of help from Burgundy upon the speedy arrival of the Lotharingian and Tuscan forces, this delay struck at the foundation of his plans. 'Where is the help which you promised?' he wrote to Godfrey on April 7th.[1] 'Where are the troops which you promised to lead to the honour and help of S. Peter?' He broke his promises like his father before him. Even the Sardinian magistrates, whose visit to Rome Godfrey had guaranteed, had not come, and the Pope threatened to be bound to Godfrey by no promise in future, if he did not fulfil his word.

Thoughts of the Crusade were in his mind when Gregory made a grateful acknowledgment on April 13th of a letter from Philip I, professing obedience to the Roman Church.[2] The devotion of Philip's predecessors to the church at Rome—he says, thinking of Caroling days—was famous in all the world, and they had been most active in increasing and defending the churches of France. Now, although the times had changed, and the glory and power of the French kings were no longer what they had been, Philip should imitate the example of his more illustrious predecessors, especially since the power of Christian princes ought to concentrate, with the Pope, in the camp of the heavenly King for the maintenance of Christian warfare.

The most favourable prospect for Gregory in the early summer of 1074 was his relationship with Henry IV. At the beginning of the Lenten Synod envoys had

[1] *Reg.* I. 72.   [2] *Reg.* I. 75.

arrived from the King, asking the Pope to postpone consecrating Anselm to Lucca, and Hugh to the bishopric of Die, until they had been invested by Henry, on the ground of ancient custom. The Pope consulted the cardinals, and agreed to postpone the consecration of Anselm, but declined the royal request in the case of Hugh. Possibly Gregory at this stage recognized the regalian rights of Henry in Italy—he had already received the Patriarchate—but not in France, where the Emperors had no jurisdiction.

In a letter to Hugh of Cluny, on March 19th,[1] blaming the Abbot for not yet having come to Rome, Gregory announced that he had sent Gerald, the Cardinal-Bishop of Ostia, to Henry IV. On April 18th [2] he rebuked the aged Archbishop Anno of Köln for similar remissness, and complained that no letters reached him from Köln. But Anno was withdrawing from public business, and at Easter was occupied with a revolt of the people of Köln against his rule. The papal embassy to Germany included Hubert of Palestrina, Gerald of Ostia, Rainald of Como, Henry of Chur and the Empress Agnes. The original object of this legation—the reconciliation between Henry and the Saxons—had been rendered nugatory by events in Saxony. But the King was regarded in Rome as being under the ban of the Church, by virtue of his continued dealings with excommunicated counsellors, although no formal sentence had been passed on him, and although Gregory was not consistent in his application of this rule.[3]

The legates met the King at a Synod held at Nuremburg after Easter. Since the destruction of the Harzburg Henry's cause in Germany had brightened, yet, supported by the Empress Agnes' counsel, he agreed to every one of the legate's demands. He promised to refrain from all simoniacal transactions, and to aid Gregory in suppressing them. Church property received by his coun-

---

[1] *Reg.* I. 62.   [2] *Reg.* I. 79.   [3] *Cf. supra* p. 96.

sellors in recognition of their assistance in procuring ecclesiastical appointments should be restored. He would assist with the suppression of clerical marriage. The royal counsellors made a similar submission, and the King was free to associate with them. The attempt of the legates to publish the decrees of the Lenten Synod failed. Siegfried of Mainz and Liemar of Hamburg voiced the opposition of the German bishops. This did not mean that they favoured either simony or clerical marriage. There were incidents which proved the contrary. They objected to the high-handed attitude of the legates, and to the methods which they proposed. They refused to agree to a synod to be attended by all the bishops of Germany and presided over by the legates. Such, Liemar alleged, could only be assembled by the Archbishop of Mainz, the legate of Germany—he forgot that Siegfried had voluntarily surrendered his privilege to Alexander II—or by the Pope himself.

Before she left Nuremberg Agnes reconciled Rudolf with the King. The legates returned to Rome with Henry's written submission. He had completely honoured his letter to the Pope of September, 1073. Not a single request had been lodged by the King—even to secure a papal condemnation of the Saxon devastation of the Harzburg. Once again Henry had shown himself open to persuasion. Gregory, on the other hand, lodged no complaint against him for the breakdown of the discussion on the publication of the papal decrees. On June 15th he expressed his satisfaction to the Empress. She had united Papacy and Empire in the bond of charity ; her son Henry was restored to the communion of the church, and his kingdom saved from general peril. While he was separated from communion the Pope could not approach him. By the Empress's example Beatrix and Matilda had been stirred up to work day and night for the church.[1]

[1] *Reg.* I. 85.

The summer was occupied by Henry with preparations for an advance into Hungary to restore his exiled relative Salomon. No protest was raised by the King against Gregory's intervention in political matters in that land. In the autumn Henry returned to Germany without having displaced Géza from the Hungarian throne. At the close of the year, the King was preparing an expedition against Saxony, with the approval of the South German princes.

The threat of excommunication issued by the legates at Nuremberg against the German bishops who did not enforce the marriage decree was not without effect. Siegfried gave his clergy six months in which to make up their minds, and at Erfurt in October, ordered them finally to give up their wives or their orders. The Synod broke into uproar and the Archbishop's life was threatened. He only secured order by promising to remit the question to Rome. But the assembly ended in confusion when Siegfried condemned the recalcitrant Thuringian tithe-prayers. Altman, Bishop of Passau, met with the same treatment from his clergy, when he attempted to enforce the celibacy decree at the Synod of Passau (1074).

Before the good news of Henry's submission had reached him, Gregory left Rome on May 9th to summon an expedition against Robert Guiscard. Plans had been laid for the supply of troops at the Lent Synod, when Beatrix and Gisulf of Salerno were in Rome. The Pope also looked for the assistance of Richard of Capua, and expected to concentrate 30,000 men at Monte Cassino, in addition to 500 Germans. The papal standard was to be erected at Monte Cimini in Tuscany. Here the whole plan miscarried. The Pisans refused to send their contingent, and showed such hostility that Gregory returned to Rome. The vassals of Beatrix broke into rebellion. In despair of overcoming Robert Guiscard by force, the Pope turned again to diplomacy, and invited

the Norman to meet him at Benevento. But Gregory's
health had been giving way since the spring,[1] and he
was now laid low by an illness from which he did not
expect to recover.[2] This illness was not connected with
old age, as Héfélé says. The Pope was still young
enough in 1075 to greet Judith, Queen of Hungary, the
daughter of the Empress Agnes, as his own sister.[3] In
the meantime Guiscard had gone to Benevento with a
troop of horse, and waited for the Pope three days.
Desiderius of Monte Cassino seized the opportunity to
try to reconcile Robert with Richard of Capua, and, while
the negotiation broke down, Guiscard sent messages of
fidelity to Gregory, and expressed the desire to meet
him. But after his recovery the Pope hesitated to
comply, being suspicious of the Norman's motives.[4]

By August 28th, the Pope had sufficiently recovered
to resume his correspondence—no letter had been
registered in the Chancery since June 15th. On September 10th he was again thinking of the Eastern
expedition. William of Acquitaine, doubtless influenced
by reports from Burgundy, had offered his services.
Gregory accepted the offer, but informed the Count that
it would be indiscreet to put his plans in writing at
present. There was a rumour that the Christians oversea
had repulsed the attacks of the Saracens, and Gregory
was delaying his action.[5]

With hands tied against Robert Guiscard, but freed
from vexation on account of Henry IV, the Pope now
turned a combative eye again upon Philip of France.
On September 10th [6] he despatched a long epistle to
Manasseh, Archbishop of Reims, and other French
bishops, which opens with an account of the distracted
condition of France, ' formerly so famous and powerful '.
The reform movement in France was not progressing

---

[1] *Cf. Reg.* I. 62.   [2] *Cf. Reg.* II. 9.
[3] *Reg.* II. 44 ' *in loco germanae sororis.*'   [4] *Reg.* II. 9.
[5] *Reg.* II. 3.   [6] *Reg.* II. 5.

without opposition. In 1074 Synods at Paris, Rouen and Reims refused to carry out the celibacy decree, and broke up in disturbance, although an earlier synod at Rouen in the same year had passed the decree against simony. In his letter, Gregory alleges that morality and law were defied, and the royal power was content to have it so. Perjury, sacrilege and incest were rife, and pilgrims from Rome were grossly ill-treated.

' Of these things—your King—who is no King, but must be called tyrant—by the persuasion of the devil, is the head and cause. All his life has been polluted with vice and crime, and, after taking up the reins of government and bearing them ineffectively, the wretched and unhappy man not only has allowed his people, by the abandonment of his rule, to fall into crimes, but has incited them by his own example. Not content with attacks on the churches, adultery, rape, perjury and fraud, he has robbed the merchants from all lands recently assembled at a great fair in France.

Cursed is the man who withholds his sword from blood, who refrains from threatening carnal men. We fear that you pastors fly when the wolf rages. No fealty prohibits you from rebuking him, nor can fear be any excuse. Call together a synod and rebuke him to his face. If he refuses amendment, tell him that we shall no longer keep back the sword of apostolic rebuke. In the meantime you will ex-communicate him, and place the whole of France under an interdict. If he does not recover his senses, let him be in no doubt that we shall attempt by every possible means to tear the kingdom of France from his occupation. If you are luke-warm we shall depose you from your office.'

If Gregory had not within the next year or two become involved in the conflict with Henry IV, the fight between *sacerdotium* and *regnum* might have been staged on French soil. Granted that the Pope had not fully recovered from his illness, that he was irritated by news from the south, no communications had passed between himself and Philip sufficient to justify this exaggerated outburst to a subject of the King of France.

Of dignified diplomacy there is not a trace, only the thunder of an ecclesiastical bully. The tone and the method were precisely the same as those already pursued, although with less violence, towards Henry IV. The Pope issued his threats not to the King, but to his subjects, and he used the same provocative metaphor, ' Cursed is he who withholds his sword from blood'. We shall not be surprised when the thunder-clouds roll away from France and across the Rhine, and loom again over the head of the German King. The wind that will drive them will come from Rome.

This letter was not the result of a transient impulsive outburst. Its substance was repeated in another despatched to William of Acquitaine on November 13th.[1] Being sent to a lay magnate, it is framed in more dignified terms. But the same offences are mentioned, and apparently among the despoiled merchants were some Italians. The Count is to associate with himself others of the more noble magnates of France—when was the whole country so badly governed ?—to warn the King of his misdoings, to follow the example of the good kings of France. If he acquiesces, ' we shall treat him as we ought, with love '. If he remains obdurate, he will be excommunicated in a Roman synod, ' whoever shall show him royal honour or obedience we shall sequestrate ' and his excommunication shall be duly confirmed at the altar of S. Peter.

On December 8th [2] Gregory wrote again to Manasseh of Reims, still complaining about the robbery of Italian or other merchants by ' Philip, King of France—yea, rapacious wolf, wicked tyrant, enemy of God and holy church '. If he offers compensation ' we shall rejoice as over a lost and recovered sheep ', if not ' we promise to oppose him with all our power in every way '. The sufferings of France are no longer mentioned, only the complaint of the Italian merchants, which turns out to be

[1] *Reg.* II. 18.   [2] *Reg.* II. 32.

10

the occasion of the original outburst in September. So the imperial wrath of this Pope could be stirred by an incident of trifling if sordid proportions. His letters strike a new note in papal diplomatics.

While the Pope was threatening the King of France with deposition, he was claiming Hungary as a papal fief. Henry IV's expedition had failed to re-establish King Salomon, or to dislodge the intruding Duke Géza. Salomon then sought papal assistance. Gregory gave him the royal title, and so recognized him as the lawful King (October 28th),[1] but claimed Hungary as the property (*proprium*) of the Roman Church. It had been voluntarily handed over to the Papacy by King Stephen I (979–1038), and the Pope alleged that Henry III when attacking that country 'for the honour of S. Peter', recognized that suzerainty (*principatum*) over it belonged to Rome, by sending to the Pope the lance and crown which formed part of the Hungarian regalia. The right and halidom (*honor*) of S. Peter, Salomon had diminished and alienated by receiving the kingdom as a fief (*beneficium*) from the King of Germany. If he wished to have a long reign without the papal displeasure, he must correct this error, and admit that he holds the sceptre of Hungary as a fief, not of the royal but of the papal majesty, and Gregory concluded by saying that he had no intention of relinquishing the papal rights.

Gregory's claim was, of course, exaggerated. Sylvester II had blessed the foundation of the Hungarian kingdom by Stephen I, and Henry III had sent the lance and crown as trophies of war to Rome in 1045, when Peter of Hungary swore fealty for the second time to the Emperor and his heirs, for the kingdom of Hungary. Therefore, Gregory's claim was a direct challenge to the imperial rights of Henry IV, from whom he had recently received complete satisfaction for all matters at issue

[1] *Reg.* II. 13.

between them. The claim to hegemony over Hungary was based upon the same kind of flimsy precedent as the demand for suzerainty over Spain made in the year before. The head of the church was extending his ecclesiastical predominance, based on the notion of a spiritual grant of the kingdoms of the world by Christ to S. Peter, and by incorporating feudal theory into his relations with the secular princes. Not only did the kings of the earth owe submission to the Pope, like any other member of the church, but the claim was being lodged that they held their sovereign rights under the spiritual suzerainty of the Papacy. Yet in that suzerainty temporal and spiritual overlordship really merged. He to whom fealty was offered for sovereign rights was the ultimate sovereign, and the kingdoms of the world in theory were at the disposal of the Bishop of Rome.

Of the regulations made at the Roman Synod of November 30th we have no record, and there is no indication that the Pope communicated with Henry IV until December 7th.[1] The letter opens with a querulous complaint that the affair of the Milanese Church had not yet been settled, in spite of the King's promise. Surely initiative in that matter now lay with Gregory. But he expresses gratification at Henry's behaviour towards the legates at Easter, and at the reports which the Empress gave of his desire to stamp out simony and clerical marriage. He invites the King to send ambassadors for the settlement of the Milanese question to a synod, or, if that is impossible, to allow the Pope to have a free hand. Siegfried of Mainz and the Bishops of Bamberg, Strasburg and Speier had already been summoned to the Easter Synod of 1075, and the Pope asks the King to insist upon their appearance, and to send with them letters concerning their life and conduct.

About the same time he made known to Henry his

[1] *Reg.* II. 30.

plans for the Eastern Crusade.[1]   Amid the excitement of
his new plans, he addresses the King for the first time
with unqualified confidence, and in terms of unsuppressed
affection.   Restraint is thrown aside.   Evil-doers may
try to sow discord between them, but Henry is his
' dearest son '.   Gregory's psychological constitution is
patently clear.   The enmity which consumes his mind
like fire from time to time, is seldom directed towards
two people at once.   When a new subject for wrath
comes before his vision, his anger cools towards old
offenders, and amity leaps into its place.   The sword of
anathema was now directed towards Philip of France.
Moreover, he had a vast scheme on hand in which
Henry must play a certain part.

The Christians oversea had again sent imploring
messages for assistance against the pagans ; they were
daily destroyed, and the Christian race was reduced to
nothing.   Now he had succeeded in rousing the Christian
conscience of the West.   From Italy and across the Alps
40,000 men were gathering on condition that Gregory
himself led them against the enemies of God to the very
sepulchre of the Lord.   But it was to be more than a
Crusade.   ' What especially impels me to this work is
that the Church of Constantinople, separated from us
on the doctrine of the Holy Spirit, waits for union with
the apostolic see.   The Armenians who have wandered
from the Catholic faith, and almost all the East, wait for
the decision of S. Peter upon their divergent views.'   So
the Pope is compelled to embark for the defence of the
Christian faith, and, if God permits him to undertake
the enterprise, he says ' I relinquish to you the Roman
Church, that you may guard her as your holy mother,
and defend her honour.'

---

[1] *Reg.* II. 31 also dated December 7th, but although registered on the
same date, the two letters may have been sent off on different days.   The
dates in the *Register* do not necessarily or probably indicate the date of
despatch, but for the sake of convenience I have treated them so.   The
letters were not sent later than the date of registration.

Thus Pope and King are to exchange places. The great scheme of the reform of the home church is abandoned to the care of him who a few months before was regarded as one of its determined foes, while the Bishop of the West leads the army of Christendom to war. What Henry thought of this absurd proposal, we are not told, but Gregory went on with his mobilization. Nine days later (December 16th) [1] he sent the fiery cross over the Alps, calling the faithful together for the enterprise over the sea, under instructions borne by the papal courier. By such brief labour they will win eternal reward. Matilda of Tuscany and the Empress Agnes he summoned to go with him, while the Countess Beatrix remained to look after their common interests at home. He urged the Tuscan Duchess to give her advice and assistance abundantly. [2] Thus the year 1074 closed for Gregory with dreams of the most amazing expedition ever planned by the brain of man—the conquest of the East by an army led by the Pope and two women, while the heir of the Western Emperors sat upon the chair of Peter, taking counsel with Beatrix of Tuscany. The reform in Germany was handed over to the judgment of the lay folk. In December, they were bidden not to obey their bishops, if the bishops did not enforce the decrees against simony and clerical marriage. [3] Two months later they were bidden not to obey their clergy. [4] Nearly six hundred years before the Puritans claimed the right of private judgment, Gregory VII gratuitously handed it to the faithful of Germany, when hastily trying to quieten his conscience for deserting the cause of reform for Eastern battle-fields. Beside Gregory's bombastic programme the showmanship of Napoleon pales into the commonplace. [5]

[1] *Reg.* II. 37.

[2] *Ep. Coll.* 11.

[3] *Ep. Coll.* 10.

[4] *Cf. infra* p. 141.

[5] E. Voosen *Papauté et Pouvoir Civil à l'époque de Grégoire VII.* p. 70 thinks that Gregory aimed at uniting the Eastern Church with the Western at this time.

CHAPTER NINE

DRIFT (1075)

WHILE the Pope dreamed, the affairs of the church drifted. After the submission of Henry at Easter, 1074, two matters were crying out for Gregory's prompt action—the Milanese question and the imperial coronation. Decisive handling of the disputed election at Milan, before Henry attacked the Saxons, might have been followed by the exit of Archbishop Godfrey under orders from Goslar, but the Pope was dreaming of shock tactics with Guiscard; while Henry was looking for couriers from the Alps inviting him to his coronation in Rome, Gregory was hurling threats across Burgundy at Philip I, and claiming empire over Hungary. At the close of the year, instead of offering the King a crown he offered him the tiara. After that, with the new year, the course of events drifted, until the young and inexperienced hand of the King galvanized them into startling action in the summer and autumn.

The delay at Milan, which cost Herlembald, the gallant 'knight of Christ', his life, is partly explained by one of the decrees of the Lent Synod, which assembled on February 24th. Its disciplinary regulations have been lost, but their content is made known in the letters of the Pope to the three bishops, Siegfried of Mainz, Werner of Magdeburg and Otto of Constance—all wrongly dated in the *Register* [1]—and to Henry IV. [2]

[1] *Ep. Coll.* 3, 4 and 5 dated March, 1074. Brooke dates them February, 1075; perhaps March is preferable.
[2] *Reg.* III. 10 dated December 8th, 1075. Peitz assigns this letter to February, 1075. He has not noticed the reference to Fermo and Spoleto, to which the king did not appoint till the end of the year.

Clergy who had obtained their orders by simony were to
be degraded. A bishopric or parochial cure obtained
by simony was to be surrendered. No married or
incontinent clerk might say Mass, or render assistance
at it. The people were not to attend Mass said by a
non-celibate priest. The appeal to the laity to assist the
reform programme was a new step, laying open the door
to scandal, real or imagined, in every parish in Europe.
But of revolutionary character was the new prohibition
against lay election to ecclesiastical offices. The freedom of clerical election had been proclaimed at the
Council of Reims (1049). The new regulation was a
natural deduction from the Election Decree of 1059;
yet without negotiation or discussion it struck at a
universal custom in the Western Church, whereby for
centuries king and baron had exerted the rights of
patrons over churches which they had founded, and of
proprietors over the occupants of benefices on their
domains. It struck at feudal law this side of the Rhine,
and at the ancient Germanic proprietary law on its farther
bank. It was, moreover, although unnoticed for several
months, a new challenge to Henry IV. From both sides
the attack on the dignity of the German King, the heir
to the Empire, was being made. He must not invest
with lay sovereignty in Hungary; he must not invest
with ecclesiastical office anywhere. The imperial functions of the son of Henry III were being stripped off
piecemeal. In the meantime a new check upon Henry's
interference at Milan had been devised. The investiture
of its archbishop by the King was illegal in the eyes of
the Curia after Lent, 1075, no matter what precedents
may have implemented it before. But at the Lent
Synod the principle only was stated, and in general
terms. Its application to Henry's action was deferred.

If the *Dictatus Papae*, which, although undated in the
Register, appear there amid other records in the month
of March, 1075, belong chronologically to this year, not

only must the development of the idea of papal supremacy over secular princes be assigned to an early date in the pontificate ; in addition, they support the evidence for the contention that the Pope was quite early arming himself against a challenge by the German King before the latter had actually shown his hand.

A more immediate thrust at the King lay behind the threat issued against the five royal counsellors, who had been placed under the ban by Alexander II.   They had been absolved by the legates at Easter, 1074.[1]   Whether the Pope disapproved of the legates' action, or whether the counsellors had given new cause for dissatisfaction, their separation from worship in church, and the threat of excommunication without reference to Henry, were provocative.   The suspension of the Bishops of Bremen, Strasburg and Speier, and the threat of suspension issued against Herman of Bamberg had more justification. The Lombard Bishops of Pavia and Turin were also suspended, and the Bishop of Placentia was deposed. Philip I was threatened with excommunication if he did not give satisfaction to the legates proceeding to France.   Robert Guiscard and his nephew, Robert Loritello, were excommunicated.[2]   Thus no steps were taken at the Lenten Synod to settle the Milanese dispute, or to make arrangements for the imperial coronation, and the Pope complicated the drift of events by striking at his opponents elsewhere.   The proceedings of the Synod reflected the depression and aggravation in Gregory's mind, revealed already in his letter to Hugh of Cluny (January 22nd).[3]   In the East, he said, the Catholic faith was going to pieces, and

'when I look west or south or north I see no bishops lawful in their appointment, or in their life, ruling the people of Christ by love and not by worldly ambition.   Among secular princes I see none who prefers God's honour to

[1] Meyer von Knonau II.   378 n. 92.
[2] Reg. II. 52a.   [3] Reg. II. 49.

his own, or justice to gain. As for those among whom I live, whether Romans or Lombards or Normans, as I often tell them, they are worse than Jews or pagans.'

The happy settlement by the legates in Germany with Henry IV was entirely forgotten. Gregory expected the whole world to assume millennial calm and unquestioning deference at the first indication of his purpose. By his impulsive impatience he was drifting into conflict, and ruining all prospect of the gradual application of the reform programme.

Meanwhile Gregory still dreamed of extending the feudal suzerainty of the Papacy over the kings of the West. On January 25th he had written to Svein III of Denmark,[1] claiming 'universal rule' over not only 'kings and princes, but all Christians'. He said that legates had been sent to arrange for the establishment of a Danish archbishopric—a check to the ambitions of Liemar of Hamburg, who like Adalbert before him now claimed jurisdiction over the Danish bishops—but that the legation had been unable to cross Germany, owing to its disturbed condition. So Gregory requests that envoys may be sent to discuss this and other matters, and asks for armed help against the enemies of the church. A Danish bishop had reported that the king had it in mind to send one of his sons to fight for the Roman Church, and the Pope now urges that he may come, together with a force of trusty knights, for 'there is not far from us a certain rich province by the sea, which vile and dastardly heretics hold', and the king's son might become duke and prince and defender of Christianity.

The Pope, no doubt, had the Normans in view. On April 17th [2] he unfolded his claim to suzerainty over the Danish kingdom. Formerly the Pope, besides teaching all nations, had corrected all kings and princes. 'The

[1] Reg. II. 51.   [2] Reg. II. 75.

law of the Roman bishops rather than that of the Roman emperors prevailed, their sound went out into all the earth, and him whom Augustus ruled, Christ ruled.' Now the kings of the earth despised the law of the church, but the 'bold race' of the Danes showed reverence to the mother of all churches ; if there was anything which the authority of the Roman Church could endow it with, let the request be made, especially if the king desired to obtain the 'noble patronage' (*patrocinium*) of the Roman Church for himself and his kingdom, as he had himself suggested in the time of Alexander II.

Gregory's statement attributes the inception of the idea of papal suzerainty over the Danish kingdom to Svein, when the latter was on a visit to Alexander's court. It is, however, significant that when Jaropolc, the son of Dmitri of Kiev, visited Rome in Gregory's pontificate, the prince is reported to have made a similar offer, with his father's sanction, for the Russian kingdom. The coincidence suggests that Gregory let slip no opportunity, when the representatives of distant kingdoms came to Rome, of developing his vast scheme for extending the papal suzerainty. If he then influenced the young Russian prince to suggest that Kiev should become part of the papal patrimony, it is probable that, when Archdeacon, his persuasion conveyed the idea to Svein of Denmark in the days of Alexander II. However, in April, 1075, he attempted to bring both Denmark and Kiev under the papal sway. On the day that his letter to Svein was registered, the copy of another letter, despatched to Dmitri, King of Kiev, was entered.[1]

'Your son visiting the threshold of the apostles came to me, and earnestly asked to obtain that kingdom by the gift of S. Peter, through our hands, having sworn due fealty to the same blessed Peter, prince of the apostles, indubitably asserting that his petition would be ratified and confirmed

[1] *Reg.* II. 74.

by your consent, if it should be granted by the favour and guarantee of apostolic authority.'

Dmitri was an exile from Kiev, and could expect little support from Henry IV, so an appeal for assistance was sent to the Pope, who made the fullest use of his opportunity. 'We have given our consent, and we have delivered the government of your kingdom to him (Jaropolc) on the part of the blessed Peter.'

Whether Dmitri had actually offered to hold his kingdom under papal suzerainty is by no means clear, but the movements of Henry's armies were causing alarm along the eastern frontier of Germany, and the Slav princes were looking towards Rome for assistance. Boleslav II, Duke of Poland, sent presents to the Curia. In his letter of acknowledgment (April 20th)[1] Gregory emphasized the supremacy of the Roman see in the ecclesiastical organization of the church, and gave notice of a legatine commission to establish an archbishopric in Poland, and to appoint more bishops for its large population. He warned the Duke to restore to King Dmitri the money which he had taken from him.

Whether at the request of Svein and Dmitri or not, the claim for papal suzerainty over Denmark and Kiev was set forth in the spring of 1075, and we shall see attempts made to extend it over other lands. Unlike former Popes, who were content with exercising their universal executive in matters ecclesiastical, or with a general and vague appeal to the Donation of Constantine in support of their authority in a local dispute, Gregory sought to make his intervention practically effective in secular affairs in the respective areas where the fealty of kings was demanded. This tendency is plainly shown in the Hungarian correspondence of this year. On January 10th he referred to the universal rule of the Roman Church in a letter to Judith, the Queen of Salomon of Hungary.[2] In a letter, dated March 23rd,[3] to her

[1] *Reg.* II. 73.　　　[2] *Reg.* II. 44.　　　[3] *Reg.* II. 63.

husband's rival, Duke Géza, he again asserted the papal
dominion over that country : ' to the King of no other
kingdom . . . is the kingdom of Hungary . . . subject,
but to the holy and universal mother, the Roman
Church '. Salomon had by divine judgment compromised his rights, through swearing fealty to Henry
IV, and not to the Papacy. Again, on April 17th,[1]
Gregory referred to his function as peace-maker between
all earthly rulers, and expresses the desire to bring about
concord between Salomon and Géza. But Hungary at
present possessed a mere ' ruler ', not a king, since
' having despised the noble dominion of the blessed
Peter, chief of the apostles, to whom the kingdom
(of Hungary) belongs . . . he submitted himself to the
German King, and received the title of ruler '. Therefore
God had transferred the power of his kingdom to Géza,
and Salomon had lost his prior right by his ' sacrilegious
usurpation '.

But the Pope was careful not to commit himself too
far in his letters to Géza. He makes a very guarded offer
of assistance provided that Géza continues to show
deference towards the Roman Church. He consistently
refers to Géza as ' Duke ' and reserves the title ' King '
for Salomon. We shall see the same cautious diplomacy
in his relations with Henry IV and Rudolf of Rheinfelden,
Duke of Swabia. Gregory was dogged by a fatal tendency to wait upon events, which removed the confidence
of his correspondents. At the close of 1075, Géza
abandoned the effort to establish himself in Hungary by
the aid of the Papacy, and turned to the Eastern Emperor,
Michael VII, to whom he swore fealty for the Hungarian
kingdom, and from whom he received a crown as the
emblem of his title and of Michael's hegemony over
Hungary—a negotiation which brought to an end
Gregory's ambitious dream of papal sway over that land.

The vital questions of the Milanese election and the

[1] *Reg.* II. 70 (Caspar).

imperial coronation were still awaiting vigorous measures, but Gregory continued to drift on the bosom of
inertia. At Easter another fire broke out in Milan and
destroyed the cathedral. The Patarines were charged
with incendiarism, and the reactionaries succeeded in
calling back the exiled captains to Milan. In a fight in
the city the gallant Herlembald fell, pierced by five
lances, with the standard of S. Peter in his hand. The
Lombard bishops, in despair at Godfrey's ineffectiveness
and inaction, applied to Henry IV to appoint a new
candidate for the see of Milan, who would more vigorously uphold their cause against the Patarines and
against Rome. In this threat to the improved relationship between Gregory and Henry, Guibert of Ravenna
played a part. He had been summoned by the Pope to
the Lenten Synod,[1] but failed to appear. He was now
suspended from office by Gregory, and the same sentence
fell upon Hugh the White, although the cause of his
condemnation is not known.

Meanwhile the papal couriers carried despatches
dealing with the domestic affairs of the church into
distant parts of Italy, and to France and Germany. In
Germany a determined attempt was made to secure the
enforcement of the Lenten decrees on simony and
clerical marriage. In addition to the letters to Siegfried
of Mainz and to the Bishops of Magdeburg and Constance [2] issued in February, similar instructions were sent
at the end of March to Anno of Köln,[3] Burchard of
Halberstadt [4] and again to Werner of Magdeburg.[5]
The simonist Herman of Bamberg, who had attempted to
bribe the clergy in Rome, was deprived of his bishopric
in June,[6] and Siegfried of Mainz was ordered to appoint
a successor.[7] But the reform movement made no pro-
gress in Germany, save in Saxony.[8] In some dioceses

[1] *Reg.* II. 42.   [2] *Ep. Coll.* 3, 4 and 5.   [3] *Reg.* II. 67.
[4] *Reg.* II. 66.   [5] *Reg.* II. 68.   [6] *Reg.* III. 1.
      [7] *Reg.* III. 2.   [8] *Reg.* II. 12.

the bishops refrained from proclaiming the decrees, in others the clergy refused to obey them. At Bamberg the clergy supported their bishop in his quarrel with Gregory. In response to Gregory's order, Siegfried attempted to summon a Synod at Mainz in August. When it proved impracticable, he wrote an explanatory letter to the Pope. But Gregory declined his excuses and insisted upon the Synod being held, urging upon him his favourite metaphor, ' Cursed is he who withholds his sword from blood '.[1] The Synod was held in October, but so obstinate and unruly were the clergy that Siegfried determined from thenceforth to abandon the attempt to enforce the decrees.

The authority of Henry IV in Germany was notably vindicated by his victory over the Saxons on the river Unstrut, on June 9th, when the tactics of Rudolf won the day decisively for the King. In October Henry mobilized another army to complete the subjugation of Saxony, but no contingents came from the Dukes of Swabia, Carinthia and Bavaria, on the feigned excuse of their severe losses in June. Here appeared from behind the royal arras the skeleton that finally ruined his reign. The German princes were opposed to the formation of a strong central government. On this occasion the King was able to proceed against the Saxons without them. Without waiting for the issue of another battle, the Saxon chiefs surrendered, and the King disbanded his army in November. With the ravaging of the Harzburg in mind, Henry foolishly threw away the opportunity for securing an abiding peace. Saxon nobles and Bishops were exiled and imprisoned, and the domains of the princes were confiscated. The King overlooked the possibility of their appeal to Rome, and the effect of his severity upon the fears of the South German magnates.

Meanwhile, Henry supported the policy of Gregory in

[1] *Reg.* III. 4.

Germany. Simonists and the married clergy received
no support from Henry throughout this summer and he
agreed to the deposition of Herman of Bamberg. After
the victory of June 9th it was full time for Gregory to
make arrangements for the imperial coronation. But
the Curia made no move. Henry had been expecting a
courier from over the Alps since the beginning of the
year, but when the despatch arrived in the spring it
came from Milan, not Rome. The situation was week
by week increasing in danger for Gregory's policy.
However, the King sent no reply to Milan, but, while
on the Saxon campaign, and before the battle of the
Unstrut, he despatched a letter to Gregory complaining
that the German princes desired the King and Pope to
remain at loggerheads. This letter he sent secretly by
envoys authorized to promote peace with Gregory.
Henry desired the Pope not to divulge their message to
anyone save the Countess Beatrix and Matilda. If he
returned safely from the Saxon expedition, he would
send another embassy.[1] There can be little doubt that
Henry had at length made some preliminary suggestions
for his visit to Italy and for the imperial coronation.
When this proposal was widely discussed in Germany
about ten years before, many of the princes had
opposed it, and the King now wished his plans to be
kept from their knowledge until the issue of the Saxon
campaign was clear. In the meantime, on July 20th
Gregory had written to Henry, in affectionate terms,
commending his support of the reform programme in
Germany, and accepting it as an indication of the King's
desire to render greater services to the church. He
announced the deposition and excommunication of
Herman of Bamberg, and begged Henry to take steps for
the appointment of a successor, in collaboration with
Siegfried of Mainz and the clergy and people of Bamberg.[2] No doubt the Pope had heard that the King

[1] Quoted by Gregory in *Reg.* III. 5.   [2] *Reg.* III. 3.

had withdrawn his support from Herman, but, although the letter is framed in the most cordial terms, no reference is made to the imperial coronation.

The royal envoys did not arrive in Rome until after July 20th [1] when Gregory had left the City.[2] They found the Pope at his summer retreat, and unable to deal with business on account of sickness. The next incident in the tangled accounts of the events of this summer was the arrival of a courier from Henry with a message for his envoys, warning them not to be surprised or take offence because the second embassy, promised when they left Saxony, had not arrived. They were to be patient and await its arrival, for the King had not altered his intentions.[3] But Henry was wavering. His courier declined to remain with Gregory on account of the Pope's illness, which was no doubt due to the summer heat, and the Pope made use of the opportunity of his return to Germany at the beginning of September, to acknowledge the King's letter of the beginning of June. He addresses him again as ' Glorious King ' and ' beloved son ', and praises him for taking counsel with men who will endeavour to anneal the peace between them. He congratulates him on the victory over the Saxons, and describes it as a divine judgment on them, although he deplores the bloodshed involved in it. He repeats his previous direction for the election of a new bishop at Bamberg. Still there is no allusion to the coronation, unless the vague expression, ' By the favour of Christ I am prepared to offer to thee the bosom of the holy Roman Church, and to receive thee as lord, brother and son ',[4] was intended to convey to the King a general approval of the idea.

At the beginning of September, Henry's second embassy to the Pope arrived, bringing also letters to

---

[1] *Cf. Reg.* III. 1 and 2, dated from Laurentum—*Codex Udalrici* dates the former from Albano.

[2] *Reg.* III. 7.   [3] *Reg.* III. 5.   [4] *Reg.* III. 7.

Beatrix and Matilda, stating that he wished the plans, secretly sent in June, to be made public. Three of the leading princes in Germany had declined to send their divisions for the autumn campaign in Saxony, and Henry sought to check the growth of disaffection by securing the proclamation in Rome of his forthcoming coronation. Moreover, an unsafe counsellor was now beside him. Godfrey the Younger of Lorraine was making proposals to Matilda, his wife, for a separation.[1] That was a covered threat at the Pope, whose friendship with Beatrix and Matilda was daily increasing.

Gregory took offence at the change in the King's attitude, and made known his displeasure in a letter to the two Countesses (September 11th).[2] He interpreted Henry's action as an indication that he did not desire a lasting peace with Gregory. It would cause the princes, who desired discord between the King and Gregory, to rejoice. Therefore he altogether rejected the royal suggestion, but would gladly return to his former plan. On the other hand, he counselled great caution in dealing with Godfrey's proposal for a separation, since the Count had already broken a promise made to him. He left the decision to Matilda and her mother, but urged that no ' treaty ' could be made with Godfrey which could not be substantiated by the teaching of the Fathers. Matilda and Godfrey stood within the prohibited degrees of marriage, and this no doubt weighed on the mind of the devout Countess, but Gregory saw that a union which had produced a son, now dead, could not easily be dissolved. He begged that, if possible, nothing might alter the affection which existed between himself and them, and, in this case, he desired to stand by them, and would love Godfrey, if he loved them, but would resist him, if he showed animosity to them.

There is no need to throw this communication against the background of a jealous husband, although no doubt

---

[1] *Cf. Reg.* III. 5.   [2] *Reg.* III. 5.

11

as always, when a good man and a good woman, not allied by kinship, find that common interests breed a common affection, there will be slanderous tongues to pour slime on a beautiful thing. Godfrey was not jealous of Gregory, but he disapproved entirely of his wife's policy in Italy, which was entirely in favour of the reform programme, and the aggrandisement of papal power, and offered all the resources of the house of Tuscany for Gregory's support.

The one clear feature in the situation was the Pope's desire to deal with Henry and the princes separately. For this reason he welcomed a secret understanding with the King. This could at any time be modified, perhaps disowned. Until Henry, without reserve, had so proved his compliancy to the papal will in all ecclesiastical matters in Germany and Italy, no public arrangements which would bind Gregory should be made for his coronation, especially since a large amount of opinion in Germany was still opposed to it. When the King's submission was so complete that he could not withdraw from it, then would the Pope readily enough take the King's side against the princes, and he should be crowned in Rome. So the policy of the Curia drifted on, waiting for the turn of events, until the patience of the young monarch was exhausted and he broke out into natural although unwise revolt.

On June 23rd Theoduin, Bishop of Liège, had died. At the request of Godfrey the Younger, the King appointed Henry, Archdeacon of Verdun, a relative of the Lotharingian Duke, to the vacant see, and he was consecrated by Anno of Köln. The investiture decree of the Lent Synod (1075) had not been published in Germany, so the King's action did not constitute a challenge to the Pope, who did not refer to the appointment in his letters of July and September.

Early in the autumn the King took the initiative in the two vital matters outstanding between him and the

Pope. He sent Count Eberhard of Nellenburg into Lombardy. The Count had been absolved by the legates at Easter, 1074, but was excommunicated again at the Lent Synod of 1075. At a council held at Roncaglia the Milanese Patarines were declared enemies of the King. Together with Gregory, ' the devil ' of Vercelli, Eberhard sought the assistance of Robert Guiscard to promote the royal visit to Rome, and offered, in the name of the King, to recognize the territory conquered by Guiscard as a fief of the Empire. Shortly before, Hugh the White had tried to bring about Gregory's overthrow, by offering the imperial crown to Robert, if he would attack Rome and depose the Pope. On each occasion Guiscard gave a similar answer. He held his conquered lands of the Roman Church, which had blessed his enterprise.

At the end of November Henry threw down an open challenge to the Pope. He appointed Tedald, Sub-Deacon of the Church of Milan, who had accompanied him as a royal chaplain upon the Saxon campaign, Archbishop of Milan. There were now three candidates in the field for the Church of S. Ambrose : Atto the papal nominee, and Godfrey and Tedald, both nominated by the King. In Italy the King also appointed bishops for the sees of Fermo and Spoleto within papal territory. On November 30th he nominated Robert to the see of Bamberg. No offence was taken at Rome by the Bamberg appointment. Gregory had repeatedly invited Henry to proceed with the election of Herman's successor, and, although he challenged the royal nominees at Fermo and Spoleto, he had warned Count Hubert, and the clergy and people of Fermo, on December 22nd, 1074,[1] not to choose a new bishop without consulting the King. But the nomination of Tedald to Milan flouted papal authority at a most sensitive point, not so much on the ground of its being a challenge to the election decree of

[1] *Reg.* II. 38.

Lent, 1075, which may not have become public in Germany, but rather as an act of interference in an area which the Pope had consistently regarded as the special preserve of Roman influence, and as a foolish complication of the Milanese problem.   It is possible that with stupid short-sightedness Henry may have thought that his appointment of Tedald would wipe out the old quarrel concerning Godfrey, and there are indications that Gregory did consider the possibility of accepting Tedald as a compromise.   On December 1st the King filled up the vacant abbey at Fulda, and shortly afterwards nominated a new abbot at Lorsch.

The Pope's enemies were uniting.   Guibert of Ravenna opened communications with Tedald, and sent ex-Cardinal Hugh the White with messages from Milan to the new Archbishop and to the King.   On December 8th Gregory sent a conciliatory message to Tedald,[1] and summoned him to attend the Lenten Synod of 1076, or, if he chose, to come to Rome before then, under a safe-conduct to be provided by Beatrix and Matilda, when a fair judgment of his case would take place, and, if it seemed equitable, Tedald should be promoted in place of Atto.   He warned him not to receive consecration, under a threat of severe penalties.   In this letter Gregory simplified the issue by ignoring Godfrey.   Thus Godfrey was rejected by both sides, and he sank into obscurity. On the next day a letter was sent to Gregory of Vercelli [2] and the other diocesan bishops of Milan, complaining of the King's action, and informing them that Tedald had been summoned to Rome, when an opportunity of proving the validity of his appointment would be provided.   The bishops were warned against consecrating him under pain of excommunication; ' as it is hard to kick against the pricks, so is it provocative to oppose the holy Roman Church.'

Whether Gregory was sincere in offering to promote

[1] *Reg.* III. 8 (Caspar).   [2] *Reg.* III. 9.

Tedald if he could prove his case is not clear. In the letter to Gregory of Vercelli he modifies his statement, and in his letter to the King of the same date [1] (December 8th) he makes no reference to it. In his long despatch, the last ever addressed by him to Henry, the Pope summarizes the issues at stake between him and the King. Henry, being in communication with excommunicated counsellors, must seek absolution at the hands of a bishop to be selected by Gregory, who shall make known to him the conditions of his submission. Against all his filial professions of love and devotion to the Roman Church, against his promises transmitted through his mother and the bishops, against the canons and decrees of the church, the state of affairs at Milan was in marked contrast, and now, adding blow to blow, he had appointed unsuitable and unknown persons to the bishoprics of Fermo and Spoleto. The royal dignity should have paid more honour to S. Peter, by whose authority Gregory held the power of the keys against evil-doers. Therefore he warns his Highness to show due reverence to the papal chair.

The Pope then refers to the investiture decree of Lent, 1075. This was based upon the decrees of the holy Fathers ; it was not a novelty ; it was not Gregory's invention. The decree was to be obeyed not only by Henry and the German kingdom, but by all princes and peoples of the earth. If the King had had any objections to raise against it, he should have sent accredited envoys, and it could have been modified, saving the honour of the Eternal King and danger to Gregory's own soul. If this course had not been agreeable, he should have made known in what respect the decree injured him or his counsellors, rather than violate a papal order. Let the King remember that Saul had been dispossessed by God, when, puffed up by pride in victory, he despised the counsel of Samuel. The discussion of the contents of

[1] *Reg.* III. 10.

the letter brought by a royal embassy Gregory postponed until he received an answer to this letter. But he sent a secret message to the King by Henry's envoys.[1]

The royal embassy had arrived in fulfilment of the King's promise made in June. It carried, no doubt, the formal application for the imperial coronation. Instead of an answer to this urgent question, the secret message of the Pope threatened the King with excommunication if he did not do penance for his personal crimes ; some of them, ' horrible to mention ', deserved deposition from the throne ' without hope of recovery '. If he continued to associate with excommunicated people, he would thereby place himself under the same ban. Legates also were sent into Germany warning the King to restore the Saxon bishops to their sees. Three months before, the Pope had hailed Henry's victory as a divine judgment upon a recalcitrant people, and had raised no protest against the repressive measures then adopted. The King's reply now was to become reconciled with Otto of Nordheim, the chief of the Saxon princes ; but he postponed the trial of the bishops, and allowed them to return to Saxony.

Apart from the excitement created in his mind by the threat of deposition, three legitimate objections might have been raised by Henry to three points in the Pope's letter. First as to the moral charges—there had been no ground for these since 1069. Secondly as to the charge of associating with excommunicated friends— they had been absolved at Easter, 1074. Thirdly as to the appeal to the investiture decree—this struck at one of the most ancient rights and practices of the German monarchy. For the rest, the appointment at Milan was an act of provocative hostility, and, although less serious in their affects, the nominations at Fermo and Spoleto, in the papal territory, were unwise, in view of the Pope's attitude. But for these things Gregory's Fabian policy,

[1] *Ep. Coll.* 14 (p. 538).

watchful, suspicious, grasping in what it sought to acquire, backward in what it offered, must be held responsible. When the impulsive young King cut himself clear from his political difficulties on the Unstrut, the latest moment had arrived for Gregory to do the generous and the just thing. But instead of offering Henry the imperial he threatened to take away the royal crown. The coronation of Henry as Emperor of Rome in September, 1075, might have reconciled him to Gregory once and for all. The King's nature was generous, and responded readily to generous treatment. More than once in his life he was reconciled with enemies who had struck at his crown and dignity.[1] But Gregory treated him with the unbending severity merited only by a hardened sinner of the Pope's own age. Spring passed into summer, and summer into autumn, and still the Pope allowed events to slide, so that the young King's patience was exhausted, and a year which was merely critical at its beginning had become fatal at the end. It was not the events of 1076, so full of dangerous portent and of hostile action against the King, which formed the crisis in Gregory's relations with Henry IV, but the events of 1075, when the Pope allowed the Roman Church to drift into stormy waters, from which sound seamanship might have preserved her ; and from these seas he was never afterwards able to bring her to the haven of peace.

Before the year closed the Pope was to receive a reminder that the gaunt hand of faction, which had prevented his predecessors from sitting easily on the papal chair, and which had torn the peace of Milan into shreds for more than ten years, had not been rendered innocuous in Rome. Gregory's administration of the marriage decree alienated a number of the clergy and

---

[1] Villemain *Hist. de Grégoire VII* II. (1873) 17 adopts a similar view of Henry's character, and (p. 256) refers to Gregory's exorbitant claims. Voigt *Hildebrand als Papst Gregorius der Siebente* (1815) p. 198 also refers to Gregory's ambitions at the beginning of his pontificate.

their relations, by compelling them to surrender either their wives or their emoluments.   At S. Peter's cathedral, he dismissed sixty doorkeepers who imposed upon ignorant visitors by dressing up as cardinals, and obtaining money from them, and who committed robberies in the church by night.   He forbade the saying of Mass at very early hours in the morning, and prohibited the opening of the cathedral before daylight, in order to check the avarice of the priests.   Among the unruly elements of the City, who took advantage of the unpopularity created for Gregory by these measures, was the son of Stephen Cencius.   After the Pope's illness in 1074 he had been convicted of forging in his own interest a will drawn up in favour of the church.   Compelled to disgorge his gains, he retired to his tower but continued his depredations in Rome.   In 1075 he was committed to prison by the City Prefect under sentence of death, and was only released by Gregory at the intercession of Matilda and the leading citizens of Rome.   On Christmas Eve Gregory was celebrating the midnight Mass in the crypt of Santa Maria Maggiore.   The rain was descending and few worshippers were present.   Cencius entered the church with an armed following and seized the Pope as he was consecrating the bread.   Gregory's robes were stripped off, and, with blood streaming from a severe wound, he was bound to a horse, and carried away to a castle outside Rome.   When dawn came the citizens surrounded the stronghold, and Cencius, realizing that he could not withstand a siege, with sword drawn, extracted a promise of safety from Gregory, who prevented his rescuers from doing justice on him.   The Pope returned to Santa Maria, and completed the Christmas Mass.

In scenes of this kind, the courage and self-possession of Gregory had long ago been tried.   As a commander of armies, amid the stress of battle and the excitement of campaigns, he might have found the place for which nature and temperament intended him.   He might have achieved for his own day and generation results as permanent as those secured by his tragic death for generations that followed.   Cencius fled away from Rome and promptly allied himself with the Pope's more distant enemies.   From first to last Gregory treated him with dignity and forbearance.   If but a fraction of the same magnanimity had been extended to the young Henry IV, the devastating war between Papacy and Empire, which set back the civilization of Europe for five hundred years, might have been avoided ; the Rome of the Cæsars might have survived the spoiling hand of the Renaissance Popes, who would themselves have been free from the demoralizing results of that conflict ; and against the greatest builders since the Romans would not lie the charge of having destroyed the greatest of the Cæsar's works.

CHAPTER TEN

INVICEM VULNERA (1076)

IF Henry's action at Milan was a challenge, Gregory's letter was an ultimatum, and 'blow for blow' was to be interchanged between King and Pope throughout this year. It did not end with the total rout of the King as so many writers have maintained. Henry was never routed by Gregory, and, although he died wretched, forsaken and defeated, long years after the Pope, it is doubtful whether Gregory's hammer blows would ever have brought him to this.

The King received the papal letter at Goslar on January 1st. All hope of an imperial coronation with the goodwill of the Pope was shattered, unless Henry had placed his hands in shackles while Gregory placed the crown upon his head. Before a month was out the King had in fierce anger scorned the Pope's terms, and retaliated with heavier blows than he had yet received. These outbursts were not usual with Henry, nor were they natural to him. On this occasion his own resentment was kept at white heat by the hate of others. Eberhard of Nellenburg and the other banned counsellors were there, and so was the twice perjured traitor, Hugh the White. The iron of the royal wrath became hotter in the fire of their spleen. On January 24th the lords of church and state met at Worms. Archbishops Siegfried of Mainz and Udo of Trier, and twenty-four diocesan bishops, among them Burchard, the Saxon Bishop of Halberstadt, were present. Godfrey the Younger of Lorraine headed the lay lords, but he alone of the leading magnates appeared. The ground had been well prepared by Hugh the White with garbled accounts of Gregory's election, scandalous reflections on his relations with the Tuscan Duchesses, and magnified reports of the Pope's difficulties with the Normans. No doubt the tale of Cencius was told, with the central piece left out—the fidelity of the Romans to their bishop. In full session of the Council the bishops signed individually a declaration withdrawing all future submission and obedience to Gregory.[1] Burchard of Halberstadt, ' the brother ' who had been commended by Gregory nine months before for ' putting his hand continuously ' to the work of reform,[2] signed the condemnation. It is reported that Adalbero of 'Wurzburg and Herman of Metz hesitated to sign on the canonical ground that a bishop could not be condemned in his absence, but they were persuaded by William of Utrecht, the friend of Godfrey the Younger. The bishops' covering letter was addressed to ' brother Hildebrand '. His election, it said, was unlawfully obtained ; his provocative policy towards the Churches of Italy, Germany, France and Spain had robbed the bishops of their power, and handed it over to the common people ; the episcopal condition was depressed, and the Pope had claimed exclusive right to judge them. So he could be no longer Pope, nor had he ever had any right to the chair of Peter. He had sworn to the dead Emperor Henry III never to become Pope himself, nor to assist in the promotion of anyone else, without the Emperor's consent or that of his son, and the first of these oaths he had rejected on another occasion. He had violated the Election Decree of 1059. His relations with Matilda were such that they could not mention them, and he took the counsel of women in the administration of ecclesiastical affairs. So they will not obey him—they never had offered to do so. He had said that he would not recognize

[1] Bruno 65. Pertz *M.G.H. Leges* II. 46.
[2] *Reg.* II. 66.

them as bishops, they would not recognize him as Pope.[1]

Fact and fiction are cunningly woven together in this concoction. It clearly shows the hand of Hugh the White, with his knowledge of the Election Decree and of Gregory's partiality for the counsel of the Tuscan ladies. A similar attempt to twist some details of Gregory's election and of the papal administration appears in the King's letter, although it is mainly occupied with the threat to depose the King. It opens and closes with phrases verging upon vituperation. 'Henry, not by usurpation, but by God's holy ordinance King, to Hildebrand, not Pope, but false monk.' This greeting Gregory had deserved because he had left no order of the church, whether archbishops, bishops or priests, untouched but had trampled them under foot, gaining favour with the people by humiliating them. The King had tolerated these things out of respect for the apostolic chair, but now the Pope had set himself up against the royal power granted to the King by God—'Thou hast threatened to take it from us' as if the kingdom and empire were the Pope's to bestow and not God's. 'Our Lord Jesus Christ, who called me to the throne, did not call thee to the Papacy.' Cunning and fraud accompanied his appointment; by money, by favour, by the sword, he had secured the chair of peace, and he now armed subjects against their rulers, and taught them to despise the bishops. Laymen had been placed over the bishops with power to depose them. 'Me also, consecrated to the kingdom, unworthy though I may be among the anointed, thou hast attacked', although by the tradition of the Fathers God alone was the judge of the King, who could only be deposed for heresy. 'Do thou . . . condemned by the judgment of all our bishops, and by our own, come down and give up the apostolic see so

[1] Pertz, *M.G.H. Leges* II. 44 ff.; Weiland *M.G.H. Constitutiones et Acta* I. 106 ff.

that another may mount the chair of Peter . . . I,
Henry, by the grace of God, King, with all my bishops,
say unto thee " Come down ", " Come down ".' [1]

Entirely misinformed on the attitude of the clergy and
people of Rome towards the Pope, and perhaps under
the influence of a garbled account of the attack of
Cencius, Henry also addressed a letter to them. He
thanks them for their fidelity to himself, and begs that
they may continue to be friends to his friends and
enemies to his enemies. Among the latter is Hildebrand
the monk, and the King ' stirs them up ' to enmity
against him, as a depredator and oppressor of the church,
and one lying in ambush against the Roman City and
the German Kingdom. This Henry had made clear in
a second letter to Hildebrand, enclosed in the despatch
to the Romans, beginning ' Henry, by the grace of God,
King, to Hildebrand '. The King contrasts his own
obedience with the Pope's enmity. Gregory had dared
to deprive Henry of his hereditary dignity, and had
attempted to alienate from him the Italian Kingdom.
He had attacked the bishops and expelled them with
insults. ' You have said, to quote your own words,
that you will die or else deprive me of life and kingdom.'
This unheard of contumacy the King had judged in a
general council, and from the bishops' letter the Pope
would see that he had been deposed. ' I give my consent and I pronounce against you the renunciation of
all right to the Papacy which you appear to have, and
demand that you come down from the chair of the City,
of which the Patriciate belongs to me by a divine grant,
and by the sworn assent of the Romans.' This letter,
says the King, had been sent to the ' monk Hildebrand ',
and continuing his appeal to the Romans, he says : ' Rise
therefore against him, liegemen, and may the first in
loyalty be first in condemnation.' The King forbids

[1] Bruno 67 ; Pertz *M.G.H. Leges* II. 47 ; Weiland *M.G.H. Constitutiones et Acta* I. 110 f.

the shedding of Gregory's blood, for life will be a greater penalty to him than death, after his deposition, but they are to compel him to resign, and to receive another Pope elected by the King with the consent of the bishops and themselves.[1]

Whether a copy of the King's denunciation of the Pope to the Romans was sent to Gregory, together with the letter especially addressed to him, is not clear. The letter enclosed in the appeal to the Romans may be a free summary of the contents of the letter sent directly to Gregory, adjusted so as to appeal more especially to civic instincts and loyalty. But it seems clear that both letters addressed to Hildebrand were despatched at the same time and not, as it has been suggested, at different periods.[2] If the language of the bishops and of the royal letters is couched in insolent and violent terms, and if the truth is twisted, especially in the former, none the less the grounds on which the attack upon the Pope is made are valid enough. No doubt his messages to the clergy and people of Germany [3] had damaged the influence of the bishops and clergy in the minds of lay-folk, and the threat to depose the King was without precedent—apart from the threat to Philip?—although the pamphleteers on Gregory's side attempted to find historical antecedents for the Pope's action.[4] No great shock was produced in popular opinion by the royal edict. The memory of Henry III's depositions in 1046 was still vivid, and the readiness with which the bishops agreed to the measure indicated the absence of any idea that a revolutionary step was being taken. That it was resented by the clergy and people of Rome

[1] Bruno 66. Pertz *M.G.H. Leges* II. 46. Weiland *M.G.H. Constitutiones et Acta* I. 109 f. Brooke suggests that this letter was not sent until 1080 (*C.M.H.* X. 137 n. 1).
[2] *Cf.* Mirbt *Wahl Gregors VII.* (1892) p. 13 n. 6 ; Meyer von Knonau II. 662 n. 71 ; and Fliche II. 291, who maintains that the letter reported in Bruno 67 was sent by Henry to Hildebrand from Utrecht. Martens I. 94 says that it was sent from Worms.
[3] *Cf. supra* p. 141.   [4] Mirbt *Publizistik* p. 238.

is not evidence to the contrary. Ever since the intervention of Henry III they had been sensitive to German
interference; moreover, the outrage committed by
Cencius had rallied popular opinion in Rome to the
Pope's support. Among the German princes the king's
action would not have been criticized in the absence of
their own political quarrel with him, and of their desire
to prevent the centralization of authority in his hands.
They made use of the opprobrium cast upon Gregory
solely on behalf of their own self-centred policy.

The delivery of the letters to Gregory and the Romans,
together with bribes and messages for the Italian nobles
and the Roman people, was entrusted to Bishops Huz-
man of Speier and Burchard of Basel, accompanied by
Count Eberhard as an escort. A council was held at
Piacenza, where the Lombard bishops swore to depose
Gregory and adopted the resolutions of Worms. While
Eberhard negotiated to unite the discontented elements
in Italy against the Pope, the two bishops handed over
their letters to a priest of Parma named Roland, a royal
official, and the embassy went on to Rome, and appeared
at the Lenten Synod, which assembled on February 14th.

The letter for the Pope may have been handed to
Gregory on the day before. After the singing of the
opening hymn, Roland read aloud one, if not both, of
the despatches, almost certainly that addressed to the
Romans, which contained one of the letters to Hildebrand. The Cardinal Bishop of Porto shouted for his
arrest. The City Prefect drew his sword in fierce anger
and a rush was made for the royal envoy. With danger
to his own person, the Pope dragged Roland to the foot
of his chair and appeased the tumult with a dignified
address reported by Donizo and extended by Paul
Bernried. Leclercq maintains that no address was made
by the Pope at this point,[1] but, while no doubt the
speech preserved by Donizo is an invention, the Synod

[1] Héfélé-Leclercq *Conciles* V. Pt. I. (1912) 161 n. 1.

would not have ended the first day's session without a pronouncement from Gregory.

On the next day Gregory lodged his counter-blow, and the condemnation of Henry was proclaimed in the midst of a prayer to S. Peter:

' Blessed Peter, Prince of the apostles, incline thy reverend ears I beseech thee to me, and hear thy servant, whom from infancy thou hast cherished, and to this day hast delivered from the hands of enemies, who hated and hate me for my loyalty to thee. Thou art my witness, and my Lady the Mother of God, and the blessed Paul thy brother, among all the saints, that thy holy Roman Church dragged me against my will to its government—that I did not think it robbery to ascend thy chair, and that rather did I desire to finish my life on pilgrimage, than to seize thy place with a worldly mind for the glory of the world. So through thy favour and not through my actions, I believe it pleased and pleases thee that the Christian people, committed especially to thee, still obey me. Especially was committed to me in thy place, with thy favour, the power given by God of binding and loosing in heaven and upon earth. So relying on this conviction, for the honour and defence of the church, on behalf of Almighty God, Father, Son and Holy Spirit, by His power and authority, do I prohibit to Henry the King, the son of Henry the Emperor—who against thy church has risen with unheard of pride—the rule of the whole kingdom of Germany and of Italy. I absolve all Christians from the fealty they have sworn or shall swear to him, and I forbid anyone to serve him as King. It is fitting that he who tries to diminish the honour of thy church, shall himself lose the honour which he seems to have. And since as a Christian he scorned to obey, and did not return to the Lord whom he disgraced by associating with the excommunicate—by doing many iniquities—by spurning the warnings which, thou art witness, I sent to him for his salvation—by separating himself from thy church, and attempting to divide it—I bind him, in thy stead, with the chain of anathema. Thus, confident in thee, I bind him, that the nations may know and acknowledge that thou art Peter, and upon thy rock the Son of the living God built his church, and the doors of hell shall not prevail against it.' [1]

Within less than three years from his election to the Papacy, the threat of deposition which had already been sent to Philip I of France, and to Henry IV himself, was formally pronounced against the German King. Although occasioned by Henry's provocative conduct, and still more by his own sentence of deposition against Gregory, this ' blow for blow ' was a natural consequence of the ambitious theory of the *imperium* set up already by the Pope over five Western lands, and regarded by him as the basis of his relationship with the whole of Europe. By the power of the keys inherited from S. Peter, and received when he mounted the papal chair, Gregory asserts dominion over the German and Italian kingdoms, and deposes their ruler, not in a fit of resentful anger, heightened by the promptings of angry counsellors, but as a pronouncement issuing from a vast conception of the range of papal hegemony. Although in the next few years, realizing that there was no suitable king to elevate into Henry's place, he may have stressed rather the excommunication than the deposition of Henry, the sentence promulgated at the Lenten Synod of 1076 was always an active factor in his mind, and a pawn in the long-drawn-out negotiations with Rudolf and the German princes. [2]

The sentence of excommunication and suspension was passed upon Siegfried of Mainz and the signatories of the bishops' letter, but those who had signed it unwillingly might escape deprivation if they gave satisfaction before August 1st. The offending Lombard bishops

[1] *Reg.* III. 10a.
[2] Much discussion has arisen over the significance of the deposition of 1076. The latest writer, Voosen (p. 260), following Mirbt, holds that it was irrevocable and declines the conclusion of Hergenrother, Martens and Fliche that it was a mere suspension. This is too emphatic ; all Gregory's later policy up to 1080 was based on the assumption that a reconciliation with Henry was possible.

shared in the sentence of Siegfried and his unprompted supporters.[1]

Sitting in the Synod was Agnes, the mother of Henry. Not for the first time did Gregory degrade an opponent in the presence of his mother. Writing in reply to Altman, Bishop of Passau, she said,

' The lord Pope has deprived my son the King of the royal dignity, on account of the declaration made against himself in the Synod, and because he associates with the excommunicate, and refuses to do penance for his sins, and has stricken him with the sword of anathema and released all who had sworn fealty to him from their oaths.'

At the beginning of her letter the gentle woman had lamented : ' With the greatest pain am I smitten, for I see the greatest danger threatening the church and especially my son, who trusts in the words of fools.' Truly, as a contemporary annalist says, the sword had passed through her own soul also.

To the faithful of all lands Gregory broadcasted the King's excommunication with sentences of burning dignity, which he was so well able to frame :

' Ye have heard, brothers, of a new and unheard of presumption. Ye have heard of the execrable garrulity and audacity of the schismatics, and of those blaspheming against the name of God in the blessed Peter. Ye have heard of the pride, which has risen up to the injury and insult of the holy and apostolic chair, such as your fathers never saw or heard, and, as history shows, has never emerged from pagans and heretics.—Wherefore, if ye believe that the keys of heaven were delivered to the blessed Peter by our Lord God Jesus Christ, and if you desire that through his hands a gate should be opened for you into the joys of eternal life, how much ought you to grieve for the injuries now inflicted on him.—In what manner, and for what reasons the blessed Peter hath bound the King in the chain of anathema, you can fully realize from the document enclosed herein.' [2]

[1] *Reg.* III. 10a.　　　　　　　　　[2] *Reg.* III. 6.

On February 26th died Henry's stoutest supporter among the German princes, Godfrey the Younger of Lorraine, murdered through the intrigues of Robert the Frisian. Early in March, Henry invested Hildulf, a priest of Goslar, in succession to Anno at Köln, and Poppo, Provost of Bamberg, to the see of Paderborn. At Easter, at Utrecht, he invested Godfrey's youthful son Conrad with the duchy of Lorraine. Here the sentence of the Pope reached him. An outburst similar to that of Worms took place at the Court. On Easter Day, William, Bishop of Utrecht, repeated the excommunication of the Pope, and declared the deposition of Henry void. But the papal ban upon the King and bishops at once began to take effect; Theodoric, Bishop of Verdun and several of the clergy secretly left the Court.

In a letter of the King to Altwin of Brixen, summoning him to another council at Worms to be held at Whitsun, Henry shows a clear grasp of the politico-ecclesiastical theory of the day. The *regnum* and *sacerdotium* each had its part to play; both were elevated above the church, but she had now been humiliated and widowed on both sides, for Gregory by usurping both had destroyed both. He had torn up the unity of *regnum* and *sacerdotium*. Christ had compared them to two swords, to be carried not by one bearer, but two. God had given Henry the kingdom, while Gregory sought to take it away. The Pope threatened to take away his life and kingdom, although he had given him neither the one nor the other. Doubtless this statement has a Cæsaro-papalist bias, but it was a view of church and state which Henry III would not have allowed to be challenged. While it provided scope for the papal supremacy over the church, it incorporated the ancient Germanic theory of the proprietary rights of the King.

On April 27th Henry lost another stout supporter by the death of William of Utrecht, and Altwin of Brixen was imprisoned in Swabia by Hartman, Count of Dillingen. At Easter the open defection of the bishops began. Adalbero of Wurzburg, Herman of Metz, Altman of Passau, Adalbert of Worms, and Archbishops Gebhard of Salzburg and Sigehard of Aquileia joined the following of Rudolf of Swabia, Welf of Bavaria and Berthold of Carinthia who began to form a party against Henry. They charged him with misuse of the Saxon victory, and of acting without their counsel.   Some of the Saxon hostages were surreptitiously released without the King's consent.   Only in North Italy did the royal cause remain firm.   At Easter in a council at Pavia, Guibert excommunicated Gregory.   The Council at Worms at Pentecost proved abortive.   The three princes stayed away, on the ground that they could no longer communicate with their excommunicated sovereign.   A like result accompanied the Council of Mainz on June 29th.   The leading magnates were absent.   Gregory was again excommunicated, but no reference was made on this occasion to the election of a new Pope.   Another batch of Saxon prisoners escaped, and the Saxon people began to prepare for renewed hostilities.

While the tide was slowly rolling up against Henry in Germany, the papal fulminations had produced but little change in Italy.   If the death of Godfrey the Younger removed all hindrance to the development of the alliance between Gregory and Matilda, movements among the Normans were again causing anxiety. Richard of Capua and Robert Guiscard ended their hostility to each other, and formed an alliance, assisted by Desiderius, the Abbot of Monte Cassino.   In May they attacked the Pope's ally Gisulf of Salerno, and Jordan of Capua advanced against Spoleto, which together with the Mark of Fermo had been confirmed to the Papacy by Matilda, after the death of her mother on April 18th.   Gregory felt the necessity for conciliating his enemies and concentrating his supporters.   Already

on March 14th [1] he had offered to make terms with
Robert Guiscard and to absolve him from excommunication, and in April he informed Wifred, the successor
of Herlembald at Milan, of his hope of peace with the
Normans. [2] Even with Henry he professed that he was
willing to make peace, in response to many urgent
requests, and he fixed August 1st as a date by which
Henry might secure absolution from the ban. [3] Nothing is said during this period of the deposition and he
continues to give him the title of ' King '. Henry,
Bishop of Trent, who had been reconciled with the Pope,
is urged to send a military contingent to Rome through
the territory of Matilda. [4] Even in Germany, where the
excommunication of the King had produced its effect,
Gregory found it necessary to justify the ban by an
encyclical drawn up to meet the objections of those who
held it to be unjust. The legality of the censure had
been questioned. [5] He recapitulates his relations with
Henry, going back to the reports of his evil life, which
reached him when Gregory was Archdeacon. After he
became Pope his warnings were still unheeded, and
through the influence of evil counsellors the King became guilty of simony. During the stress of the first
Saxon campaign Henry wrote a submissive letter, and
he was absolved by the legates in Germany. After his
victory over the Saxons he broke his promises, and
associated again with excommunicated persons. Repeated warnings were disregarded, together with the
threat of deposition, and he made shipwreck of the
Church of Christ by compelling the bishops in Germany
and Italy to withdraw their allegiance from the apostolic
see. For these reasons he had been excommunicated.
The letter closes with an appeal for assistance to persuade
the King to repent.

On July 25th the Pope sent out another encyclical to

---

[1] *Reg.* III. 11.
[2] *Reg.* III. 15 (Caspar).
[3] *Ep. Coll.* 13.
[4] *Ibid.*
[5] *Ep. Coll.* 14.

all the faithful, shorter but framed in similar terms, except that, as August 1st was drawing near, and no sign of submission had been received from Henry, the letter closes on a threatening note which does not appear in the German encyclical. It repeats the well-worn threat that the spiritual sword will not be withheld from blood.[1] A remarkable feature in both these letters is the absence of any allusion to the deposition. Although bishops and princes in Germany were withdrawing from the King's society in obedience to the anathema, the proclamation of the deposition had so far not been followed by a demand for the election of another King. But that Gregory was pursuing his policy of waiting upon events is made clear by his return to the question of deposition, when he saw that a movement in that direction had been started in Germany in the autumn.

These encyclicals constituted an able statement of Gregory's case, but as impartial estimates of the issues at stake they are ruined by their omissions. The omission of all reference to the deposition was, of course, the result of political vigilance, if not craft. The omission of all reference to the imperial coronation, the real centre of Henry's antagonism, was not intentional, because all along the Pope was blind to the urgency of this question, but that does not alter the fact that it rendered valueless the justification of the Pope among the supporters of the King in Germany, and still more so in the King's own eyes.

In the summer of 1076 Gregory was free to take a hand again in the affairs of distant churches. He wrote in a spirit of confidence to a Spanish bishop,[2] contending that by God's aid the Roman Church remained firm as from the beginning, and would continue to do so. Therefore, let her decrees be obeyed, especially must steps be taken to promote the use of the Roman order

[1] Reg. IV. 1.   [2] Reg. III. 18.

of the Mass in Spain and France. An oath of fealty was sworn by Swonimir, Duke of Croatia-Dalmatia to Gregory as suzerain, in the presence of one of the legates.[1] Cyriac, Archbishop of Carthage, was ordered to send a nominee to Rome to be consecrated as bishop, so that at least three bishops might be available for consecrations in Africa, and Gregory reveals an accurate knowledge of church history by reminding Cyriac that in ancient times the episcopate in the province of Africa was very numerous.[2] The clergy and people of the province of Mauritania were urged to obey the new Archbishop of Hippo, whom they had sent to Rome for consecration, in order that the Saracens might desire to imitate and not despise the Christian faith.[3] A charming letter was despatched to Anazir, Emir of Mauritania, thanking him for desiring the consecration of the Archbishop of Hippo, and for his generous manumission of Christian slaves. This kindness had been inspired in the Emir's heart by ' God the Creator of all, who illumines every one who comes into the world '. The Pope says that love is due to the Saracens more than to any other race because, although in a different way, they believe and confess the one God, and daily praise and reverence Him as the Creator of the universe and Governor of the world. This grace of God in the Emir many noble Romans recognized and made known. Among them Alberic and the Prefect Cencius were sending messages to him desiring to share in his friendship, and to be of service to him. May God lead him, after a long life in this world, into the bosom of the blessed and most holy patriarch Abraham.[4]

The despatch might be that of a British resident to an Indian prince. There is not a word that could offend the sensitiveness of oriental punctilio, no reference to

---

[1] Deusdedit *Collectio Canonum* III. 278, ed. Wolf von Glanvill (1905) pp. 383-5.
[2] *Reg.* III. 19.   [3] *Reg.* III. 20.   [4] *Reg.* III. 21.

the Man of Nazareth for the eyes of the son of the
Prophet. If but a fraction of this generous tact and
charming courtesy had been shown to Henry IV, the
young King's opposition would have dissolved before
the Pope's advances.

CHAPTER ELEVEN

CANOSSA (1077)

THE victorious pilgrimage of Henry IV to Canossa began in the autumn of 1076, not in January, 1077. August 1st came and went, and Henry made no sign of submission. By August 25th Gregory knew that the Saxons were in arms again, and he heard of the disaffection of the princes. The tone of his letters completely changed. 'The excommunicated priests and laity,' he says in reply to Herman of Metz,[1] 'are those who are known to communicate with the excommunicated King Henry—if it is right to call him King.' Against those who were challenging the legality of the King's excommunication by the Roman bishop he quotes patristic statements. A forced interpretation of one of the Forged Decretals is introduced to support an alleged opinion of S. Peter, when conducting an alleged consecration of Clement, to prove that Christian people ought to reject an unworthy candidate. Pope Zacharias deposed the Frankish King, Childeric, and absolved all the Franks from their oath of allegiance. Gregory the Great had said that all kings and dukes who opposed his teaching were excommunicated and deprived of their dignities. Ambrose excommunicated the Emperor Theodosius and forbade him to enter the church. No one is excepted from the binding and loosing power of Peter. 'If the holy apostolic see, with princely power divinely conferred on it, may judge concerning spiritual things, why not secular?'

[1] *Reg.* IV. 2.

'If religious men are judged when necessary, why not, much more, secular men, for their depraved conduct? Perhaps they think the royal dignity exceeds the episcopal. From the very fundamentals they can discover how much they differ. The one human pride procured, the other the goodness of God instituted. The one strives for vainglory, the other aspires always to eternal life.'

Then he refers them to the letter of Pope Anastasius to the Emperor of the same name, and to a letter attributed to Ambrose, in which the episcopal and regal dignities are compared with lead and gold. Constantine the Great took not the first seat, but the last, among the bishops. Gregory VII then gives licence to certain bishops to absolve the offenders in Germany from excommunication, but not the King until he has unreservedly repented, and—yet again—'Cursed is he who withholds the spiritual sword from blood.'

If the Pope had been supplied with some reliable knowledge of church history in Africa, his information concerning the church in Europe was widely inaccurate, if not wilfully garbled. Ambrose did not excommunicate Theodosius. The tale about Zacharias is a myth—the Pope merely agreed to Pippin's change of government. Gregory the Great may have vaguely said that a refractory ruler should lose his dignity, but in no case did he attempt to depose a king. The letter of Pope Anastasius had nothing to do with the question raised by Gregory VII, and as for the alleged statement of Ambrose, it merely compares the kingly and episcopal dignities, and on spiritual grounds gives precedence to the latter.

But Gregory was warming up again, not only for the fight with Henry, but for the renewal of the proclamation of the universal *imperium* of S. Peter. Four days later he issued his fourth encyclical of this year, addressed to all the faithful, warning them that the King was attempting to sever the Pope from them, through the instrumentality of ecclesiastical and secular persons. He repeats the prohibition against the absolution of the King before he had done satisfaction.[1] On September 3rd appeared the fifth encyclical, in which he significantly refers them to the first encyclical sent out in February from the Lenten Synod.[2] This contained the promulgation of deposition as well as the anathema, and he says that it gives sufficient reasons for both. It was not quoted by the Pope in his more conciliatory letter of the summer, because he then desired to keep the deposition in the background. He now adds that if the King repents, he is to be received, not only with justice ' which prevents him from reigning ', but with mercy, on account of the pious memory of his father and mother. But the oil of piety must be mingled with the wine of discipline, lest the honour of Holy Church and of the Roman Empire be ruined. On no account may he be absolved without the further consent of the apostolic see. If he remains obdurate, some one else must be found to govern the kingdom. If their election of a new King proves valid, it shall be confirmed by papal authority, and supported by a new coronation at the Pope's discretion. They must supply him with careful details of the person and behaviour of the elected King. With regard to their oath to the Empress Agnes, no question will arise if the King dies before her. But if, on account of her great love for him, she resists justice, or if she submits to it, then, when they have certainly ascertained that the deposition has taken place, the counsel of the Empress as well as that of the Pope must be taken, concerning the selection of another king. Either she will consent to their common counsel, or the authority of the apostolic chair will remove all bonds which appear to hinder justice.

While Gregory appeals to the deposition pronounced in Lent, he attempts to shift the responsibility for the

---

[1] *Ep. Coll.* 15.   [2] *Reg.* IV. 3.

initiatory steps taken to make it effective upon the German people. The Lenten Synod had stated the principle. It is for them to work it out. Thus, if during the summer he realized that the Papacy could not carry through the transaction by its own power, he does not in any sense suggest a deposition *de novo*. Yet he applies the title 'King' to Henry, but that his policy of the preceding months compelled him to do.

Gregory has been charged with fomenting the Saxon revolt. There is no evidence for this in the first Saxon war, and, although no communication between the Pope and the Saxon leaders can be traced in 1076, yet undoubtedly the papal encyclical produced effect in Saxony, as elsewhere, in quickening discontent which was already latent, even when it was not already active. When autumn came, Henry had lost almost entirely the fruits of the victory on the Unstrut. Otto of Nordheim fell away from him again, and together with Burchard, Bishop of Halberstadt, who was certainly receiving the Pope's circular appeals, organized a new Saxon uprising. The attempt of the King to coerce them by the aid of Brâtislav and the Bohemian army failed. In September the princes met at Ulm and arranged for the diet which met at Tribur on October 16th. Here representatives of the Saxons were present, and the papal legates. The Pope had been invited to come, or to make his wishes known through ambassadors. The Saxon delegation advocated the deposition of Henry and the appointment of a new king. To this proposal the princes were not yet inclined. Jealousy among themselves would complicate the election, and they were anxious to secure the full support of the Pope. Gregory was therefore invited to attend a council at Augsburg on February 2nd, 1077, where the affairs of the kingdom would be finally decided. Henry, who remained at Oppenheim near by, was notified that he must secure absolution from the Pope within a year and a day from the Lenten excom-

munication, or lose the kingdom.   In the meantime he
was to remain quietly at Speier without exercising royal
functions.

When the princes set up the Pope as the adjudicator
in German affairs they threw away the results of Tribur.
In spite of his asseverations, Gregory did not intend to
undertake the responsibility for the actual deposition of
the King.   He was no more certain of the continued
submission of the princes than of Henry.   When they
themselves had effected the deposition, and had become
responsible for the new candidate to the throne, he was
prepared to intervene, in order to grasp whatever fruits
were possible for the papal policy.   That had been made
clear in the encyclical letters.   The princes and bishops
must   elect   their   own   candidate.   Gregory   would
approve.   But by appealing to Gregory the princes
threw away the initiative, as later events showed, and
made it possible for Gregory to play off Henry against
their candidate, when he had been selected.

Still worse, the conclusions of Tribur opened the door
for the King's escape.   To the Pope had they appealed ;
so would he.   Henry's statesmanship was never more
effective than when he tore a leaf from the book of his
adversaries.   And again, the royal action could not be
criticized, since they themselves had urged upon the
King submission to the Pope.   In each case, both in
relation to their own policy and the future policy of the
King, they forgot Gregory and the possibility of papal
action   which   would   neutralize   their   plans   in   either
direction.

The policy of submission which Henry now instituted
was the first step towards his victory at Canossa,[1] and
the final cancellation of the findings of Tribur.   He sent
a promise of 'due obedience' to Gregory.   He would
at a convenient time expurgate the grave faults com-

[1] It is difficult to reconcile Fliche's conclusion that at Canossa Gregory
lost all his advantages, and yet did not meet with defeat (pp. 307 f.).

mitted against the apostolic see. Then he issued an
Edict to the subjects of the realm. By the advice of
some the Lord Pope Gregory had been stealthily deposed;
now by the advice of faithful men the King had changed
his former opinion and offered to the apostolic see and
the Lord Pope Gregory due obedience in the manner
of his ancestors, and would give full satisfaction for
presumptuous conduct towards him. Others must do
the same, and secure absolution, if they were under the
ban. Both the *Promissio* and the Edict are non-com-
mittal; they are concerned with the excommunication,
and the King makes no reference to his own deposition
already pronounced by the Pope.

Apart from the attempt made by the princes to foist
the responsibility for the election of a new king upon
him, events were shaping in a direction desired by
Gregory. By the action of both King and princes he
was apparently regarded as having the controlling hand
in German affairs. On October 31st he wrote confi-
dently to the leaders of the Patarines in Milan that the
pride of the Normans would soon be repressed, they
would not for long be able to prevail against the Papacy.
The conspiracy of King Henry and the simonists was
being openly contested by the German bishops and
princes. Numbers of faithful men who came to Rome
avowed that, unless the King did satisfaction, they would
publicly elect another king. As for the dispute at Milan,
the power of S. Peter, which had already expelled Guido
and Godfrey, would overcome Tedald.[1] Then arrived
Udo, Archbishop of Trier, the royal envoy, stating that
Henry was coming to Rome to make his submission.
At this juncture nothing would contravene Gregory's
wishes and policy more than the visit of the King. The
responsibility for humiliating Henry must be thrown
upon the princes, and his submission must take place
before their accredited representatives. So the Pope

[1] *Reg.* IV. 7.

promptly accepted the invitation of the princes to attend the Council of Augsburg, and gave notice in a sixth encyclical that he would be at Mantua by January 8th.[1] He professed to be ready to shed his blood, if necessary, on behalf of the church, and asked them to prepare for his reception, especially by promoting peace in Germany. The bearer of the letter would inform them of the refusal to treat with the King, which had been given to the royal envoys. In a seventh encyclical [2] he repeats his previous statement that he was coming to Germany, against the advice of opinion in Rome, but he was prepared to go, and he lays emphasis upon the necessity for their taking adequate steps to assist his journey. Before the end of the year he left Rome, and reached Florence by December 28th.

The attempt of Hugh, Abbot of Cluny, Henry's godfather, who had travelled to Italy to persuade Gregory to interview the King in Rome, had failed. The period of a year and a day from his excommunication at the Lenten Synod, within which Henry must secure absolution, was running out. The papal ban weighed far more heavily upon him than the papal deposition. Absolution would have a double political effect. It would enable him to open communication with a large number of those who were still loyal to him in mind, though severed from active relationship with him by the excommunication, and so enable him to reconcentrate armed forces. It would cancel the future political effectiveness of the princes' resolution at Tribur. So the King determined, at all risks, to extract absolution from the Pope. Before Christmas (1076) he left Speier, accompanied by his Queen, Bertha, and three-year-old son Conrad. The Rhine passes were guarded by Rudolf, Welf and Berthold, so he passed through Burgundy and secured the support of William of Burgundy at Besançon. He crossed the Rhône at Geneva and

---

[1] *Ep. Coll.* 17.   [2] *Ep. Coll.* 18.

passed through the territory of Adelheid of Susa, his wife's mother. Although allies of Popes, Adelheid and her son Amadeus joined the King's following. They entered Italy by the Mont Cenis Pass. The winter was one of extreme cold on both sides of the Alps. The Rhine and the Po were frozen over for many weeks. In the slippery descent, the men were frequently compelled to go upon hands and knees, the women being carried by oxen. Horses could not keep their feet. On his arrival in Italy, the royal supporters in Lombardy began to come in. Entirely opposed to any submission to Gregory, they expected Henry to lead them in an attack on the Pope, and at Pavia he might have opened hostilities. But Henry's statecraft, always more clear-sighted and more prompt than Gregory's, realized that the political necessity of the moment was the absolution.

Meanwhile Gregory, with difficulty, had crossed the snow-clad Apennines on the way to Mantua. At the Po he received a warning from Gregory of Vercelli, the German Chancellor, entrusted with the duty of accompanying the King to Germany, that Henry was in Italy. Gregory at once retired to Canossa, the mountain fastness of Matilda, encircled by a triple wall. Here he was entirely secure from any force that the King might bring against him. Here the excommunicated bishops and laymen from Germany began to arrive, and received absolution, on condition that they separated themselves from the King. From Reggio Henry opened negotiations with the Pope, through the agency of Adelheid, Amadeus and the Margrave Azzo, and through Hugh of Cluny, who was at Canossa. On January 25th, he arrived outside the castle gate, and then for three days, garbed as a penitent in woollen shirt with bare feet, he waited in the snow. The Pope was in a political quandary, largely created by himself. By failing to insulate the quarrel with Henry from external political influences, he had placed himself under an obligation to the princes.

Apart from the question of the deposition, absolution from excommunication would free the King from many difficulties, and if granted without the princes' consent might estrange them from the Pope. Yet by separating the questions of excommunication and deposition, it was possible for Gregory to find a way out which would at least save his dignity.

At this time the Pope was the victim of his own policy in more than one respect. He had been rightly charged with relying on the counsels of women. His negotiation with Henry was now biased by the weighty influence of Matilda, who added her intercession on the King's behalf to that of Adelheid and Hugh of Cluny. On January 28th Gregory gave way, and proposed to the King three conditions. He must agree to submit to the judgment of the princes on the charges brought against him by them, or defer to their counsel within a period to be fixed by the Pope. If any hindrance arose to postpone the adjudication, he must still be ready to submit to it when arranged. He must give a safeguard for the Pope's journey across the Alps, and for that of his envoys.[1] To these terms Henry agreed, and the doors of the castle were opened to him. Under stress of emotion, partly the result of reaction on a mind suddenly released from intense anxiety, the King broke down. But they were the tears of satisfaction with the success of his manœuvres, not the tears of penitence. In the castle chapel the King was received back into the communion with the church; he was offered the kiss of peace, joined in the Mass, and sat at the Pope's table at the meal which followed. Before he left Canossa he was warned to be true to his promises and to avoid the society of the Lombard bishops.

At Canossa there could be no discussion concerning the imperial coronation. Gregory's negotiations with the princes had made that impossible, and they soon

[1] *Reg.* IV. 12a.

13

realized that, if their attempt to dethrone Henry was compromised, it had not been shelved by the Pope. Moreover, the question of the Lombard crown was at this point rendered difficult by the same contingency. Yet it was not unnatural that Henry, regarding the Italian coronation as a possibility without prejudice to the German dispute, should have looked for a favourable reception of the idea of the Pope. But again the possibility of making a tangible concession to the King was allowed to pass, and hostile demonstrations on the part of the Lombard bishops against papal interests and personalities were readily seized by Gregory as an excuse for declining the King's request for the Lombard crown. No doubt the real reason was the ill-effect such a step would have had upon the Pope's relations with Germany.

While in Milan the papal policy scored a marked success, through the submission of the hostile clergy, who surrendered their allegiance to Tedald, and obtained absolution from the legates, Anselm of Lucca and Gerald of Ostia. In other north Italian towns the legates were attacked, and at Piacenza Gerald was imprisoned by Dionysius the Bishop. Doubtless as the outrage was committed by an ecclesiastic, Henry did not intervene, and left the matter to the ecclesiastical authorities. But his inaction gave Gregory a concrete excuse for refusing the Lombard crown. In the meantime the King had again assumed the royal executive, and was performing royal functions at Piacenza and Verona. Although failing to grasp the political significance of his action, and refusing to approve his negotiations with Gregory at Canossa, his friends among the Lombard bishops and magnates began to gather to his court, including the Empress Agnes. But so closely intertwined were political and ecclesiastical affairs in Lombardy, that while Henry remained in Italy he could not avoid giving offence to the Papacy. For example, Guibert of Ravenna came to the Court.

Henry's descent upon Italy was marked by another political consequence of supreme importance for the King. It made impossible the Pope's journey to Augsburg, with the further result that the council arranged for February 2nd did not take place. An explanatory letter was despatched by Gregory to the German princes immediately after the absolution of Henry at Canossa.[1] Gregory says that he had reached Lombardy about twenty days before the princes' escort was due to arrive. Then he received word that the escort could not get through, and in the meantime Henry had appeared in Italy, and immediately sent envoys to him, promising satisfaction and obedience, in return for absolution. Gregory says that he delayed concession for a long time, kept the King three days at the castle gate in a penitent condition, and finally at the intercession of others, who accused him of unnecessary severity, granted the King's request, on the conditions which were enclosed in the Pope's letter.[2] But he still desired to come to Germany to settle the affairs of the kingdom with them.

The Pope's letter encouraged the princes to resume their arrangements for the assembly of a council, especially when they heard that the question of Henry's rule was still open.[3] At Ulm in the middle of February they arranged for a diet at Forcheim to meet on March 13th, and, according to one report, invited Gregory to attend. Towards the end of February Gregory sent them another letter.[4] He desired to come to Germany, although his counsellors, with the exception of Matilda, were opposed to the project. Indeed, he would already have arrived if the princes had sent the promised escort. Henry's penitent attitude had extracted absolution from the Pope, but no other negotiations with him had been conducted, save what appeared to be in their interest. The Lombard bishops, enraged when they heard that a

[1] *Reg.* IV. 12.
[3] *Cf. Reg.* VII. 14*a* (p. 402).
[2] *Reg.* IV. 12*a*.
[4] *Ep. Coll.* 20.

definitive settlement had been reserved for the German princes, had broken out into renewed attacks. He was not happy about the King's behaviour, for the offenders were allowed into his presence. He desired to come to them with the King's consent if possible, if not, without it. But, if it should prove finally impossible, he would pray that they might be guided to a happy settlement of the affairs of the kingdom.

If at the beginning of the year Gregory's policy was to keep Henry out of Italy, it was now Henry's policy to keep Gregory out of Germany. The King received a message from Rudolf warning him not to return before sending either Gregory or the Empress to arrange the preliminaries of peace. On March 1st Rudolf's envoy informed the Pope of the intention of the princes to elect another king. Gregory then requested the King for an escort to Germany, but was answered with the excuse that the interval before the Council of Forcheim met was too short to enable the King to comply. From now onwards drift, delay and hesitation, which prevented a decisive policy in 1075, descended like a blanket on Gregory's actions. The legates, Bernard the Cardinal-Deacon, and Bernard the Abbot of S. Victor, were sent to Germany with instructions to delay the appointment of a new king until Gregory could take part; but, if the kingdom would thereby be endangered, they were to proceed with the election. With this doubtful guarantee of Gregory's approval, the princes at Forcheim nominated Rudolf of Rheinfelden, Duke of Swabia, who complied against his conscience, but not against his ambition. He was crowned at Mainz on March 26th, but two days later was compelled to flee, owing to an uprising of the people of Mainz. The townsmen of Worms made a similar demonstration on behalf of Henry. Meanwhile, Rudolf sent a message of submission to Gregory [1] inviting him to come to

[1] *Reg.* VII. 14*a*.

Germany for the final settlement, and promising an escort.[1]

At Pavia, where Henry was still cherishing the idea of receiving the Italian crown, news reached him that Rudolf had been offered the German crown. He at once demanded Rudolf's excommunication by Gregory, who refused to comply until he had formally inquired into the merits of the case, and warned Henry that nothing could be done until his legate, Gerald of Ostia, was released from imprisonment. So great matters were intermingled with small, and the latter were allowed, as formerly, to confuse the Pope's judgment at a critical juncture. Henry determined to return to Germany. Shortly before he left Italy, he lost the support of Gregory of Vercelli, who was thrown from his horse and died soon afterwards. Before this Cencius had died, but the King had wisely declined his offer of support. Henry crossed the Alps by way of Fruili and entered Carinthia. In Bavaria he was well received by the people of Augsburg, and at Regensburg secured the adherence of the lesser Bavarian and Bohemian nobles, and raised a military force. The war on Rudolf began. The King had a large following in Bavaria, Swabia and Burgundy. Swabia was overrun, and at Ulm the anti-King was deposed.

Hearing of the hostile movements in Germany, Gregory made an impulsive attempt to check hostilities. On May 31st he ordered the legates to warn both ' Kings ', Henry and Rudolf, to provide the escort for his passage over the Alps, that he might hold a council in order to decide the dispute between them. If either of them opposed the Pope's will, the legates, making use of papal authority, were to resist him ' even to

---

[1] Martens I. 142 describes the decision of Forcheim as a blow at Gregory. On the contrary it agreed with the Pope's disinclination to select a new candidate. Gregory desired to approve him, and then decide between the two claimants to the throne.

death ', depriving him of the right of governing the
kingdom, and excommunicating him. Whoever obeyed
must be confirmed in the royal dignity, by the authority
of the Papacy, at a properly convened council. All
possible support should be offered to him, and all clergy
and laity were ordered to obey him.[1]

Similar directions were given to the German people
in an encyclical of the same date,[2] in which the Pope
emphasizes in stronger terms the threat to the Christian
religion and to the ' Roman Empire ' created by the
warring candidates. Clearly the Pope was becoming
unnerved by the course of events. His stability was
shaken. Still clutching at the possibility of adjudicating
in Germany, he yet hands over his authority to the
legates as at the Diet of Forcheim. Still worse, he was
unable to make up his own mind between the claims
of the two ' Kings '. He was groping after events to
supply a decision. When the position became clearer
he reproved the legates for acting on his own hasty
instructions. By June 9th, Gregory's vacillation had
taken another turn. In a letter to the Hungarian Archbishop of Gran, he complains that the disturbance of
the times made impossible his long expected visit to
Germany.[3]

At Nuremberg, towards the middle of June, Henry's
supporters agreed to attack Rudolf in Saxony, and the
King, who had little to gain by Gregory's appearance
in Germany, declined to provide an escort for the Pope.
Rudolf, cut off from the Alpine passes, was unable to
do so. By August the two armies were encamped
against each other on the Neckar, and the princes on
either side made an abortive arrangement to meet on
the Rhine on November 1st, without Henry and Rudolf,
in the presence of the legates, to decide between the
two Kings. The position of the legates had been
neutralized. The Abbot of S. Victor was imprisoned

[1] *Reg.* IV. 23.   [2] *Reg.* IV. 24.   [3] *Reg.* IV. 25.

by Udalrich of Lensburg, one of Henry's supporters, and the Cardinal-Deacon had gone over to the side of Rudolf.

By the middle of September Gregory was back in Rome, and news from the south forced him to attempt a more active intervention in Germany. Robert Guiscard early in the year had captured Salerno, and, when Richard of Capua joined Guiscard in an attack on Naples, Gisulf of Salerno fled to Rome. On September 30th the Pope despatched a remarkable letter to Udo, Archbishop of Trier,[1] one of Henry's supporters, in which Rudolf is not mentioned, but Henry is referred to in a tone of conciliation. Gregory forwards a copy of the King's oath at Canossa, in order to emphasize his own clemency on that occasion, and while complaint is made that the legates Gerald of Ostia and Bernard of S. Victor were imprisoned in Lombardy and Germany, and that Henry had taken no steps to secure their release, the Pope protests that he has done nothing hostile to the 'King' by way of retaliation, and has no intention of doing anything unjust. He closes the letter with a vague admonition to the Archbishop and his suffragans to take steps for the freedom of the church and the common good, but not a word is said about his own visit to Germany.

Through the intervention of Hugh of Cluny, Henry, with bad grace, secured the release of Abbot Bernard. Meanwhile the other legate, Bernard the Cardinal-Deacon, on November 11th, had excommunicated Henry with the consent of Siegfried, and seven other bishops, at Rudolf's council at Goslar.[2] This sentence was not confirmed by Abbot Bernard, who towards the end of the year summoned Udo and other German bishops to

[1] *Reg.* V. 7.

[2] Martens I. 168 denies that Henry was excommunicated at Goslar, on the ground that Gregory does not allude to it. But the legate's action had compromised the discussion of the case at the forthcoming diet, and on grounds of policy Gregory was silent.

meet on January 14th (1078) at Hirschau, in order to condemn Henry, and also Rudolf, if he ever made peace with him. Meanwhile, the fighting in Germany continued, in Swabia and Bavaria. At the close of the year Rudolf went on building up his power in Saxony.

Before the end of the year of Canossa the grandiose scheme, whereby the Pope was to sit in judgment upon the heir of the Cæsars at the head of a German diet, had come to nothing. On both sides of the Alps after the autumn of 1077 little more was heard of a papal visit to Germany. The idea was conceived a year before, when Henry was a fugitive from his kingdom, because he was an outcast from the church. But after he had regained the sceptre by his victory at Canossa, there was never any possibility that a German escort would come, short of the total rout of Henry's forces by Rudolf. But with more than one-half of South Germany behind him, together with the Rhine towns, this was not probable, and Henry's power set up a barrier against Rudolf in the north, and cut him off from Gregory. With the Normans again in an aggressive mood in the south of Italy, and the Lombards still hostile in the north, it was impossible for Gregory to obtain an escort from Matilda, and the project of Tuscan aid in this form never materialized. Even his delegated authority in Germany had broken in two, and the legates were pursuing, at the same time, contrary policies, and always went further than the Pope intended, though not further than his written instructions warranted. So the princes, save those of Saxony, paid less and less attention to Gregory and his legates, and gave themselves intermittently to war and council, dividing themselves between Henry and Rudolf as self-interest decided.

In the summer, with the prospect of dictating terms to two warring kings before him, the Pope not unnaturally sought elsewhere to confirm the papal hegemony in one direction and to extend it in another. In

the first year of his pontificate he had lodged a claim
to suzerainty over Spain on the ground of Constantine's
Donation, but no despatch sent to that country set forth
the claim so definitely as the letter to the Spanish princes
of June 28th, 1077.[1]   'We wish you to know . . . that
by an ancient constitution the kingdom of Spain was
delivered to S. Peter and the holy Roman Church for
law and ownership' (*in jus et proprietatem*).   The rights
of the Papacy had been lost sight of partly through the
Saracen invasion, partly through the negligence of the
Popes.   Now that God was giving them the victory,
he urged them to revive and restore those rights.   On
the same date an encyclical letter was sent to Narbonne,
Gaul, Gascony and Spain, claiming the right, by primitive custom, to send legates into every Christian land,
who should act in the place of the 'governor and ruler
of the Roman Church' by virtue of the legatine commission.[2]

In 1074 Gregory had attempted to establish a footing
for the oversight of the island of Sardinia, but seems to
have been checked by the combined policy of the Pisans
and Godfrey the Younger.   On September 16th, 1077,[3]
after a preliminary despatch on September 1st,[4] he
instituted a more direct and dictatorial policy towards
the Corsicans.   'Ye know, brothers, that the island which
you inhabit belongs by right of law and ownership to
no mortal, to no power, save the holy Roman Church.'
Those who had hitherto held it had been guilty of
sacrilege.   He rejoices at the report that they wish to
return to allegiance to the Papacy.   If they maintain
their resolution 'we have through the mercy of God in
Tuscany large contingents of the counts and nobles prepared, if necessary, to come to your aid and defence '.   He
sends to them Landulf, the Bishop-elect of Pisa, 'to
whom I commit my power among you in spiritual
matters, that he may receive the land on behalf of S.

[1] *Reg.* IV. 28.   [2] *Ep. Coll.* 21.   [3] *Reg.* V. 4.   [4] *Reg.* V. 2.

Peter and myself, and that he may . . . devote himself
to all causes whatsoever pertaining to S. Peter, and to
me through him.'

If the legate's powers are confined to ecclesiastical
affairs, secular rulers hold their authority under the
suzerainty of the Papacy. On this theory the margin
between spiritual and secular control becomes small, and
the door is always open to ecclesiastical interference in
the secular sphere. Corsica was claimed for the papal
hegemony in exactly the same terms as Spain. Meanwhile, the new rulers in Hungary and Denmark—
Ladislas the brother of Géza and Harald (Acon) the son
of Svein—were urged to maintain the reverence and
obedience shown by their predecessors to the Papacy.[1]

Not a year had passed since Gregory became Pope
without the extension of this claim to some new area,
and we shall see it lodged again against another realm
newly conquered by the Pope's allies.[2] It is necessary
to emphasize this department of Gregory's policy, because it has often been alleged that his suzerain claims
did not develop until after the quarrel with Henry IV
broke out—a conclusion which has been confirmed by
the habit of surveying his relations with other princes
and other lands, when the story of that dispute has been
completed.

[1] *Reg.* IV. 25, V. 10.
[2] Again Fliche's conclusion is uncertain. He admits that Gregory
claimed suzerainty over Corsica, Sardinia, Spain, Hungary, Croatia-
Dalmatia and Kiev, but not over Bohemia, Denmark or England
(pp. 326 ff.). But if Gregory was dilatory in diplomacy he was emphatic
in the application of principles, and there can be little doubt that his
attitude to all these kingdoms was the same. Voosen 194 f. denies
that Gregory claimed suzerain rights over other countries, save where the
affairs of the church were concerned (*cf.* p. 312). O. Gierke *Political
Theory of the Middle Ages* is a better guide ; *cf.* pp. 11 ff. and 105 ff.

CHAPTER TWELVE

TRIFLING IN THE SYNODS (1078–1079)

IN December, 1077, died Gerald of Ostia, lately released from captivity, and the Empress Agnes. These losses were partly counterbalanced by the removal of Sigehard, Patriarch of Aquileia, one of Henry's counsellors, who had died in August. But the relative positions of Pope and King had been entirely changed by the events of 1077. However wrongly posterity may have interpreted Canossa, neither Gregory nor Henry was under any illusion as to its significance as a royal victory. The King's position was restored, and he was again at the head of a fighting force. Gregory had lost the initiative in Germany and was once more on the defensive. There he remained during the rest of the conflict. Until his position had been strengthened in Germany, Henry allowed the question of the imperial coronation to fall into abeyance. For eighteen months he negotiated with Rome, trying to secure not arbitration by Gregory, but the open condemnation of his adversary. The policy of Rudolf was similar. Neither of the principals in the contest for the throne desired the practical settlement of the dispute by Gregory or his legates. Each desired a pronouncement against the other. After the failure of the Pope to appear in Germany in 1077, the South German princes lost confidence in Gregory. The Saxons, on the contrary, continued with increasing querulousness to appeal to him for direct intervention. During 1078, and in the spring of 1079, the negotiations assumed a new character. The breakdown of the legatine commissions in Germany

during 1077 was followed by a transference of the
negotiations to Rome, and in these synods at Rome the
dispute was carried on by the envoys of Henry and
Rudolf, while the Pope hedged, and trifled away the
King's forbearance.   Gregory realized, in spite of his
repeated protests against the iniquity of war, that only
an appeal to the sword could decide the issue, and he
continued his old policy of waiting on events.   He overlooked the fact that if Henry took the field for a decisive
battle, without the papal condemnation of Rudolf, he
would turn with exasperation against the Pope, and the
sword which had smitten the King's enemy in Germany
would be turned next against Gregory.

The year 1078 opened for Gregory with an attempt
to insinuate the papal hegemony over Serbia, by the
well-worn device of sending a papal banner—in addition
to a pallium—in answer to a request for assistance from
King Michael, together with the usual claim for reverence to be shown to the apostolic see.[1]   Meanwhile the
influence of the Curia in Italy had declined.   No Synod
had been held in 1077, and the attitude of the Normans
had again become worse than threatening.   Towards
the end of the previous year Richard and Robert had
attacked Naples, and on December 19th Robert began
the siege of Benevento, within papal territory.

The Lent Synod of 1078 met on February 27th.
Without specifying their leaders by name a general
excommunication was issued against the Normans, who
were at one and the same time preparing to invade
Fermo and Spoleto, besieging Benevento, threatening
to invade Campania, Sabina and the maritime province,
with the final object of marching on Rome.   Bishops
or clergy who admitted the Normans to divine service
were threatened with deposition—a warning directed
against Desiderius of Monte Cassino, whose dealings
with the already excommunicated Norman chiefs had

[1] *Reg.* V. 12.

given offence in Rome. Against the refractory bishops in Milan and Lombardy a series of depositions and excommunications was issued. Tedald and Guibert of Ravenna were deposed and placed under the ban. Arnulf of Cremona and Roland of Trevisa, and the twice perjured traitor, Cardinal Hugh the White, were condemned in similar terms, together with some other ecclesiastical and lay-magnates. Bishops who were absent from the Synod without leave were placed under the ban. The effects of excommunication were tightened in one direction and relaxed in another. The ordinations of clergy performed by excommunicated bishops were declared to be ' ineffective' (*irritae*) [1]—the view of Humbert, not the milder one of Damiani. Oaths made to people under the ban were pronounced void. On the other hand, since the rule cutting off an excommunicate from the society of other people often inflicted hardship upon humble folk, and upon those placed in special circumstances, women, children, servants, slaves and countrymen, all belonging to the lower ranks, as well as those who unknowingly communicated with people under the ban, were declared to be exempt from the regulation which prohibited them from contact with those under the ban. Envoys, pilgrims and travellers were declared free to buy the necessities of life in countries lying under an interdict. Acts of humanity to an excommunicated person were also permitted. Shipwrecked persons were to be protected against robbery, under pain of excommunication. [2] Berthold adds that decrees were passed against lay investitures, simony and clerical marriage.

A resolution on the German dispute was forced upon the Synod by the action of Henry and Rudolf, who sent envoys, without the invitation of the Curia. Henry was represented by Benno, Bishop of Osnabruck, and by

[1] *Cf.* Mirbt p. 441 on the significance of this expression.
[2] *Reg.* V. 14a.

Theodoric, Bishop of Verdun; Rudolf's difficulties prevented him from sending representatives of the same rank, and their names are not reported. The royal envoys professed obedience and submission to the Pope and asked for justice, at which the embassy of Rudolf ironically applauded.[1] They alleged that Rudolf had tried to eject the King from his throne, and, although Henry could have overpowered him, he preferred to submit the dispute to Gregory. So Henry's supporters in the Synod called for Rudolf's excommunication. Gregory then began the policy of trifling which characterized his pronouncements in the synods and despatches of the next twelve months. The Pope said he could not pronounce immediately upon the question, especially without details of the ban passed on Henry in November at Goslar. He must have guarantees of obedience from each side, together with securities for embassies and conferences. In the meantime, he postponed his answer until the close of the Synod, and in the interval called upon all to pray for a right judgment. On the Saturday he declared his decision. Either he or his legates would come to Germany to hold a conference in the absence of both kings, in order to discover the way to a solution, and a threat of anathema was directed against all who should hinder the fulfilment of this resolution.[2] Then, with the showmanship which he loved, the Pope and his following threw themselves on the ground, and allowed the lighted tapers in their hands to be extinguished.[3] *Tenebrae* of this kind might impose upon a Roman synod, but histrionic symbolism and vague procrastination had no effect on any question across the Alps, and the dispute was immediately on fire again. Gregory had simply reverted to the methods adopted after Henry's return to Germany.

The arrangements for the council in Germany were left in Henry's hands, and he was instructed to cease

[1] *Reg.* VII. 14*a* (p. 403).   [2] *Reg.* V. 14*a*.   [3] Berthold.

hostilities in the meantime. To Rudolf Gregory sent the apostolic blessing, an act which was interpreted by Rudolf's followers as a renewed condemnation of Henry. A circular letter to the German nation gave notice of the proposed council, and issued a warning against all who might hinder its assembly. The council would be convened by the bearer of the letter, in collaboration with Udo of Trier, 'who favours Henry', and by another convener to represent Rudolf, and it would be presided over by legates to be chosen in Rome for the purpose.[1]

On the same day (March 9th) Gregory ruined all prospect of a German council by recommencing his customary haggling for a safe-conduct. Udo of Trier and a delegate from Rudolf were summoned to Rome to discuss the time and place of the conference, and to give the Pope a clear idea of the prospect of peace, and of the security of the legates who were to return with Udo. If he could not obtain a representative from Rudolf, the Archbishop of Trier must come alone, and, if the legates already in Germany wished to accompany him, he must procure a safe-conduct for them from the King.[2]

In addition to the disappointment created by the procrastinating resolution of the Lent Synod, the report now went round Germany that Gregory was negotiating with Henry's supporter, Udo. Indeed a growing preference for Henry is indicated in this letter. He is 'the King'. In Saxony the disappointment became vocal, and was made known in a letter sent by the Saxon clergy and people to Gregory. They charge him with delay in coming to their assistance. By his own action Gregory had deprived Henry of the throne, and had prohibited them from serving him, at the same time excommunicating him. They had obeyed the Pope's injunctions, and yet, without consulting them, Gregory

[1] *Reg.* V. 15.   [2] *Reg.* V. 16.

had absolved Henry, who was now free to molest them. Even so, they had understood that the absolution did not affect Henry's deposition, but now this was altered, for the Pope's communications refer to ' two Kings ', and he who by a papal judgment had been deposed was now restored by the papal authority. Henry's followers, disobedient to the commands of the synods, were now received at Rome, and when they returned to Germany were set up in a position of honour. The Saxons expostulate on the devastation and ruin being caused by continued delays.[1]

Very little can be found for criticism in this respectful but damaging communication. That Gregory realized he had lost influence in Germany is shown in the weary letter sent to Hugh of Cluny on May 9th,[2] but the wrong-headed Pontiff never seemed to possess a glimmering of an idea that his troubles were created originally by his own overbearing policy, and latterly by trifling and procrastination, if not by double-faced negotiations.

When Henry's envoys returned to him at Köln just before Easter, the King realized that the Goslar ban of the preceding November had been disregarded at Rome. Both he and Rudolf proceeded by steps which were deferential to the Papacy. At Mainz Rudolf declined to invest Wigolt, his own candidate for the vacant see of Augsburg, with the ring and staff, and left that duty to Siegfried. Henry supported the efforts of Udo, who was not able to obey the Pope's citation to Rome, to assemble the proposed council at Fritzlar. But Henry's chief supporters stayed away, and further delay occurred through the action of the Saxon delegation, which obtained the postponement of a decision to a future council, to be attended by the papal legates. This was entirely in accordance with Gregory's plan, but then

---

[1] Bruno c. 108. Martens without sufficient grounds rejects the Saxon letters as forgeries.

[2] *Reg.* V. 21.

Henry showed his hand, by declining to give his consent. The Saxons concluded that *ipso facto* he again fell under the papal ban, and according to the terms of Gregory's encyclical of March 9th they had a semblance of justification. But Gregory did not take this view. As no legates appeared at Fritzlar, he could afford to brush its conclusions aside, and regard the proposed council as still to be convened. On July 1st he issued another encyclical to Germany, drawing attention to the obstruction of the council which was to decide whether Henry or Rudolf should rule, and reminding the faithful that such action came under the anathema of the Lenten Synod.[1]

Although the Saxons are not mentioned by name, they alone as a body had made known their objections to the Pope's plans, but, before their reply reached Gregory, the warring Kings engaged in heavy fighting. Since the revolt of the princes in 1075 no field action had taken place between Henry and the rebel forces. The armies had marched and counter-marched, burned and devastated, faced each other and retreated. The result of this manœuvring was that Henry had been turned out of Saxony and Rudolf out of Swabia, and each occupied the base of the other. On August 7th (1078) the two armies met in a sanguinary battle at Melrichstadt, fought in two sections. The division under Rudolf was defeated, and broke in rout before Count Eberhard of Nellenberg. But Otto of Nordheim and Frederick of Saxony dealt with Henry's division in a similar way. Rudolf retired to Saxony and Henry to Bavaria, each side claiming victory, but as Henry was first in the field again, and ravaged Swabia in November, his freedom of action was less hindered by the battle than Rudolf's.

The significance of the battle for Gregory's policy was nugatory, and he proceeded with his plans for

[1] *Reg.* VI. 1.

14

another synod in Rome in the autumn. The Norman menace was for the time being withdrawn. Jordan of Capua and Roger of Sicily had been brought to submission by the ban issued in Lent. In April Richard, Jordan's father, died. Jordan gave up the siege of Capua, and his reconciliation with Gregory forced Robert to raise the siege of Benevento. At Capua in July, and at Monte Cassino in August, the Pope was near the scene of these movements, but by the beginning of October he had passed to the north of Rome into Tuscany. In the reports of Melrichstadt received from both sides, the Pope was able to judge that the battle was indecisive. In September he received another reminder of his waning influence in Germany, in the form of a reply from the Saxons to his encyclical of July 1st. They alleged that Gregory's proposal for a council in Germany was impracticable, because all the bishops obedient to him had been expelled. Besides, why discuss who should be king when he had already deposed Henry, who had also been excommunicated by his legate, at the same time that the election of Rudolf was confirmed? If Henry's rule was still valid, what became of the oaths which his subjects had broken at Gregory's order, and what became of the allegiance of Rudolf's followers? What a state of affairs! Was there ever such confusion in the church? [1]

This unanswerable northern logic received no reply from Gregory, but its effect can be detected in two letters belonging to this period. Henry, Bishop of Liège, is cautioned against those guilty of ' contempt of the synod '—Lent, 1078—which had directed a council to be held in Germany to decide whether Henry or Rudolf should reign. [2] In a citation to the Bishops of Gaul to attend the forthcoming synod in November, Henry is described as ' so-called King '. [3] Had the Saxon shaft gone home? In this letter the French bishops were

[1] Bruno c. 114. [2] *Reg.* VI. 4. [3] *Ep. Coll.* 23.

rebuked for their tardy support of the Papacy in its contest with the *regnum*. Was Gregory beginning to realize that the dispute was insoluble without the intervention of public opinion in the rest of Europe ? After the indecisive action at Melrichstadt both sides in Germany were again clamouring for the condemnation of their adversaries. Moreover, the question of investiture, which became a matter of burning controversy upon Gregory's death, was emerging into prominence and called for attention, while the Saxons gave him no rest. In October another closely reasoned complaint reached the Curia.[1] Why was justice denied to them when it was not denied to their enemies ? Why did he not proceed against those disobedient to his directions ? How could that be lawful for them, which was not lawful for those who obeyed him ? Their enemies supported the King whom Gregory had deposed, and whom the legate had excommunicated. So, unrestrained by papal authority, they relaxed the reins for the Saxons' destruction. Why did the Pope dissimulate this disobedience, while for the slightest offence ' you proceed against us poor miserable sheep ' ?

When the Synod assembled on November 19th, the envoys of Henry and Rudolf attended, each protesting that the settlement of the affair in Germany, arranged at the last synod, would not be hindered by his principal, and each demanding a judgment against the other. Henry claimed the excommunication of Rudolf, and the anti-King asked for the confirmation of the Goslar ban against Henry. Still waiting on events, Gregory postponed the decision of Henry's case to the Lenten Synod of the next year.[2] Rudolf's claim was gracefully deferred, but Gregory warned his envoys that, unless the archbishop and bishops who had crowned him could justify their action, they would be deposed, and Rudolf would lose the kingdom.[3] The threat of excommunication

[1] Bruno c. 115.   [2] Berthold.   [3] *Reg.* VIII. 51.

against those who had hindered the assembly of a council in Germany was renewed.

When Gregory postponed the decision of Henry's case to the next synod, he was playing for time, since a circular letter went out to Germany and Saxony, giving notice of a forthcoming visit of the legates to hold a council for the arrangement of peace, and threatening the ban against those who opposed them.[1] So the November Synod did no more than repeat the dilatory resolutions of the Lenten Synod of that year.

From the standpoint of the reform programme and the general administration of church affairs, the decrees of November, 1078, were far more effective. The clergy were forbidden to receive investiture to churches, abbeys and bishoprics from the hands of the emperor or king or from any lay person, but no penalty was imposed on the laity who invested. Usurpation of the territories of the Roman Church was declared to be sacrilege. Definitive pronouncements were made against simony, the secularization of church lands—especially in Germany and South Italy—against those withholding payment of tithes, and against unjust penances, breach of the Sabbath, and of the celibacy laws. Ornaments were not to be removed from the churches save under extreme necessity. Schools were to be maintained at all cathedral centres, and the laity were to make an offering at Mass. Some dignitaries in high station were excommunicated, among them Nicephorus III (Botaniates) who, in the spring of the year, had ousted the Eastern Emperor Michael VII from the throne. Guibert, Archbishop of Ravenna, was deposed without hope of restoration, and a letter to the people of Ravenna notified them of the deposition.[2]

After an interval of nineteen years Gregory was again involved in the eucharistic controversy, which was still

[1] *Ep. Coll.* 25.　　　　　[2] *Reg.* VI. 10.

raging in the French Church. As this case was regarded at Rome as a merely local dispute, it was dealt with separately at a special council convened on November 1st before the Synod. In 1077 Gregory had warned Berengar to desist from teaching until his views could be examined before the Pope, but letters from Berengar and Hugh of Cluny kept the matter before the Pope's attention, and in 1078 Berengar was summoned to Rome. At the Council of November 1st a statement on eucharistic doctrine, similar to that presented to Berengar at Tours (1054), was drawn up and recited by the Archdeacon. Gregory, whose views on the Eucharist were outlined to Matilda in 1074,[1] pronounced him free from heresy, and contended that his views coincided with those of Damiani. Berengar's enemies in the Council urged that the case should be postponed to the Lenten Synod of 1079, and, after ordering the case to be settled next day through the ordeal by fire and then countermanding the order, the Pope agreed.[2]

On December 15th, the Pope sent a long despatch to Olaf III of Norway, epitomizing the creed and promising to send instructions on the Christian faith. He invited him to allow young men to come to Rome to be educated in theology—a request which he had made to Harald of Denmark. Olaf was warned to give no assistance to the brothers of Harald, who were attempting to persuade him to divide the kingdom with them.[3] Liemar, Adalbert's successor at Hamburg, was attempting to revive his predecessor's claims over the Scandinavian churches, and Gregory's letter seems to have been issued to check this development. To Welf, Duke of Bavaria, and to the Bavarian bishops, he wrote emphasizing the authority of the Papacy, directing them to carry out the resolutions of the Lenten and November Synods concerning the arbitration in Germany.[4] As the Bavarian Duke and

[1] Reg. I. 47.   [2] Cf. my Berengar p. 176 ff.
[3] Reg. VI. 13.   [4] Reg. VI. 14.

bishops were supporters of Rudolf, the papal letter can have brought them little satisfaction.

The Lent Synod of 1079 assembled on February 11th. The German question was deferred until the case of Berengar was settled. Throughout his pontificate Gregory's devotion to the Virgin Mary was frequently made known,[1] and before the Synod opened he ordered intercession to be made to her concerning Berengar's teaching, and believed that he had received an answer favourable to him. Three cardinals were sent into retreat for three days, and a fast was imposed on the clergy. By these measures the Pope hoped to prepare for the acquittal of Berengar at the Synod. But Berengar's adversaries insisted on a full discussion, and he was compelled to swear to a new formula.[2] The Synod objected that he was interpreting the word *substantialiter* in his own sense, and Berengar impulsively appealed to Gregory's former interview with him, at which he alleged the Pope had agreed with his views. Gregory, whose mind was anxiously preoccupied with the German dispute, wrathfully rebuked him and compelled him to submit. It appears that, as at the Lenten Synod of 1076, only when flouted face to face was he able to issue a definite decision. Berengar was threatened with imprisonment if his submission was not sincere, but he received absolution and was sent back to Tours, after some delay, under the Pope's safe-conduct,[3] and Gregory made Radulf, Archbishop of Tours, responsible for his security against the attacks of Fulk, Count of Anjou.[4] By pronouncing judgment upon Berengar, Gregory did as great a disservice to the church and to the liberty of European thought, as by attempting to deprive Henry and the laity of a definitive voice in ecclesiastical appointments. He missed the opportunity of instituting a

---

[1] *Cf. Reg.* I. 15, I. 47, III. 10*a*, IV. 2, VII. 14*a*, VIII. 8.
[2] *Reg.* VI. 17*a*.   [3] *Ep. Coll.* 24.
[4] *Ep. Coll.* 36 ; *cf. Berengar* pp. 190 ff.

reform of dogma which might have been combined with the practical reform of clerical life. The two were closely related. Many of the practical abuses of the later Middle Ages issued from the hardening of church doctrine. A vigorous support of Berengar's programme might have instituted a movement in ecclesiastical thought which would have rendered the Reformation unnecessary.

No decrees on church reform have been handed down from this Synod, but in June of this year an important modification of the law of simony was announced by Gregory. Clergy, who without knowledge and without payment had received ordination from simonist bishops before the pontificate of Nicholas II, might be confirmed in their office.[1]

At the Lent Synod of 1079 the case of Rudolf was for the first time adequately presented, and Henry's envoys were outmatched. Henry now seems to have been under the same disadvantage as Rudolf at the time of the two earlier synods. The royal envoys said that Henry would send a more weighty embassy in the near future. They referred to the legal difficulty of judging the King in his absence, especially as the charges brought against him were mendacious, and they appealed to the Synod to advise the Pope in this sense. For the rest, the King had hitherto been unwillingly prevented from sending a safe-conduct for the legates to go to Germany. But this was mere finesse—their real object was to secure the postponement of a judgment against Henry.

A greater impression was made by the Cardinal-Deacon Bernard, and Bishops Altman of Passau and Herman of Metz, representing Rudolf and the Saxons. They described the sufferings of the people in Germany, caused by Henry's operations, and presented a letter from the Saxons. The Saxons had heard that in a recent Roman Synod the doubt had been expressed whether

[1] *Reg.* VI. 39.

Henry lay under excommunication. Indeed, he had been many times placed under the ban. Gregory had himself excommunicated him and then conditionally absolved him. Henry had broken his promise and ill-treated the legates. For this reason Bernard had excommunicated him again, deposed him, and by apostolic authority confirmed another in his place. Henry then attacked the bishops, removed the goods of the churches and ravaged the kingdom, especially Swabia. Therefore Siegfried of Mainz and seven bishops excommunicated him, and the Bishop of Wurzburg and the legate Bernard had anathematized all concerned with him. If the Pope did not add another sentence, at least he should not recognize those who were under the ban until they had done satisfaction.[1]

Yet no decision was issued by Gregory at the Synod. The envoys of Henry were compelled to take an oath that the King would send an embassy by May 2nd to conduct the legates to Germany, and that the King would obey their directions. The messengers of Rudolf swore on his behalf that he would attend or send representatives to the council to be held in Germany, when judgment prepared by the holy Roman Church should be given on the dispute. He would then observe the terms of peace arranged.[2]

There can be little doubt that Gregory once again had no intention of arriving at a definitive conclusion at the Synod, and that he opened the case with the purpose of transferring for the third time the final judgment to a council to be held by the legates in Germany. Yet he was clearly influenced by Rudolf's advocates. Rudolf is referred to in their oath as ' King ', and a tendency to adopt a more favourable policy towards Henry, which had been growing throughout the preceding months, and of which the Saxons repeatedly complained, was checked. At the close of the Synod,

[1] Bruno c. 112.　　　　[2] Reg. VI. 17a.

Peter, the Cardinal-Bishop of Albano, and Udalric, Bishop of Padua, were sent to Henry announcing its results, and urging him to uphold them. In the meantime he must maintain peace towards his enemies and restore the deprived bishops to their sees. He must send seven envoys to Rome to assure the Pope that he would give a safe-conduct to the legates for the German council. The despatch of this embassy constituted a breach of the terms agreed to by Henry's envoys at the Synod. It left Rome before the King was given an opportunity to send the messengers promised in the oath of his envoys. The Pope's altered tone is also indicated in the letter sent to Rudolf and the Saxons at the same period. He addressed Rudolf as ' King ' and this title is omitted in the case of Henry. Gregory says that he had not been influenced by lying statements ; let them strive ' more and more ' to defend themselves and to bring an end to their labour. The findings of the Synod might be ascertained in an accompanying letter, and from the statement of the bearers, Herman of Metz and Altman of Passau.[1]

Henry, Patriarch of Aquileia, was selected to preside at the forthcoming council in January, and his oath of allegiance to Gregory was recorded among the decrees of the Synod. He swore especially to defend the regalian rights of the Papacy.[2] By this submission the new Patriarch repaired the defects in the investiture already received from Henry, which the Curia regarded as invalid. This and the despatch of Udalric of Padua, a Gregorian but also a supporter of Henry, to Germany are the only indications at the time of special consideration for Henry's case. The excommunication of Tedald and the Lombard Bishop, Richard of Tarvisa, was confirmed, and the intruded bishops of Fermo and Camerino among others were condemned.

During February, Henry made an unsuccessful attempt

[1] *Ep. Coll.* 27 ; Bruno c. 120. [2] *Reg.* VI. 17*a*.

to arrange a peace with the Saxons, without reference to the Pope, but they declined to act without the Curia. Then the King despatched Benno of Osnabruck to Rome, in order to counteract the effects of the reports which had been lodged against him at the Lent Synod. The legates met Henry at Regensburg on May 12th. A second conference at Fritzlar arranged by them again failed, partly through Henry's absence, and partly through the Bohemian attack on Saxony, stirred up by the King. Yet the legates' action caused dissatisfaction to Rudolf and the Saxons. The legates were constantly in the neighbourhood of Henry, and the Patriarch and Udalric soon came definitely under his influence. He persuaded them to call another conference in the middle of August at Wurzburg, too far from Saxony to form neutral ground. Here, in the absence of an adequate delegation from Rudolf, the legates declined to pronounce judgment against the anti-Pope as Henry wished ; and they emphasized their terms of reference, which left that decision to a future council, after report had been made to Rome, and when Gregory's wishes had been made known. Although Henry's envoys at the Lent Synod had agreed to this procedure, it was a procrastinating policy and continued the delays of the last eighteen months. Henry now gave up the idea of negotiation and renewed hostilities, which were continued intermittently till the end of the year.

Gregory realized that events in Germany had taken the wrong course. In the summer he wrote to 'King Rudolf' and complained of the frequent embassies of 'Henry' which attempted to attach the Pope to his cause, but Gregory said that he would not depart from 'the middle way of justice'.[1] Yet on June 16th he expressed approval of Henry's treatment of the legates.[2] Within a few weeks unfavourable reports about them had reached him, and he then wrote warning Peter of

[1] *Ep. Coll.* 26.   [2] *Reg.* VI. 38.

Albano and Udalric of Padua that he had heard that they
were exceeding their orders, and cautioned them to
abide by them.   They were to pronounce no judgment
between the two Kings, nor on the Bishops of Trier,
Köln, Augsburg and others who had accepted lay
investiture; they were to send messengers to Rome on
these matters.   The judgment on the royal dispute lay
in S. Peter's hands.[1]   By October 1st he had realized
that the legates had been guilty of mismanagement.   In
a letter to the German nation he refutes their suspicion
of his impartiality, and says that he is vigorously maintaining it, against Italian opinion, which almost entirely
supported Henry.   He expresses regret if the legates
have acted to the contrary, and admits that a report had
reached him that they had been coerced and deceived.
He could do nothing further until the legates returned
to Rome with their own report.[2]

The legates arrived in Rome at different times.   Udalric's report, entirely in favour of Henry, was received
first, but failed to impress Gregory, who learned the
true state of affairs from Peter of Albano some time afterwards.   Henry was then charged with disobedience,
falsehood and subterfuge, and his case was thoroughly
discredited at Rome.   In a letter to Rudolf the Pope
deplored the fruitlessness of the legatine commission,
protested his impartiality and avowed that he had done
everything possible to procure peace.[3]

If sincere it was indeed a confession of defeat.   Yet
no other result ought to have been expected.   Three
times had the Roman Synod met, and three times pursued the same broken and discredited policy of assembling a council in Germany, which was not even then
to be empowered with authority to settle the question
at issue.   Gregory was throughout awaiting the issue
of events by battle, but, as no decisive action was fought,

---

[1] *Ep. Coll.* 31.   [2] *Reg.* VII. 3.
[3] Meyer von Knonau III. (1900) 225.

he was gradually being forced, by Henry's defensive measures, to incline more and more towards Rudolf, who consistently professed submission to Rome, and took no steps to vitiate his position. Yet Rudolf was doing nothing practical to provide a settlement in Germany, short of the sword. Moreover, at the end of 1079, when circumstances were drawing Gregory and Rudolf closer together, an effective alliance had already been rendered doubtful owing to the distrust created in the minds of the Saxons by Gregory's dilatory policy of the preceding year. At every critical juncture in the long dispute the Pope was dogged by his own previous policy.

CHAPTER THIRTEEN

CÆSAR TURNS (1080)

THERE were two critical periods in the pontificate of Gregory VII—the year 1075 and the year between Lent, 1078, and Lent, 1079. In 1075 he wore out Henry's patience by refusing to place on his head the imperial crown which had not yet been denied to him; in 1078-1079 he embittered him by refusing to restore the German Crown which had been taken away. In each case the year of drift and procrastination was followed by swift and dramatic developments, concluded in the earlier period by the reconquest of half Germany by Henry, and in the later by his conquest of Italy. On January 27th at the battle of Flarcheim near Mülhausen, the King, masked by a snow blizzard, crossed the river and assaulted Rudolf's forces all day long. In the evening, when the rout was beginning, the troops of Otto of Nordheim came up, and Henry was finally repulsed. It was Waterloo without the overthrow of the imperial army. The royal army and fortunes were still. intact after the battle, and Rudolf suffered a heavier loss than the heaps of dead on the field, by the defection of the Saxon Billungs, Herman and Magnus, and of the Margrave Egbert of Meissen to the royal standard.[1]

Whether the action was decisive or not, the King proceeded on the assumption that it was. Liemar, Archbishop of Hamburg, and Rupert, Bishop of Bamberg, were despatched to Rome, with the demand for the anti-King's excommunication without further judgment,

---

[1] On the significance of Flarcheim *cf.* Fliche II. 377 and Hauck *Kirchengeschichte Deutschlands* III. (1906) 820.

and with the renewed threat to appoint a new Pope if Gregory declined. German gold was handed out to the Romans by the envoys. Rudolf also announced the battle to Gregory and his embassy brought a letter from the Saxons. They complained that no definitive answer to all their appeals had been received, ' but everything was suspended in the uncertainty of the future '. King Rudolf had triumphed and Henry as usual had fled. They admitted that the Pope's visit to them was impossible, but in so far as the conflict which they had undertaken at his behest had not been composed by the Pope or by his decrees, but was left to the arbitrament of the sword, they begged him to confirm the action of the legate Bernard—who had condemned Henry at Goslar.[1]

The surest means of bringing Gregory VII to a decision was to offer to him a personal affront, and this Henry had again done. The Pope replied to the threat of deposition in the Lent Synod of 1080, which opened on March 7th. Possibly, fearing a repetition of the affront of 1076, the royal ambassadors were not admitted to the Synod. In an assembly convened by themselves they appealed to the canons on the King's behalf, and issued threats in his name. With difficulty they left the City. Rudolf's embassy demanded justice against a King already deposed, who was ravaging the kingdom and desolating the church. It complained of the investiture of bishops by Henry. The charge was true, but the investiture question had not so far been linked up with lay election in the findings against Henry at the synods. Gregory now dealt with it in the first decree. In addition to the penalty, imposed in November, 1078, on spiritual persons who received investiture from laymen, a specific threat of anathema was now issued against emperors, kings, dukes, marquises and counts who disobeyed the injunction. Another decree strengthened the law against lay election, and outlined the procedure when a bishopric

[1] Bruno c. 110.

became vacant. A suitable candidate was to be sought out by a visiting bishop, sanctioned by the Pope or the Metropolitan, and then elected by the clergy and people with the consent of the Pope or Archbishop. Where a canonical election was not possible, the appointment was to be made by the Pope or Archbishop. Lay election was excluded, and the door was closed to old proprietary custom. Tedald, Guibert and other bishops were again condemned, and a general excommunication was pronounced against the Norman invaders of church lands in South Italy, but with a safeguarding clause against unjust judgments at ecclesiastical tribunals. Feigned penances were to be prevented.

As in the Lent Synod of 1076, Gregory again cast the condemnation of Henry into the dramatic form of a prayer to S. Peter. He recapitulated the events of his own life from the time that he left the City with Gregory VI, emphasizing the validity of his own election. Chief among the enemies who had tried to eject him was Henry, ' whom they call King ', who had planned a conspiracy with many German and Italian bishops. He lays stress on the fact that at Canossa Henry had not been restored to the German kingdom, nor was the allegiance from which his subjects had been released restored to him. Gregory asserted that he had intentionally kept this question open in the interest of the German bishops and princes. But they ' without my counsel ' elected Rudolf as King. Thenceforward he had tried to act impartially between them. But Henry had prevented a definitive council from meeting in Germany, and so involved himself in condemnation ; therefore,

' I subject to excommunication and bind with the chain of anathema . . . Henry whom they call King, and all his supporters. Moreover, . . . forbidding to him the kingdom of Germany and Italy, I remove all royal powers and dignity from him, and I forbid any Christian to obey him as King, and all who have sworn to him or shall swear allegiance I

absolve from the oath. May Henry—and his followers—
have no power in war and no victory while he lives.'

He consigns Rudolf, ' whom the Germans elected for
themselves as King ', to S. Peter's care ' that he may
rule over and defend the German kingdom ', and grants
absolution to all his followers. ' As Henry, for his
pride, disobedience and falsehood is justly deposed from
the dignity of the kingdom, so to Rudolf, for his humility,
obedience and truth, the power and dignity of the
kingdom are conceded.' The prayer to SS. Peter and
Paul continues.

' Act now, I beseech you, most holy fathers and princes,
that all the world may understand and know that if you can
bind and loose in heaven, you can on earth, according to merit,
remove and grant empires, kingdoms, principalities, duchies,
marquisates, counties and the possessions of all men. You,
indeed, have frequently taken away patriarchates, primacies,
archbishoprics and bishoprics from the depraved and unworthy, and given them to religious men. If indeed you
judge spiritual matters, what is to be believed of your power
concerning secular affairs ! And if ye shall judge angels, who
bear rule over all proud princes, what can ye not do to their
servants ! Let all kings and princes now learn how great
you are and what you can do, and may they fear to weigh
lightly the order of your church. And respecting the afore-
said Henry, may you carry out your sentence so swiftly that
all may know that not by chance, but by your power he falls.
He shall be confounded—would to penitence that his spirit
may be saved in the day of the Lord ! " [1]

When Rudolf and the Saxons read this judgment they
might well be satisfied. They might also justly ask why,
if Henry had already involved himself in the anathema
by hindering a decision in Germany, the Pope had not
months ago agreed. This had been one of their arguments all along, but, while Saxon blood might flow in
battle after battle, it was not until the pontifical dignity
was personally flouted that the logical course, from their

[1] *Reg.* VII. 14a.

standpoint, was taken. The vague phrase imposing upon Rudolf allegiance to S. Peter—to the Papacy— suggests that at length Gregory was applying to Germany the claim for papal suzerainty already extended over so many Western lands. However, it is clear that he made no offer of the Italian Crown to Rudolf. Did he hope to offer this to Robert Guiscard, in order to set him up as a permanent barrier against Teutonic aggression ? If so, he might have laid the foundation for Italian unity, and have achieved a more lasting benefit for Europe than could ever come from the grounding of the medieval Papacy. Moreover, a German nation would have issued from the event, and with Germany and Italy looking to their own affairs, the principle of nationality would have been established on the mainland of Europe four hundred years before it began to be effective. The Popes would have been free to check the Hundred Years' War between England and France, with all the evil results attendant for both lands upon that useless struggle, and they might have been saved from the Avignonese captivity and the Great Schism.

Gregory cannot be acquitted of a tendency to in-sincerity in his speech before the Synod. Henry had made no attempt to challenge his election to the Papacy. The Pope emphasized the fact that at Canossa he did not restore the German kingdom to Henry, yet he had continued to address him as King, and only during the last few months had he used the royal title when referring to Rudolf. He had waited to ascertain whether events in Germany would justify the risk of a final breach with Henry. After 1076 Gregory was content to lay chief stress upon Henry's excommunication ; after 1080 the emphasis was laid upon the deposition. In 1076 his appeal to S. Peter, made in the Synod, was little more than an attempt to invest his judgment of the King with mystic dignity ; in 1080 addressed to S. Paul, as well as S. Peter, it was an appeal for doom and destruction

15

upon Henry's head, shot through with flashes of the Pope's rancour and enmity. The satanic zeal of holy men had been seen in history more than once since the sons of Zebedee called for fire upon the heads of the Samaritans, and long years before the shrewd Damiani had called Hildebrand ' my holy Satan '. He was right, Gregory was ' holy ' in his purposes and motives and personal character, yet satanic in his methods and policies. The hammer blows of his anathemas were wielded with the zeal of Elijah, but when he also imitated the sons of Zebedee, he forgot the repulse which fell upon the ears of those over-zealous saints.

The balance of Gregory's judgment was completely shaken at the time. On Easter Monday he declared, in the Church of S. Peter, that if Henry had not repented by August 1st he would be dead. Perhaps his emotion was stirred, not only by the threat of his own deposition lodged by Henry's ambassadors, but by the most magnificent bequest ever made to the Roman Church which came to it at this period. Since her mother's death the widowed and now childless Matilda had more and more devoted herself and her resources to the Papacy. The youngest child of Boniface and Beatrix, she had inherited a vast domain in the north of central Italy, on both sides of the Apennines. Like Elizabeth of England she spoke many languages, but was as beautiful [1] as the latter was plain ; and instead of devoting her gifts to intrigue she turned them to religious exercises. She signed no death warrants, but interceded even for her enemies. Her dislike of the Germans dated from the time when, a child in the early teens, she had been taken captive with her mother to Germany by Henry III. Now when Henry IV was threatening to invade Italy she made over her territories to the Roman Church, and held them henceforth under papal suzerainty. The bequest was confirmed twenty-five years later to Urban II, and vastly

[1] Amédée Renée *La Grande Italienne* (1859) p. 33.

extended the temporal power of the Papacy. Gregory's part in the transaction has not been revealed. It is certain that he would do nothing to hinder it, and, if he suggested it, he was merely applying to Northern Italy the policy already applied to the South. One of the most fixed features in Gregory VII's policy was the extension of the patrimony of the Papacy, and the affirmation, wherever possible, of papal suzerainty in the West.

The fulminations of 1076 dissolved the royal campaign in Germany, and forced Henry to check his adversary by the political manœuvre of Canossa. They had encouraged his enemies, and detached many of the bishops from his cause. No such results followed the anathemas of 1080. Bishops changed sides again, but they now went back to Henry. There was another royal journey over the Alps in the next year, but the King now came to organize war, not to confess sins. Moreover, Henry's pamphleteers began to publish a better case than the Gregorian writers. If the sentence of 1076 had put an instrument into the King's hands with which to begin the reconquest of Germany, the sentence of 1080 opened the way to a conquest of Rome. Italian opinion, which before had been divided between King and Pope, now turned increasingly in Henry's direction. In Lombardy where the King had always had a large following, the royalist sentiment was stirred to a pitch of excitement, not so much on account of loyalty to Henry as of hatred towards Gregory. The politically minded Lombard episcopate, and especially the canon lawyers of Ravenna, saw that the Pope had over-reached himself, and that nothing but war now lay between him and the German King. On the way back to Germany, Henry's envoys had lost no opportunity of stirring up antagonism which was latent, and adding fuel to malice which was burning both in Tuscany and Lombardy. Benzo, the Bishop of Alba, who, since being driven out of Rome with Cadalus, had been writing caustic verses against Gregory, again assumed the rôle of a papal pamphleteer and demagogue, but with far more danger to Gregory. Peter Crassus, the learned canonist of Ravenna, put forth a reasoned statement of Henry's case which retained a high place in the flood of polemical literature now appearing. Henry was King by divine appointment and by hereditary right. It was his duty to defend the Roman Church and Italy, like his predecessors Charles the Great and Otto I. Against him had risen the mqnk Hildebrand whom the Roman people had originally made Pope—an enemy of law, peace and the Christian religion. Contrary to the canons he had wrongfully summoned Henry before his tribunal and had illegally deposed him. Peter Crassus urges the King to call a council, at which Hildebrand should be deposed, and he and his followers excluded from the church.

The work was sent to the King in June, 1080, and was revised in 1084.[1] It presents a good case for the early medieval theory of imperial rights, but its appeal to the authority of Roman Law and the canons is of doubtful validity. Its theory of divine right goes farther than the ideas of the Caroling and succeeding periods. Yet the historical significance of the work lies in its whole-hearted defence of the German kingship against Gregory's claim to exercise over it the papal hegemony, and Peter Crassus was only one of many writers who came forward to defend the King. On the other hand, an equally large number of publicists defended the Pope. The polemical writers reflect the disordered opinion of Europe at the time. Opinion was aligned not only between Pope and King on the great political issue at stake, but also between the two branches of reviving legal studies. The canon lawyers, on the whole, were supporters of the Gregorian claims, while the civilian lawyers, influenced by old legal theory, were inclined to defend the Emperor. To this large body of opinion loyal to the King must be attrib-

[1] Mirbt pp. 18 f. ; Voosen p. 80 n. 47.

uted, in some measure, the success of Henry after the year 1080. His grasp upon the sword was strong, but in Gregory's lifetime he did not obtain a decisive issue by battle in Germany. He crossed the Alps more than once, leaving unconquered enemies in his rear, but the weight of North Italian public opinion was sufficient to turn the scale in his favour. On the papal question Rome was conquered, as in the days of Frederick II, without the aid of a large German force.

At Whitsun at Mainz no less than nineteen German bishops agreed to the royal decision to hold a council for the deposition of Gregory. This assembled at Brixen, near Chur on the German side of the Alps, on June 25th. Among the thirty bishops present, the Germans were headed by Liemar, Archbishop of Hamburg-Bremen, Rupert of Bamberg and Benno of Osnabruck. A large delegation of Lombard bishops included Guibert of Ravenna, Henry of Aquileia and Tedald. Hugh the White drew up the charges against Gregory in exaggerated terms, but with effective results. No serious moral offences were alleged, as at Worms (1076), but he was accused of necromancy and of poisoning four of his predecessors, as well as holding the heresy of Berengar. The main attack centred upon his treatment of Henry. Gregory's deposition was proclaimed, and Guibert of Ravenna, an ecclesiastic of unimpeachable character, a sympathizer with church reform, yet a consistent opponent of Gregory, was elected Pope. He readily promised to crown Henry in Rome at Whitsuntide next year. Rudolf and his followers were excommunicated.

Gregory perceived the storm gathering over the Alps, and took active measures in his own defence. By the spring of this year Robert Guiscard had overcome his rebellious vassals, and had made peace with Jordan of Capua, who was already reconciled with the Papacy. He was now free to exploit the quarrel between Gregory and Henry for his own purposes. Although Gregory had again excommunicated the Normans at the Lent Synod (1080), he hoped to check the advance of Henry upon Rome by the aid of Guiscard, and negotiations began in which each side sought to over-reach the other. Desiderius of Monte Cassino was ordered to absolve Robert, and Count Sion de Crépy, a Frenchman, was sent to develop the new *rapprochement*. On June 10th at Ceprano the Pope received from Robert a confirmation of the oath of submission made by Richard of Capua in 1059, and on June 29th renewed the terms of the Treaty of Melfi of the same year.[1] But the Pope was compelled to allow the Norman conqueror to retain his gains in South Italy. Salerno and Amalfi and part of the Mark of Fermo were expressly excluded from the patrimony of the Roman Church, which Robert swore to defend.[2] To this concession the Pope unwillingly gave consent,[3] it was a surrender of claims long maintained by the Curia against the Norman Duke, and indicated the stress of Gregory's position. Although Robert had declined to share in the measures taken by Henry and the Lombards for the deposition of the Pope, his depredations against papal territory and the lands of papal allies far exceeded anything that Henry had attempted. The new treaty therefore represented a sorry surrender of principle on the part of Gregory. It deprived his claims against Henry of any remaining cogency. Up to this point his attitude to all who contravened his principles had been one of considerable dignity, but, once he had surrendered to the Norman depredator, the question leaps to the fore —why not also to Henry years before ? With crafty insincerity Robert Guiscard kissed the Pope's foot, and was then reinvested with the land for which he had sworn allegiance. If Gregory in 1075 had invited the young King Henry to Rome for the imperial coronation, the Milanese question and other outstanding issues

---

[1] Cf. *supra*, p. 57 f.   [2] *Reg.* VIII. 1*a*, *b*, *c*.
[3] *Reg.* VIII. 1*b* (June 6th, Caspar).

might have been as easily settled, for the Pope had no concession to make to Henry such as he allowed Robert.

Yet the hollowness of the new alliance immediately began to appear. The Eastern Emperor Michael VII had been dethroned by Nicephorus III (Botaniates) ; Michael applied to Gregory and Robert Guiscard for assistance. Already a bond between the dethroned Emperor and Robert had been established, when Guiscard's daughter was sent to Constantinople to become the bride of the Emperor's son, Constantine. But she was now a prisoner in the hands of Botaniates. One of Robert's vassals, Abelard, had fled to Constantinople, and was under the protection of the usurper. Robert's attention was therefore preoccupied with the preparations for an attack upon Constantinople, and the Pope was forced to agree to his plans. He called upon the bishops of Apulia and Calabria to summon the knights of the south to join Robert's army for the war.[1] There is a report of a consecrated banner handed by Gregory to the Norman, which seems to show that a crown was in contemplation for Robert Guiscard—but which crown, that of Constantinople or of Italy ?

Gregory's confidence in the new Norman alliance is reflected in the correspondence of this period. Old papal claims were re-asserted, and new demands were put forth. In October, 1079, he warned an enemy of Swonimir that the Dalmatian magnate was under papal suzerainty and therefore under papal protection.[2] In the same month the Pope had commended Alfonso of Aragon and Castile for his loyalty to the papal suzerainty.[3] Two days after the new pact with Guiscard, he threatened the Spaniard with excommunication for provocative treatment of a legate.[4] The King submitted and was again commended.[5] On January 3rd (1080) Gregory refused

[1] Reg. VIII. 6.   [2] Reg. VII. 4.
[3] Reg. VII. 6.   [4] Reg. VIII. 2 and 4.
[5] Reg. VIII. 3.   The date of this letter must be after June 27th.

to accept the excuse of Manasseh, Archbishop of Reims, that Philip of France had hindered him from attending the Roman Synods [1]; on April 17th he confirmed a sentence of deposition against the Archbishop, already issued by the legate Hugh, Bishop of Die. [2] The Pope sought to strengthen the good understanding existing between the Curia and Denmark. In October, 1079, he praised the devotion of King Harald (Acon) to the Roman Church, [3] and on April 19th, 1080, wrote in glowing terms of his father Svein, who had not been surpassed by the Emperor Henry III in loyalty to the Roman Church. [4] But Gregory's attention, apart from the German and Italian question, was chiefly devoted towards England during the period.

Between March, 1079, and May, 1080, no less than six letters were despatched to England. While in May, 1077, Gregory had declined to accede to William's intercession on behalf of the deposed Bishop of Dol, [5] in April, 1078, he wrote commending William's uprightness of life, and ' liberal wisdom '. [6] Yet the English King, by constant appointments to English sees and abbeys, was guilty of one of the leading offences in the list of charges against Henry IV. A year later (March, 1079) William's regulations, which prohibited the bishops from visiting Rome, were giving offence to Gregory, and Lanfranc was rebuked for not coming to Rome for fear of the King, and a warning was issued against William. [7] In September the Pope was still complaining of William's action. [8] On April 24th, 1080, when the conflict with Henry was looming ahead, Gregory wrote to William, reminding him of his services to him at the time of the Conquest, and appealed to him for aid, praising the King as ' the jewel of the princes '. The Pope does not specify the nature of the assistance required, but confides

[1] *Reg.* VII. 12.   [2] *Reg.* VII. 20.   [3] *Reg.* VII. 5.
[4] *Reg.* VII. 21.   [5] *Reg.* IV. 17.   [6] *Reg.* V. 19.
[7] *Reg.* VI. 30.   [8] *Reg.* VII. 1.

that issue to William's envoys.[1]   On May 8th the legate
Hubert left Rome with another despatch—together with
letters to Queen Matilda and Robert of Normandy,
warning the latter to obey the King [2]—in which the Pope
compares the spiritual and royal dignities to the sun and
moon, appointed by God to rule the world.   If the royal
dignity rules under God, it is by the papal vigilance and
dispensation.[3]   Behind somewhat obscure terminology
Gregory makes plain his long-cherished notion of the
superiority of the papal hegemony to the regal.   The
legate carried with him the formal demand for the more
regular payment of Peter's Pence, and for William's
homage to Gregory.[4]   So England was placed in the
same category as Sicily, Spain, Hungary, Corsica, and
other lands.   It was regarded as part of the original
patrimony of S. Peter bequeathed by the old decretals.
This was the last attempt made by Gregory to establish
this amazing claim, and it was met with a prompt refusal
by William.[5]   What views were held by the King on
the dispute with Henry we do not know, but the utmost
he offered to do was to pay Peter's Pence regularly.

Since his return from Lombardy in September, 1077,
although distracted by the German and Norman questions, the general administration of the affairs of the
church throughout Europe never ceased to receive
attention from the Pontiff's vigilant eye.   From the
appointment of bishops down to the smallest details of
ritual observance, nothing was too general or too minute
to call forth a letter from the Chancery.   Brâtizlav, Duke
of Bohemia, was refused permission to allow the use of
the Slavonic tongue at the Mass.[6]   The Archbishop of
the Armenian Church was warned to mix water with the
wine, and to continue the use of unleavened bread, in
spite of the objection of the Greek Church.   Oil for

---

[1] *Reg.* VII. 23.   [2] *Reg.* VII. 26 and 27.
[3] *Reg.* VII. 25.   [4] *Cf.* Brooke *E.H.R.* XXVI. 225 ff.
[5] *Cf.* my *Lanfranc* pp. 220 ff.   [6] *Reg.* VII. 11.

the chrism must be made from balsam, not from butter.[1]
A Sardinian archbishop was ordered to shave his beard
according to Roman method.[2]

Encouraged by the new Norman alliance, and relying
upon the armed assistance of the Normans, Gregory announced to the bishops of South Italy in July the speedy
overthrow of the anti-Pope.[3] The attack on Guibert
of Ravenna by Robert and Jordan, by Matilda's Tuscan
army, and the papal forces of central Italy, would begin
in the cool weather, before September 1st.[4] So late as
September 18th, he interpreted the discovery of what
was claimed to be the body of S. Matthew, as a sign
that heaven was about to come to the rescue of his
cause.[5] Yet heaven had not fulfilled his prophecy of
the death of the King August 1st had come and gone
and Henry was still alive. In the middle of that month
the King held a great assembly at Mainz at which the
decrees of Brixen, and the election of the anti-Pope were
confirmed. Gregory's less boastful prophecy of the
near approach of Norman aid remained equally unful-
filled. September 1st had passed without the movement
of the Norman host to the north. In October it was
still on the coasts of the Adriatic, looking towards Constantinople. Without waiting any longer for Guiscard
and Jordan, the army of Matilda moved against Ravenna.
On October 15th at Volta, near the Lago di Garda, it
was routed by a Lombard force, led by a natural son of
Henry. On that day, also, in Germany, was fought the
battle of Hohen-Mölsen near the river Elster, between
Henry and Rudolf. The King was without the contingents of Bohemia and Meissen, but on his side fought
the young Frederick of Hohenstaufen, member of a
house which was soon to take the place of the Salian
emperors in the struggle with the Papacy. Like all
other actions of this war it was obstinately contested,

---

[1] *Reg.* VIII. 1.   [2] *Reg.* VIII. 10.   [3] *Reg.* VIII. 5.
[4] *Reg.* VIII. 7.   [5] *Reg.* VIII. 8.

with varying success on either side, and, if at the close of the day fortune had somewhat inclined towards Rudolf, victory came to Henry with nightfall, when the anti-King died of his wounds. His right hand had gone, and he had been pierced in the abdomen. The Saxon lords gathered round, and vowed that even so they would have no other king in Saxony. Yet, according to a report from a partisan of Henry, Rudolf expressed regret for his rebellion before he died. Although still barred out of Saxony, only the discouraged forces of Matilda now stood between Henry and an advance over the Alps to Rome. Cæsar's fortune had turned, and, if the factions and the walls of Rome, coupled with the insufficiency of the force which the King brought with him in 1081 and 1082, delayed for three years more his coronation in the City, that was assured so long as Robert Guiscard was thinking of a crown in Constantinople, and was detained by unruly vassals in the south.

No word of Gregory's feelings on that twice-fatal day of October is forthcoming. Yet, on the very date of the battles in Lombardy and Germany, he wrote in sobered terms to the Tuscans and to Fermo and Ravenna, exulting no more in the approach of Norman aid, content only to urge the faithful to elect a successor in Guibert's place.[1] But Ravenna was now the centre of the royalist party in North Italy, and the Pope's orders fell on deaf ears. In December he announced that he was sending Richard, one of the Roman clergy, to be the new Patriarch.[2] But of Richard's election, now or later, no word appears.

A significant indication of the effect of misfortune on Gregory's mind at the close of this year appears in his changed attitude to Philip of France. We have seen that in the autumn of 1074 he was threatening the King with the very anathemas which were hurled against Henry eighteen months later. On December 27th three

[1] *Reg.* VIII. 12 and 13.   [2] *Reg.* VIII. 14.

letters were despatched to France, demanding the
appointment of a successor to the deposed Manasseh,
Archbishop of Reims, and releasing the diocesans from
their allegiance to him.[1] On the same day a letter was
sent to Philip condoning the offences of his youth, and
urging him to assent to the arrangements made at
Reims.[2] Yet no sign of repentance such as Henry had
repeatedly given is recorded to have been offered by the
French King. But the time was past when Gregory
could afford to raise up for himself any more enemies.
When the year 1080 closed, its events showed many
resemblances to 1074. Then also had he boasted of the
mighty things to be done by the aid of Norman arms,
and then also did he experience the futility of relying
on Robert Guiscard. The Norman Duke was coming
indeed, but when he came it was too late for the rescue
of Gregory's German policy, and Robert's hammer
blows were rained, not on a German or Lombard army,
but upon the citizens of Rome.

[1] *Reg.* VIII. 17-19.   *Reg.* VIII. 20.

CHAPTER FOURTEEN

ASHES (1081–1085)

IN the last four years of Gregory's life there was a curious reversion of his fortunes to the conditions of his archidiaconate. The range of his activities shrinks again within the City walls. Armed forces encircled Rome and there were enemies within the gate. An anti-Pope was again outside waiting to mount the throne of Peter. In the old days the genius of Hildebrand had never been defeated. The gold of Benedict, the soldiery from the Trastevere, the squadrons of Godfrey, and sometimes a Norman troop or two, had always proved sufficient to overcome his enemies in the end. Perhaps also the recollection of those earlier triumphs strengthened Gregory's confidence now. If so, it was a fatal legacy from a past which could not be revived, for, although the conditions now in Rome were similar, how different were they in the world outside! No longer was the see of Peter claimed by Benzo on behalf of an anti-Pope but by the German monarch himself, victorious now in Germany, and supported by the armed contingents of Lombardy. Public opinion on both sides of the Alps had largely turned against the existing Curia, and rolled up recruits for the King's forces. The marvel is that Gregory was able to hold out so long. Perhaps even his iron fortitude would have given way earlier, save that hope in Robert Guiscard sprang eternally in his mind. Yet that trust in Norman aid not merely prevented him from bowing to necessity and coming to terms with his victorious enemy with a generous gesture in surrender, it set back the advancement of his cause after he was gone. For many years the Romans and Italy did not forget the charred ruins of Rome, and every family in the City, and many in the country around, mourned sons and fathers, as well as wives and daughters who lost life or honour in the sack of 1084. But even after the fatal October 15th, 1080, such scenes were not imagined, and Gregory still relied upon his diplomacy to bring up the Eastern army of Guiscard to match the Lombard and German forces on the plains before the City.

The Lent Synod of 1081, in the month of February, did little more than excommunicate the enemies of the Pope, and suspend bishops who had failed to be present. Henry IV and two Campanian lords, Hildimund and Land, of Lombard origin, were especially named.[1] The continued improvement in the King's fortunes in Germany, in spite of the sentence passed on him in Rome at the Synod of 1080, was causing widespread doubt in Germany as to the legality of a papal judgment of the German King. As in 1076, Herman of Metz wrote to Gregory for an authoritative statement on the legal aspect of the case. A lengthy reply, which occupies over fourteen pages in the *Register*, was sent by Gregory on March 15th.[2] It forms, like the reply to that Bishop of 1076, the Counsel's opinion of the Curia, on the new doctrine of the papal theocracy. By the authority of Christ kings are amenable to the binding and loosing power of the Papacy, and many passages in the Bible and in the decrees of the Fathers uphold the same principle ; so the decrees of the Roman Church cannot be rejected. The substance of several alleged historical and canonical precedents, already quoted in the letter of 1076, are repeated, together with some additions. The Pseudo-Isidorean letter of Julius I to the Eastern bishops, which merely bases the general power of excommunication on the grant of the keys by Christ to S. Peter, is

---

[1] *Reg.* VIII. 20a.   [2] *Reg.* VIII. 21.

brought forward as the authority for the universal judicial rights of the Pope. The threat of excommunication, issued in a letter of Gregory the Great against refractory kings, is quoted more extensively than in 1076, and is transformed into a decree of condemnation against Henry IV. A forged excommunication of the Emperor Arcadius by Innocent I is introduced, as well as the wrong interpretation of the action of Pope Zacharias, which had appeared in the earlier letter.

While the letter of 1081 is mainly occupied with proving the validity of the royal excommunication, the question of the deposition is not omitted. The pious aspiration of Gregory the Great, that offending monarchs may lose their rank, is twisted into a decree of deposition. The rebuke of Theodosius by Ambrose, the so-called Ambrosian letter, and that of Gelasius I to the Emperor Anastasius, together with the story of the relations between Pope Zacharias and Pippin, are forced, in a similar way, to support Gregory's claim to the supremacy of the papal see over the royal power. Indeed, scarcely seven good emperors and kings could be recollected among the great number of unworthy rulers. Gregory mentioned by name Constantine the Great, Theodosius, Honorius, Charles the Great, and Louis the Pious, omitting, significantly, Henry III.[1]

While Gregory was attempting in his letter to Herman to justify his treatment of Henry, he took measures not only to conserve his gains in Germany, but to proclaim and enforce there the principle of papal suzerainty already set up at the Lent Synod of 1080. In a letter to Altman, Bishop of Passau, and William, Abbot of Hirschau,[2] he admits that he was being advised to make peace with Henry, if the latter proved conciliatory. Now that Rudolf was dead, and while Robert Guiscard

[1] Martens II. 51 ff. gives a tabulated comparison of the letters to Herman of 1076 and 1081.
[2] *Reg.* VIII. 26 (dated by Caspar March, 1081).

was still under the ban, this was the obvious course for
the Pope to take, but in place of instituting a wise and
generous peace policy, he urged caution in the selection
of a successor to Rudolf.   When a suitable candidate
had been found, an oath of obedience to the Pope, of
which Gregory gives the terms, must be taken by him.
He must agree to uphold the grant of lands and tribute
made to the Papacy by Constantine and Charles the
Great, and of all similar grants since that time.   Not a
word is said now, or anywhere else in the *Register*, of
Herman of Salm, brother of Conrad of Luxemburg, who
was elected by the Saxons to succeed Rudolf.   The
Pope asks for armed help in the event of Henry's descent
upon Lombardy.   He foresees that Matilda's forces will
not be sufficient to drive him back.   He seeks aid
especially from Welf, the son of the Margrave Azzo, to
whom Matilda in later years gave her hand.   With
hostilities in view, the legates in Gaul, Peter, Bishop of
Albano, and Gisulf, the dispossessed Prince of Salerno,
were ordered to gather in the tribute of the French
churches, and in the same letter a claim to suzerainty
over Saxony was set up on the basis of an alleged grant
made to the Papacy by Charles the Great.[1]   Alfonso of
Spain [2] was thanked for an ample and magnificent
donation.   Gregory again reminds the Spanish King
of the duty of displacing the Gothic liturgy by the
Roman order, and expresses regret that Alfonso allowed
Christians to be ruled by Jews in certain parts of Spain.
This was in contrast with the graceful message to the
Muhammedan Emir who ruled over Christians in Africa.
Before Easter, negotiations were also begun which
confirmed the sacrifice of principle to Robert Guiscard
already instituted in June 1080.   If this step had been
taken by the Pope when the troops of Henry were ready
to storm the walls of Rome, it might have been interpreted as a concession to necessity, and, even so, would

[1] *Reg.* VIII. 23.   [2] *Reg.* VIII. 25.

still have compared badly with his consistent hostility
to the German King. But that contingency was not
to arise for another two years. In 1074 Gregory had
declared that he would never agree to Robert's conquests of papal territories.[1] The complete change in
the Pope's attitude towards Robert is confirmed by the
fact that he selected Desiderius for the negotiation—a
prelate already under disapproval at Rome for his
friendly dealings with the Normans. In his letter to
Desiderius, Gregory spoke of accommodation and the
utility of a peace with Robert. The Romans were looking to him for help. He asked for a military contingent
to be commanded by Robert himself or by his son, to
be sent after April 4th, so that rebels against the Roman
Church might be reduced by terror or by force. The
Duke was to be persuaded to prevent his nephew,
Robert Loritello, from attacking papal territory in the
south.[2] A change of tone was also adopted towards
the French-Norman bishops and fighting men. The
suspended bishops were to be restored. Against the
Norman knights, who were under the ban for failure to
uphold the decrees against simonist and married clergy,
or for the non-payment of tithes, the rigour of the
canons was to be tempered, on account of the disturbance of the times. The same conciliatory attitude was
to be observed towards the King of England, in spite
of the fact, says the Pope, that he gave offence in some
respects,[3] and Gregory's last recorded letter to William
urges him to release his half-brother, Odo of Bayeux,[4]
from prison. A surrender of principle in all Norman
lands was being made by Gregory at this time, in order
to gain support for upholding his principles against
Henry. At the same time he attempted to detach

[1] Reg. IV. 7.
[2] Reg. VIII. 27 (Caspar dates the letter beginning of February, 1081).
[3] Reg. VIII. 28.
[4] Reg. VIII. 60 (cf. Lanfranc p. 232. Caspar dates this letter at the
end of 1083).

16

Henry's followers from him in Germany, especially Benno, Bishop of Osnabruck.[1]

By Easter Day (April 4th) Henry was in Verona with a small force, and went on to Ravenna, where he waited for Lombard reinforcements. Both sides attempted to secure the aid of Robert Guiscard. The Norman declined the King's offer of the Mark of Fermo, and a marriage between Henry's son, Conrad, and one of Robert's daughters. To the Pope Robert turned a deaf ear. Gregory warned Desiderius that the King would be before the walls of Rome by Whitsun, and said that he was prepared for death rather than surrender. The Romans would credit the report of a treaty between the King and Robert, if the latter did not send help.[2] But a new revolution at Constantinople had displaced Nicephorus III by Alexius Comnenus, and Robert's attention was preoccupied with events there. To the Pope he announced his refusal of Henry's alliance, and made the excuse that he would not have made preparations for the Eastern campaign if he had known that danger from the King was so imminent; but they must now go forward. On May 25th, he sailed for Illyria.

Henry crossed the Apennines by the middle of the month, and received the submission of Lucca in the territory of Matilda. He arrived before Rome without hindrance, and issued an appeal to the Romans, reminding them of past allegiance to his father, and posing as the peace-maker between the *regnum* and *sacerdotium*. But no German Emperor, not even Henry III, was ever popular in Rome, and, since he had elected Guibert of Ravenna as Pope without consulting them, the Romans were not in a mood to be influenced by the royal rhodomontade. On May 21st Henry encamped on the Neronian Field, and there stayed until the summer heat drove him off at the end of June. A charter granted to the Pisans marked a stage in the development of the

[1] *Reg.* VIII. 33. [2] *Reg.* VIII. 34.

freedom of that town, and so of the Italian cities of the Middle Ages, but it antagonized Florence, the enemy of Pisa. Henry's policy towards the German and Italian towns fostered the growth of civil freedom against the nobles. By contrast, the ecclesiastical demand for free election, while democratic in principle, struck at the development of freedom in the towns, because it aimed a shaft at the royal authority, the sure guarantee in the early Middle Ages against the oligarchical tyranny of bishop and baron.

In Germany Herman of Salm was elected in succession to Rudolf in August, and fighting broke out between him and the royalists, led by Frederick of Hohenstaufen. Henry's cause received powerful support from the pen of Wenrich, *Scolasticus* of Trier, who wrote a work against Gregory. On October 16th Robert Guiscard defeated Alexius, the Eastern Emperor, in a great battle before the walls of Durazzo. In reply to his letter announcing the victory, Gregory begged him, as a debtor to the patronage of S. Peter, to delay no longer in coming to his assistance against Henry.[1]

At the end of February, 1082, the King was back before the ramparts of Rome. His manifesto to the Romans this time omitted all reference to the anti-Pope, and, while it attacked 'Hildebrand' and compared his persecution of the church with that of Decius, it offered to recognize Gregory as Pope. When the City gate remained closed the siege began, and the environs of Rome were devastated, but Henry's army was still too small to make any impression on the defenders, and with the arrival of hot weather he again retreated to Lombardy. But this summer his diplomacy secured a good understanding with Desiderius, the Abbot of Monte Cassino, and with Jordan of Capua. In the royal Court at Albano the Abbot secured a privilege for the abbey, and Jordan obtained a golden bull in support of his

[1] *Reg.* VIII. 40.

tenure of Capua. Desiderius seems to have held out the hope of the imperial crown to Henry. An alliance was also concluded with Alexius against Robert Guiscard. A rebellion of his vassals in South Italy, and the report of Jordan's negotiation with Henry, brought Robert back to South Italy at the end of May, but there was no hope of his march to Rome this year.

Gregory's position was rapidly declining. No Lenten Synod could be held this year. He wrote to Lanfranc of Canterbury,[1] demanding his appearance in Rome by November 1st—a demand which was not fulfilled [2]— and possibly hoping to secure tangible aid from England. He issued an encyclical to all Christians complaining of the afflictions of the church, but exhorting them to patience, fortitude and hope.[3] Jordan of Capua was again placed under the ban,[4] and there is a report that even Desiderius was condemned. The first rift in the loyalty of the Romans appeared when Gregory gave orders for the removal of church plate for the war funds. The cardinals and clergy successfully resisted the papal demand, but Gregory's necessities were met for the time being by the receipt of treasure from Matilda in the autumn. In this year (1082) Gissurus was created first Bishop of Skalboltina in Iceland, by the order of Gregory, through the instrumentality of Hartwig, Archbishop of Magdeburg, who had displaced Liemar of Bremen as the papal agent for the North-Western area of Europe.[5]

In the first half of 1082 Herman of Salm contemplated a diversion into Italy on behalf of the Pope, but his defeat at Mailburg by Brâtizlav on May 5th made the expedition impossible. In January, 1083, Otto of Nordheim died, and Henry was released from any further

---

[1] Reg. VIII. 43 (Caspar, May–June, 1082).
[2] Cf. Lanfranc pp. 225 f.
[3] Reg. VIII. 42.   [4] Reg. VIII. 46.
[5] J. Langebek Script. Rer. Danicærum Med. Aevi III. (1774) 46.

anxiety that the new anti-King would cross the Alps. In January, Gregory left the City for the south, to secure troops from Robert Guiscard, but he was back in Rome in February before Henry reappeared. A peace-party was already organized and sent an embassy to Henry, but the receipt of 30,000 *solidi* from Guiscard enabled Gregory to defeat their efforts for the time being, although the appearance of famine caused many of the citizens to leave Rome. After three attacks made this year (1083) Henry captured the Leonine city with S. Peter's Church, and confined Gregory to the castle of S. Angelo and the old town. An ambassador from Constantinople brought 'to the King a large sum of money, with the promise of more, if Henry attacked Robert Guiscard. The loyalty of the Roman nobles was now easily purchased. They promised that Gregory should hold a synod in November, at which the dispute would be settled. When the King again withdrew from the City, taking with him hostages, some of the nobles promised that at the end of fifteen days he should be recalled, when either Gregory should crown him, or, if he were dead, or had left Rome, another Pope should be elected for this purpose. A similar proposal had been made by the King the year before, and it is remarkable that, although he secured the control of S. Peter's Church in the early summer of 1083, he made no attempt to be crowned by Guibert. Henry was ready to abandon the anti-Pope and the resolutions of the Synod of Brixen. If the Pope had responded by agreeing to recognize Henry as King, a basis for agreement would have been reached, but this last opportunity was also allowed to pass. The Pope was compelled by opinion in Rome to accede to the request for a synod to be held on neutral ground, and he made a gesture in favour of a more reasonable treatment of the German question by denying that Rudolf had been elected by his order or advice ; yet he still fixed all the blame for the dispute upon

' Henry, the so-called King '.[1] Gregory was playing for time, and for the arrival of Guiscard's army.

Amid the heat of the summer, Henry's garrison in Rome lost ground, and its Captain Udalrich of Godesheim died. Gregory secured the assembly of the Synod within the walls on November 20th. Irritated by the failure of his attempt to negotiate a peace, Henry prevented many bishops from attending, and arrested Otto of Ostia. A long and moving speech by the Pope had only a transient effect,[2] and his proposal to excommunicate Henry again was defeated by the peace-party among the cardinals. When the King returned to claim the fulfilment of the promise made by the Romans, he made a last overture to Gregory, who put the last nail into the coffin of negotiation by demanding penance from Henry.

In February, 1084, in accordance with his pact with Alexius, Henry marched into Campania and made a demonstration against Robert Guiscard. On his return to Rome he disbursed another subsidy received from the East among the nobles and citizens. Gregory's followers were falling away rapidly. Thirteen of the cardinal-clergy, including the Chancellor Peter, and the chief official of the Chancery clerks, deserted him. All his overtures having been refused by the captive in S. Angelo, only one course was open to the King. On March 21st, he seized the Lateran Church. At a Synod held in S. Peter's, Gregory VII was deposed and excommunicated. On Palm Sunday, Guibert was enthroned as Clement III, and on Easter Day (1084) Henry and his Queen received the imperial crown. Cæsar had triumphed. To the very end he had hoped for an accommodation with Gregory, who, true to the policy of the last ten years, had allowed the initiative to pass to the anti-Pope Clement. In Henry's three sieges of the City between 1082 and 1084 no wanton act of destruc-

[1] *Reg.* VIII. 51 (Caspar, summer 1083).   [2] *Reg.* VIII. 58.

tion is recorded, and before his coronation he had won the respect of many in the Curia. The vindication of his case, which appeared in the anonymous *Dicta cujusdam de discordia papae et regis*, reflected the opinion of more than half Germany and Italy. While his triumph in Rome was brief, and if in Germany he was destined to be defeated by the local ambitions of the German magnates from restoring the fallen fabric of his father's empire, in Rome itself no reproaches were raised against him. That was not merely due to the events which issued in his coronation ; it reflected also the revulsion of feeling, which finally turned against Gregory, among the Romans and Italians of his own generation, on account of the calamity which now fell upon the City.

After his coronation Henry failed to take S. Angelo and other fortified places in Rome, and from the humiliation of capture by the Emperor, Gregory was finally delivered by Guiscard. Only six months before, that far-sighted warrior missed the greatest opportunity of his life by not marching on Rome to dictate terms to Pope and King alike. No power in Europe, save that of his distant countrymen in England, could have opposed the might of the Duke of Apulia, Calabria and Sicily. But, although Guiscard had robbed S. Peter's patrimony, he always stood in awe of Gregory, and he seems to have been badly informed of the strength of Henry's army. By the spring of 1084 his rebellious vassals had been repressed, and at Gregory's final appeal he marched on Rome with 30,000 foot and 6,000 horse. The peace-making Desiderius warned both Pope and Emperor of his intention. Henry retreated on May 21st. Three days later Guiscard's advance-guard of 1,000 horse and 3,000 foot approached the City, expecting to make contact with the Emperor's army. Henry's force was well on the way to the Apennines, yet the gates of Rome remained closed to the Pope's deliverer. It was a curious situation, and reveals the full extent of Henry's victory in Rome. When he retreated the Romans manned the walls against the King's enemy and the Pope's friend.

For three days Guiscard reconnoitred. He placed a large force on the northern bank to watch for Henry. At dawn on May 28th, the Duke himself advanced with the storming ladders against the Porta San Lorenzo, and by six o'clock he was on the ramparts, and had unlocked the gates. Thirteen hundred men were admitted. They joined Gregory's guard around S. Angelo and made contact with Robert's army on the northern bank across the Milvian Bridge with the cry ' A Guiscard ! A Guiscard ! ' Gregory was rescued and carried to the Lateran, but, while the Norman was making a formal submission to the Pope, the loot of the City had begun. During the next forty-eight hours the Romans recovered their spirit and rallied their forces. The Norman troops were attacked in the streets, Roger Guiscard dashed in with 1,000 horse, but failed to make headway against the frenzied citizens. The order to fire the buildings was given, and the flames, fanned by a rising storm, destroyed the northern and south-eastern parts of Rome. The Roman soldiery were hurled across the Tiber, churches and houses were ransacked, and, against the Duke's orders, the women—nuns among them—were marched with hands tied behind their backs into the tents of the Norman and Saracen fighting men. Hundreds of the citizens were sold into slavery, and others were led back with the retreating army into Calabria. No distinction was drawn between the Pope's friends and his enemies.

No such destruction of Rome and of its ancient glories is laid to the charge of Goth or Vandal. Yet such was Gregory's legacy to the City. He succeeded in preserving his own hands from placing the imperial crown on the head of his enemy, but the hands of his allies laid the imperial City in ashes. The first round of the great conflict between Church and Empire was won by the secular power, but while some inevitable destruction, which included the columns of the Septizonium, had accompanied the attacks of Henry's troops, Rome was not left in ashes by the imperial victor.

Gregory dared not remain in the ruined city. He went with the army of Guiscard, laden with the spoils of Rome, first to Benevento, and then to Salerno. On the way, the army passed the stronghold of Tivoli, where his rival, Clement III, defied the hasty attempts of the Normans to take the castle. By Christmas Clement was sitting on the chair of Peter in Rome.

In the autumn Gregory's last Synod was held at Salerno. Here the ban was issued for the last time against Henry and Guibert. Peter, the Cardinal-Bishop of Albano, was sent to France with the Pope's last encyclical.[1] It was written with all his former spirit and defiance. There are still those who are faithful to S. Peter, he says, whom no terror or bribe can seduce. Yet there is a note of hysteria in this letter which has not appeared before. ' I cry, I cry and I cry again, but the time of anti-Christ approaches——' So he pronounces his final confession of faith. He had always striven that the church might be free, pure, and catholic. ' The blessed Peter, prince of the apostles, is the father of all Christians, and the chief pastor after Christ ', and ' the holy Roman Church is the mother and mistress of all churches '.

In October, Robert Guiscard left Italy to rejoin his army at Durazzo. He died on July 7th of the next year. The Emperor spent Christmas at Köln, while Goslar was still held by the anti-King Herman. In January (1085) an abortive peace conference was held by the princes at Gerstungen. At Easter the legate Otto of Ostia, whose influence was exerted against the desire for peace in

---

[1] *Ep. Coll.* 46. Voosen p. 83, following J. Gay *Les Papes du XI⁰ Siècle* (1926) pp. 284, 332, brings Gregory back to Rome for the Synod held there in Nov., 1084. This is not probable.

Germany, convened a synod at Quedlinburg in Herman's presence. Decrees were passed announcing the supremacy of the Bishop of Rome, whose judgment no man could question. The ban against Henry was confirmed, and the reforming decrees were re-issued. At the end of April the Synod of Mainz replied for the Emperor with a condemnation of Gregory, and with the confirmation of Clement III's election. The Truce of God was declared operative throughout Germany. The faithful supporter of Henry in all his German wars, Brâtizlav, Duke of Bohemia, was promoted to the dignity of kingship.

When the hot weather approached in South Italy the Pope became ill. In the month of May it was clear that his end was near. The cardinals and bishops gathered round asking him to name his successor. He suggested Anselm of Lucca, Otto of Ostia, and Hugh the Archbishop of Lyons, whom Gregory had made primate of the dioceses of Lyons, Rouen, Tours and Sens. One report says that Desiderius was also named, but this is hardly likely. Of these, only Otto of Ostia, who became Urban II, was destined to reach the chair of Peter. Before the end came, Gregory absolved all his enemies, save Henry and Guibert. He died on May 25th, 1085, and was buried in the crypt of S. Matthew at Salerno.

' I have loved righteousness and hated iniquity, therefore I die in exile ', he said before his ardent spirit departed. But they were the words of a vanquished man. Nor was the logic sound. The premise was true, but not the conclusion. He had loved righteousness, and as a man and as a bishop had lived righteously, but, while he lived for righteousness, he did not die for it, even though what was golden in his convictions survived him. His doom was formed by his own unwisdom. Like Charles I he was no martyr. In all his relations with Henry one thing needful was lacking —charity. Against a young man's sins and impulsive headiness Gregory hurled the papal thunders. Charity united with righteousness might have wooed Henry to the Pope's wisdom, for the lasting peace of both, long years before the danger of a Norman assault approached the City. The ashes of Rome ought to have covered Gregory's tomb, even as they lie on his memory, for when he called Guiscard up to the walls he knew the man and his methods. Among his many quotations from Scripture, Gregory forgot one text! 'All they that take the sword shall perish with the sword', even though they draw the sword of the Spirit, for that is to be wielded by God alone.

CHAPTER FIFTEEN

THE PHŒNIX

THE conflict between Empire and Papacy was an illustration of the attempt to solve the relationship of an irresistible force and an immovable mass; yet the ship of Gregory's personal fortunes foundered upon a rock of his own creation. The claim for papal suzerainty, first applied by him under Nicholas II, and extended to almost every country in Europe, was Gregory's creation, and it places him in the category of European dominators of the Napoleonic stamp. But if on this principle his fortunes shivered, it remained and became the foundation of the power of the medieval Papacy. Reinforced by feudal notions, standing clear as an assertion of the ecclesiastical hegemony of the bishopric of Rome over every Western see, Gregorianism was handed on as an abiding result of Gregory's work. Herein lay the germ of every later papal claim, even of its latest practical manifestation, infallibility itself. Before his death the Synod of Quedlinburg proved to the world that his principle would not die with him, and the papal pamphleteers battled for his case against the royalist writers. Although his immediate successors wisely moderated the application of the principle in relation to the Empire, they kept it pretty well in evidence in all ecclesiastical administration, so that, when the second phase of the great contest between church and state appeared with the investiture question, they were able to secure a compromise in which the balance inclined rather to the church; and when the third stage came in the conflict with the Hohenstaufen, the Papacy was able to take its revenge for the humiliation of Gregory VII by the overthrow of that house.

Yet if Gregory framed Gregorianism in its chief aspect—papal suzerainty over kings—most of the ideas behind his scheme were not his own.[1] The supremacy of the Bishop of Rome over other Western churches had been proclaimed from the ninth century onwards. Hincmar described him as the ' Vicar of Christ ', and Nicholas I was one of the founders of the papal monarchy. The conception of the patrimony of Peter was taken from the Forged Decretals, and the claim to depose kings and unbind their subjects from allegiance—the latter first formally announced by Gregory—seems to have been deduced from the idea of the authority of Peter, which the Pope inherited. The claim to excommunicate a monarch was not an innovation.[2] No leading branch of Gregory's work was motived by an idea created by himself, and perhaps this explains some of his failure. There is always more danger of disaster in applying the principles of others than in working out a self-created idea. The reform of clerical life, by the uprooting of simony and the re-establishment of celibacy, was the programme of the Papacy from Leo IX onwards, supported by Cluniac influences ; and during Gregory's pontificate the policy was especially successful in England and Normandy and also in France. In these countries the work of the legates was effective, with the support of the King in one case, and in spite of him in the other. The reform of church-life, by checking lay election, and the framing of the Election Decree for papal appointments, issued from the Lotharingian school, and received formulation in the hands of Humbert. While the widespread Romanization of the church of the West was the work of Gregory,[3] the development of papal administration, the citation of

[1] *Cf.* Fliche II 409 ff., and Voosen 35 ff.
[2] Carlyle II. (1909) 204 f.   [3] Mirbt p. 610.

bishops to Rome, the foundation of the system of appeals, the legatine commissions, which weakened the power of the Metropolitans—all features of the centralizing policy of the reformed Papacy—were in operation in the days of his predecessors. Gregory accelerated the process already in motion. He held synods every Lent, save in 1077 and 1082, while in 1074 and 1078 an additional synod assembled in the autumn. His legates more frequently crossed the Alps, and there were many more citations to Rome during his pontificate. But not one of these activities was devised by Gregory.

The promotion of the study of canon law was already strong not only in Lorraine, whence Gregory himself derived his interest in canonical principles, but in Normandy and England,[1] South Gaul and Italy.[2] If the sack of Rome involved the destruction of the old Roman school of law, and left the way open for the schools of Ravenna and Bologna, yet Gregory's promotion of the canon law was one of the most abiding features of his work. Many of his letters, and especially the two famous despatches to Herman of Metz, illustrate his knowledge of the canons, and in the *Dictatus Papae*, now assigned to the year 1075,[3] he drew up a number of principles later embodied in the textbooks of canon-law. None of the Pre-Gregorians sketched such a centralization of ecclesiastical authority as the *Dictatus Papae* reveals.[4] The Roman Bishop alone is by right called universal. His legate takes precedence of all bishops in council, and can issue sentence of deposition against them. The Pope cannot be deposed in his own absence. He alone can make new laws, found new churches,

[1] Brooke *The English Church and the Papacy* (1931).
[2] Fournier *Mem. de l'Inst. Nat. de France XL.* (1916).
[3] *Cf.* Peitz, Casper, Fliche and Voosen *op. cit.* and Jules Gay *Les Papes du XIe Siècle* pp. 343 ff. ; Blaul *Studien zum Register Gregors VII. (Archiv. f. Urkundenforschung* Bd. IV. (1912) pp. 113 ff.).
[4] Fliche II. 197 f.

create abbeys, divide or unite bishoprics. He alone
may use the imperial insignia. His feet only are kissed
by princes. He may depose emperors. He may trans-
late and consecrate bishops. No book may be held
canonical without his authority. He only can revise a
papal sentence. He can be judged by no one. All
greater causes are to be referred to Rome, and no one
may condemn an appellant to his judgment sent. The
Roman Church has never erred and never will err.
When canonically consecrated, the Roman bishop possesses the sanctity of S. Peter. He is not catholic who
does not agree with the Roman Church.[1] The researches
of Peitz and Caspar, and their predecessor, Löwenfeld,
have removed the doubt concerning Gregory's author-
ship of this collection of maxims, some of which were
taken from earlier canons and from the decretals. If
they date from 1075, they reinforce the evidence supplied
by the claims already at that time exerted by him over
Sicily, Spain, France and Hungary, for the early conception of hierocratic ideas. In the middle of his pontificate the canonists were busily at work under Gregory's
inspection. That which Damiani had failed to do
during Hildebrand's diaconate was taken up, at the
Pope's request, by Anselm of Lucca, Bonizo of Sutri
and Deusdedit, and there is some ground for the view
that the collection of Cardinal Atto, Archbishop of
Milan, was made during this time.[2] For the Chancery
Gregory's pontificate was not eventful.[3]

---

[1] *Reg.* II. 55a.
[2] Fournier *Mem. de l'Inst. Nat. de France* XLI. (1920) 271 ff. (*Cf.
Mélanges d'Archéol. et d'Hist.* XIV. (1894) pp. 98 ff.) Fournier (p. 282)
assigns the collection of 74 Titles to Hildebrand's influence. This is
rightly contested by E. Caspar *Hist. Zeitschrift* CXXX. p. 21. If the
collection dates from about 1050, Hildebrand was too young and not
sufficiently prominent at Rome at that date to have been entrusted
with the work of drawing them up, although he may have taken them
with him to Gaul in 1054.
[3] Lane Poole *Lectures on the Hist. of Papal Chancery* (1915) 71. But
Peitz *Das Orig. Reg. Greg.* VII. (1911) p. 219 takes the opposite view.

Another feature [1] among the minor details of the papal programme appears to have issued from Gregory himself —the revision of the constitution of secular canons. So early as 1059 he urged the reform of prebendal tenures and of the remuneration of secular canons, and applied his rule to the canons of S. Martin at Lucca in 1077,[2] and S. Mary at Lucca in 1078.[3] In the following year he drew up rules to shorten the hours of worship observed by secular canons, but increased the days of fasting and silence.[4] For the rest, his career was a conflict on behalf of the application of principles inherited from others, and he lost the first phase of the dispute between Church and Empire because these principles were brought into contact with another set of principles and customs derived from ancient German church law. The views of Gfrörer and Delarc, modified by Giesebrecht and Hauck and Meyer von Knonau, require further readjustment, in the light of the studies of Stutz and Scharnagl and Imbart de la Tour on the one hand, and of Fliche [5] and Voosens on the other. The most original enterprise undertaken by Gregory, apart from his claim to suzerainty over the kings of the West, was the Eastern Crusade. When Urban II preached the First Crusade in France in 1095, his stirring words fell on hearts already prepared by the messages sent to Burgundy twenty-one years before. The Crusading idea originated in the martial spirit of Gregory VII, and he first planned the counter-stroke of Europe against Saracen aggression, when he called the armed hosts of the West to advance to the aid of Constantinople, and to march on the tomb of the Redeemer.

[1] H. Mann *Lives of the Popes* VII. (1910) 13 suggests a revival of ecclesiastical art and especially painting under Gregory VII.
[2] *Reg.* V. 1.　　　　　　　　　　[3] *Reg.* VI. 11.
[4] Morin *Revue Bénédictine* XVIII. 177 ff.
[5] Although here with caution.

INDEX

17   247

DATE DUE